COMPETITION AND PRODUCTIVITY GROWTH IN LATIN AMERICA
AND
THE CARIBBEAN

Scan to go to this publication online.

COMPETITION AND PRODUCTIVITY GROWTH IN LATIN AMERICA
AND
THE CARIBBEAN

*Ekaterina Vostroknutova,
James Sampi, Charl Jooste,
and Jorge Thompson Araujo*

WORLD BANK GROUP

Contents

Boxes

Figures

Map

Tables

Foreword

The Latin America and Caribbean (LAC) region continues to grapple with depressed growth and job creation rates that are among the lowest in the world. A long-acknowledged cause is the lack of competitive pressure on firms, the related high degree of concentration in domestic markets, and the barriers to international competition. This situation leads to the poor allocation of factors of production and low levels of innovation that impede productivity growth. To date, however, the evidence making the case for a renewed effort to enhance competitive forces has been elusive.

This report fills that gap by employing case studies, new data, and novel empirical analysis to make the case that increasing competition should be part of the region's growth strategy. It highlights how market concentration continues to be high by global standards and how barriers to entry and expansion rooted in regulations or uncompetitive strategic behavior protect inefficient firms and prevent the entry of the new higher-productivity firms critical to growth. It provides some of the first documentation of how actions by national competition authorities to enhance competition do, in fact, increase output, productivity, and job creation; and it argues that these agencies need to be strengthened and given more autonomy.

However, the report also warns against a simple "more is better" recipe for competition policy. In line with the thinking of Philippe Aghion and coauthors, it documents how, faced with increased international competition from the China shock, most LAC firms were not near the technological frontier and thus were unable to innovate to confront new competition. Thus, greater competition internationally needs to be complemented by policies to strengthen firm capabilities and support national innovation systems.

Competition and Productivity Growth in Latin America and the Caribbean provides a fresh window into the troubled growth dynamics of the LAC region. Still, the lessons complement the work seeking to enhance growth and job creation more globally, like the World Bank Productivity Project and *World Development Report 2024: The Middle-Income Trap.* As such, it provides an invaluable resource for policy makers and analysts globally on the critical role of competition in driving economic transformation and growth.

William F. Maloney
Regional Chief Economist,
Latin America and the Caribbean Region
World Bank

Acknowledgments

This report was prepared for the regional vice president of the Latin America and the Caribbean region, Felipe Jaramillo, and guided by William F. Maloney, regional chief economist, and Doerte Doemeland, practice manager.

We thank the report's distinguished Advisory Board, which consisted of Philippe Aghion (College de France, Institut Européen d'Administration des Affaires, and London School of Economics), Chad Syverson (University of Chicago), and Thomas Cheng (University of Hong Kong).

The team is grateful to Marcela Meléndez and other reviewers inside and outside the World Bank Group, including Martin Rama, Ivailo Izvorski, and Thomas Haven.

Preparation of the report was led by Ekaterina Vostroknutova, Charl Jooste, and James Sampi. Jorge Thompson Araujo contributed as a coauthor. Excellent research and drafting assistance from Ana Francisca Urrutia Arrieta, Dong Phuong Dao, and Anders Pinchao Rosero is acknowledged with thanks. Administrative and operational support from Anjali Kishore Shahani Moreno, Benjamin Vuilleminroy, Adriane Landwehr, and Giselle Velasquez has been invaluable. The team is grateful for the unwavering support from John Burgess, who edited numerous versions of the report.

The report could not have been written without the invaluable collaboration of Comisión Federal de Competencia Económica (COFECE, Mexico); Comisión de la Defensa de la Competencia (Uruguay); Tribunal de Defensa de la Libre Competencia (Chile); Fiscalía Nacional Económica (Chile); Ministerio de Economía, Fomento y Turismo (Chile); Organismo Supervisor de Inversión Privada en Telecomunicaciones (OSIPTEL, Peru); and Instituto Nacional de Defensa de la Competencia y de la Protección de la Propiedad Intelectual (INDECOPI, Peru).

The World Bank also acknowledges the cooperation with the Organisation for Economic Co-operation and Development (OECD) and thanks the OECD for providing the analysis supporting the assessment of competition policy in Latin America and the Caribbean.

The team is also grateful to Martha Licetti, practice manager, and her team: Graciela Miralles, Martha Denisse Pierola, Tania Priscilla Begazo Gomez, and Paul Phumpiu Chang for curating chapter 5—addressing competition policy work in the region—and for the extensive comments to the report as well as several background papers used in different chapters.

In particular, the report depended on the 36 scholars, researchers, and policy makers who produced the key papers on which the report's conclusions are based. Nine of these papers focus on analysis, as follows: Arayavechkit, Jooste, and Urrutia Arrieta (2022); Cusolito, Garcia-Marin, and Maloney (2021); Giuliano and Zaourak (2022); Iacovone, Rauch, and Winters (2013); Reed et al. (2022); Sampi, Jooste, and Vostroknutova (2021); Sampi, Urrutia Arrieta, and Vostroknutova (2024); Schiffbauer, Sampi, and Coronado (2022); and Tello and Tello-Trillo (2021).

Ten other papers focus on policy, as follows: Araujo and Meester (2023); Cheng (2022); Coronado et al. (2021); Goodwin and Villarán (2022); Lee (2022); Li (2021); Miralles, Dauda, and Zipitria (2021); Palacios Lleras (2021); Pierola (2023); and Saslavsky and Arvis (2022).

This report and the accompanying background papers are available online at https://hdl.handle.net/10986/42869.

About the Authors

Jorge Thompson Araujo is a senior collaborating researcher at the Department of Economics of the University of Brasilia, Brazil, and a senior consultant for the World Bank. Before his retirement from the World Bank in 2021, he was practice manager of the Macroeconomics, Trade and Investment Global Practice for the Latin America and the Caribbean region. Previously, he was an associate professor of economics at the University of Brasilia. He has published widely in the areas of economic growth, functional distribution of income, and public finance. He coauthored the World Bank regional report *Beyond Commodities: The Growth Challenge in Latin America and the Caribbean* in the Latin America Development Forum series. He holds a PhD in economics from the University of Cambridge, United Kingdom, and an MSc in economics from the University of Brasilia.

Charl Jooste is a senior economist in the Growth and Jobs Global Practice in the Prosperity Vice Presidency of the World Bank. Previously, he was a director at the Ministry of Finance in South Africa. He has published widely in the areas of economic modeling, fiscal policy, and monetary policy. He holds a PhD in economics from the University of Pretoria.

James Sampi is a senior economist in the Prosperity Vice Presidency at the World Bank. He has worked extensively as a country economist in the Latin America and the Caribbean region. His research interests encompass macroeconomics in developing countries, productivity dynamics, the interplay between economic growth and fiscal policy, and applied econometrics. His work has been published in leading scholarly journals, including the *Review of Economics and Statistics*, *Economics Letters*, and *Electricity Journal*. He holds a PhD in econometrics from the Vrije Universiteit Amsterdam, a master of research in economics from the Universitat Pompeu Fabra, and a master of science in economics and finance from the Barcelona Graduate School of Economics.

Ekaterina (Katia) Vostroknutova is a lead economist in charge of the Growth Team in the Economic Policies Global Practice at the World Bank. She joined the World Bank as a young professional as a core team member of *The World Development Report 2005*. She has worked extensively in the East Asia and Pacific, Europe and Central Asia, and Latin America and the Caribbean regions.

Her research, analytical, and operational work at the World Bank has focused mainly on the microfoundations of economic growth and economic policy and growth strategies in developing countries. She holds a PhD in economics from the European University Institute, an MSc in economics from the European University at St. Petersburg, and a degree in mathematics from the Moscow State University.

Overview

Summary

There are many potential reasons for the decades of slow growth in Latin America and the Caribbean, including macroeconomic volatility, low savings and investment rates, underdeveloped institutions, and resource misallocation across sectors and firms. However, one significant factor stands out: the lack of competitive pressure on firms, which hinders creative destruction and results in inadequate incentives for innovation. This issue has not received sufficient attention from policy makers and analysts.

Creative destruction in the region is limited by barriers to entry that protect inefficient and unproductive firms from competition, allowing them to accumulate rents. Many of these barriers are rooted in local and national government regulations. These regulations reduce competitive pressure, leading to low entry rates, high markups, slower growth among firms, and limited efforts to innovate, all of which contribute to low productivity growth.

Could more intense competition accelerate productivity growth in the region? Empirical evidence suggests that national competition authorities have promoted greater competition, resulting in higher productivity and improved market outcomes. Both new entrants and established firms have benefited.

This report underlines the importance of competition policy in preparing countries—and the firms in them—for external shocks through import liberalization. It also notes that the success of competition policy in raising productivity depends on other complementary policies that amplify the benefits of competition for productivity. The competition-innovation nexus is crucial. Countries need coordinated progress in competition policy frameworks and national innovation systems.

The region requires deliberate measures to boost productivity at the firm level. Competition policy plays a key role by leveling the playing field for market participants, unblocking the creative destruction process, and providing highly productive enterprises with new incentives to grow and innovate, while enabling unproductive enterprises to exit. Yet competition in domestic markets must be accompanied by complementary policies that enhance worker and firm capabilities to increase the share of firms that are closer to the global technological frontier and able to benefit from increased foreign competition.

Chapter 1. Competition, Innovation, and Productivity in Latin America and the Caribbean

Latin America and the Caribbean is characterized by low average growth. On average, countries in the region have not converged to the income level of the United States. The region's relative average income per capita has stagnated for over a century, at about 25 percent of the US benchmark. Given the ample factor endowments of land, labor, and capital, output per worker in the region should be about 60 percent of the US level. For a few decades in the twentieth century, the region outperformed emerging peers, thanks to factor accumulation, mainly fixed capital and skilled labor. However, since the 1980s, output per worker relative to the United States has steadily declined.

Economic growth in the region, when it has occurred, has not resulted from improved productivity or good productivity dynamics capable of sustaining future growth. Overall, productivity has contributed little and often negatively to economic growth. This low contribution to economic growth relative to factor accumulation distinguishes the countries in the region from other emerging markets and developing economies.

Aggregate productivity depends on the productivity of firms, and firm-level productivity is driven by innovation that increases firms' capabilities (the within-firm or innovation channel of productivity). Firms in the region introduce new products less often, hold fewer patents, and use less sophisticated managerial practices, compared to firms in other regions. Compared to countries in the Organisation for Economic Co-operation and Development (OECD), firms in the region invest less in research and development and rely more on non-frontier activities for innovation. Some countries are better at innovating than others; however, they primarily engage in catch-up innovation by introducing products or processes established elsewhere but new to the firm.

Productivity growth depends on how well capital, labor, and other factors of production are allocated across firms and sectors. If they are not allocated to more productive units, aggregate productivity will suffer. Productivity also depends on the rates at which more productive firms enter the market and less productive firms exit. The survival of low-productivity firms reduces aggregate productivity.

Competition is crucial to the operating environment that contributes to productivity growth. It forces less productive firms to exit the market while more productive firms enter, survive, and grow. It is an incentive for innovation. In its absence, firms may operate at higher costs and fail to upgrade to more efficient technologies. Less intensive competition enables rent-seeking behavior. Firms with high market power often divert resources from productive activities to engage in rent seeking to maintain or boost their market power.

Markets in the region operate at low levels of competition and high average market power. Latin America and the Caribbean has a great number of tiny firms that employ a large share of workers. Approximately 70 percent of the workers are active in businesses with fewer than 10 employees, compared to 23 percent in the United States. The number of microfirms is also much higher: in Colombia and Mexico, almost 90 percent of establishments are microfirms, compared to 50 percent in the United States. A small number of firms dominate most markets. A typical manufacturing sector in the region has a dominant firm with a market share between 20 and 60 percent, and average markups—the difference between the cost and the selling price of a product—have been historically high, far above those in other regions.

Chapter 2. Removing Barriers to Entry and Expansion

Markets featuring low levels of competition are characterized by high entry barriers. There are different types of entry barriers, and they vary in their effects on markets. Natural or structural entry barriers result from industry structural characteristics, like economies of scale (when average production costs decline as the quantity produced increases) and network effects (when the number of consumers using a product or service affects the value of the product faced by other users). Meanwhile, incumbent firms intentionally erect strategic barriers to deter entry and protect market share. Often, government policies or regulations restrict entry by establishing exogenous barriers, such as tariffs and operating licenses. This report presents evidence on the potential impacts of removing these barriers.

In Peru, following a competition authority intervention, the removal of local market entry barriers across 1,800 municipalities led to an 11 percent rise in firm-level productivity. A reform in 2013 granted legal authority to the Peruvian national competition authority, the National Institute for the Defense of Competition and the Protection of Intellectual Property (Indecopi), to investigate local and regional market access rules and publicly label as illegal or irrational those that did not align with the national framework or did not make economic sense. If a municipality persisted in imposing an offending rule, firms could use a reporting mechanism, which prompted swift sanction by Indecopi. Alongside a

400 percent increase in fines, this approach effectively removed local regulatory entry barriers. The impact of the reform was felt across 13 major sectors, a quarter of the country's municipalities, and 16 percent of the formal firms. Firms in areas where entry barriers were removed saw a boost in productivity growth compared to similar firms in nonreform areas.

Another example from Peru is that ex ante regulations aimed at raising quality standards for the provision of information and communication technology services increased firm-level revenue productivity by about 20 percent. This example demonstrates the potential of regulatory frameworks to complement competition policy as a driving force behind innovation and productivity. The improvement was driven mainly by firms in the telecommunications industry and those in the top 5 percent of the productivity distribution. Regulations that weaken quality requirements or make entry easier reduce average product quality at the bottom of the productivity distribution. They do so because lower quality standards reduce the entry barriers facing low-productivity firms that may produce lower-quality products and services.

Chapter 3. Antitrust Enforcement

Competition agencies in the region are still weak on average. In recent years, the competition authorities in some countries have become more autonomous, operating as specialized bodies with strengthened sanctioning capacity. However, these agencies have remained small and underresourced for the massive tasks they must carry out. International best practice has not yet been fully adopted. Agencies have struggled to enforce competition laws. Mexico has a competition law that dates back to 1917, but the authorities operated with inadequate funding until 1992, when an independent body was established to investigate anticompetitive behavior. Overall, competition law reforms have lagged behind other reform programs.

Competition agencies are understaffed and underfunded relative to peers in other regions. The average competition budget in Latin America and the Caribbean is lower than in the OECD and significantly affected by a few larger jurisdictions with particularly high competition budgets (OECD 2022). Although the ideal staffing and budget sizes are justifiably tied to the size of the local industry, budget and staffing data offer insights into agency capacity and positioning within government policy priorities.

According to several measures, competition agencies in the region underperform compared to peers, despite progress over the past three decades. For example, countries in Latin America and the Caribbean significantly underperforms relative to almost any other group of countries as measured by the average number of cartel investigations launched by the competition authority on its own initiative (ex officio investigations) each year. Although this lower number might indicate a smaller industrial sector, it suggests that many cartels continue to operate undetected. The region also makes less use of leniency programs and performs fewer unannounced inspections to investigate competition law infringements, compared to Asia, Europe, and the OECD. Likewise, dawn raids are less common. The average value of fines imposed on cartels by competition authorities in countries across the region is low relative to the sanctions in OECD jurisdictions. However, the elevated sanctions imposed in some recent cases hint at progress among regional competition agencies.

Sound competition policy could lead to improved market outcomes in the region. Evidence of the impact on productivity of stronger competition laws and authorities has been limited. This report contributes fresh evidence on the impact of competition laws and agencies in enhancing market conduct and performance in Latin America. Country case studies reveal the largely positive impacts of these competition authorities even though these authorities are underfunded and understaffed.

In Mexico, antitrust penalties in 2020 increased sector-level sales by 1.3 percentage points annually (Reed et al. 2022). The impact of the antitrust penalties imposed by the Mexican competition authority, the Federal Economic Competition Commission, from 1993 to 2018 was evaluated using 90 cases from a total of 261 investigations into suspected anticompetitive practices, for which a suitable control group was identified (Reed et al. 2022). About 40 percent of Mexico's economic activity was investigated for anticompetitive practices during this period. Monetary sanctions in antitrust cases translated into an increase of 5.8 percent in sales in the affected sectors. The identification and penalization of anticompetitive practices were effective in reversing declining sales in sectors that had previously been monopolized. Contrary to expectations, wage rates increased by 1.4 percent per year after the sanctions were imposed, alongside increased employment and a larger wage bill, challenging the idea that antitrust enforcement harms labor markets.

Enforcing antitrust rules is crucial for promoting competition, safeguarding consumers, and boosting productivity growth. Novel data highlight the effect of competition policy enforcement on relevant markets in Chile, Colombia, and Uruguay. Given the absence of systematic information to study competition policy enforcement in the region, the analysis builds on an effort to construct databases for these three countries, comprising a universe of 89 cases of collusion and abuse of a dominant position in Colombia in 1999–2020, 114 cases in Chile in 2009–19, and 87 cases in Uruguay in 2009–15. The agencies in these countries are well trained to identify cases appropriate for intervention. Preliminary econometric results suggest that firms in the affected industries experience increases in productivity following antitrust enforcement actions addressing collusive practices and cases of abuse of market power, such as predatory pricing and refusals to deal.[1]

Chapter 4. International Competition, Complementarity, and Capabilities

The economic literature provides empirical evidence on the effects of increased import competition on productivity and innovation. There is a consensus on the positive impact on productivity of the greater competition fostered by trade liberalization. Foreign entry into a domestic market equates to increased competition that reallocates resources in favor of more efficient producers and incentivizes firms to innovate to escape competition. The wider availability or reduced cost of intermediate foreign inputs may also help to improve market outcomes.

Competitive shocks associated with imports have been shown to generate diverse impacts across firms. For instance, firms in the United States that are exposed to competition from countries with relatively lower wages, such as China, are less likely to survive or grow. Capital-intensive and high-skill-demanding plants are less affected. Similarly, a trade shock may lead to reallocation decisions at the product level. Although the evidence on this result is scarcer, it reveals that firms are likely to drop products that generate lower sales to increase the weight of their core products in output.

Studies on the impact of imports, mainly of Chinese origin, on producers in Latin America and the Caribbean have focused chiefly on sector-level outcomes. Across the region, the competitive force of Chinese imports has favored producers and exporters of raw materials while hindering industries specializing in commodity chains, electronics, automobiles, and auto parts. For instance, the influx of Chinese goods into the United States has crowded out Mexican exports to that country. It has also led to greater innovation in Mexico, such as quality certification training and worker participation and training programs. Similarly, industry exposure to trade liberalization in Argentina stemming from the Southern Common Market (MERCOSUR) agreement has incentivized firms' investments in innovation. In Chile, imports from China and India have stimulated firm-level quality upgrading.

The forces at play in the relationship between the greater competition arising from trade and the incentive to innovate as the vehicle for long-lasting productivity enhancements are more nuanced. The relationship between increased import competition and innovation is mediated by a firm's proximity to the technology frontier. Findings in countries across the region indicate that firms' responses depend on their productivity level. Highly productive firms upgrade product quality to set themselves apart from foreign producers of competing goods, whereas less productive firms that cannot raise the quality of their products react by reducing prices, or they may shrink and exit altogether.

In Mexico, rising exposure to products of Chinese origin in 1995–2004 led to an expansion among larger firms (by sales) and the contraction or exit of smaller firms. Greater import competition elevated the likelihood that firms would restructure their output portfolios to focus on core competencies by prioritizing products with larger output shares and halting the production of marginal goods with lower relative weights in their portfolios. Larger firms and core products were shielded from the increased competition. These outcomes are considered to have led to higher aggregate productivity despite an overall contraction in sales as the exit of less productive businesses outweighed the expansion of more productive ones.

In Chile, increased Chinese imports in 2000–07 contributed to a reduction in average markups and an improvement in average product quality, as well as a decline in overall spending on innovation and the likelihood of engaging in process and product innovation. Frontier firms, defined as the top 10 percent of firms in the productivity distribution, sought to escape the new competition through investments in innovation that allowed them to become more competitive and productive. However, the bottom 90 percent of businesses, which were farther from the technological frontier, exhibited a decline in innovation. On average, the effect on aggregate productivity was null.

In Peru, the effect of tariff reductions under the US preferential trade agreement (PTA) varied across domestic producers, depending on whether the reductions applied to final products or production inputs. Tariff reductions on final products under the China and European Union PTAs hurt productivity growth among non-exporters but helped to boost productivity growth among exporters. In contrast, the tariff reductions on final goods hurt all domestic exporters and non-exporters. However, tariff reductions on production inputs acted in the opposite direction under the US PTA, boosting productivity growth among all domestic producers and contributing to higher average productivity growth. Tariff reductions on production inputs under the European Union PTA also contributed to higher productivity growth among businesses that do not export.

This evidence points to the heterogeneous effects of import competition across firms. Only firms at the top of the productivity distribution—those that were exporters—were able to reap the benefits of lower trade barriers that affected both input and final output markets.

The remaining critical question is how to spark the engines of innovation and productivity at the firm level. Increased import competition fails to boost economic growth if the productivity distribution is skewed to the right because only a few firms are sufficiently close to the global technological frontier to survive and benefit. The challenge in creating the conditions for innovation and productivity improvement at the firm level lies in developing complementary policies and better innovation systems. This challenge is closely connected to the challenge of establishing and supporting sound institutions to defend competition in local markets.

Chapter 5. Getting It Right: Making Competition Work

The interface between competition policy and the broader regulatory framework is critical. Ill-conceived product market regulations, for example, may reduce contestability and dampen competition by creating barriers to entry, facilitating collusion, and tilting the playing field. To succeed, competition policy reform may require prior or accompanying regulatory reform.

Competition and innovation are generally mutually complementary, but there are also trade-offs that must be considered. The distribution of firms according to productivity or distance from the technological frontier matters for the success of competition-innovation reform. The desire to escape competition will be triggered only among firms that have the capacity to innovate, and innovation policy can lead to productivity growth only if there is also a competition policy. Development policy design thus becomes more complex if the complementarities and trade-offs are considered.

Capabilities matter for both private sector firms and public sector competition authorities. Strong organizational and managerial capabilities are necessary among firms if pro-competition policies, such as import liberalization, are also to be pro-innovation. Government enforcement capacity will determine the scope and prioritization of competition and innovation policies in each country.

Institutional independence and political support are vital for the success of pro-competition reform. Reform is more likely to succeed if there is a robust political consensus in favor of it and the competition authorities are beholden to no one in the political or business world. The popularity of anticartel enforcement among populations can provide momentum for competition policy reform.

Note

1. The estimated effects on productivity depend on the methodological approach to productivity estimation. Refer to Sampi, Urrutia Arrieta, and Vostroknutova (2024).

References

OECD (Organisation for Economic Co-operation and Development). 2022. *Competition Trends 2022*. Paris: OECD.

Reed, Tristan, Mariana De La Paz Pereira López, Ana Francisca Urrutia Arrieta, and Leonardo Iacovone. 2022. "Cartels, Antitrust Enforcement, and Industry Performance: Evidence from Mexico." Policy Research Working Paper 10269, World Bank, Washington, DC.

Sampi, James Robert, Ana Francisca Urrutia Arrieta, and Ekaterina Vostroknutova. 2024. "Antitrust Enforcement, Markups, and Productivity: Evidence for Selected South America Countries." Background paper for this report. World Bank, Washington, DC.

Abbreviations

CADE	Conselho Administrativo de Defesa Econômica (Administrative Council for Economic Defense) (Brazil)
EIU	Economist Intelligence Unit
FNE	Fiscalía Nacional Económica (National Competition Authority) (Chile)
GDP	gross domestic product
HHI	Herfindahl-Hirschman Index
ICT	information and communication technology
IDB	Inter-American Development Bank
Indecopi	Instituto Nacional de Defensa de la Competencia y de la Protección de la Propiedad Intelectual (National Institute for the Defense of Competition and the Protection of Intellectual Property) (Peru)
ISIC	International Standard Industrial Classification
ITU	International Telecommunication Union
LAC	Latin America and the Caribbean
LPG	liquefied natural gas
MERCOSUR	Mercado Común del Sur (Southern Common Market)
OBG	Oxford Business Group
OECD	Organisation for Economic Co-operation and Development
PMR	Product Market Regulations indicator
PTA	preferential trade agreement
R&D	research and development
SIC	Superintendencia de Industria y Comercio (Superintendence of Industry and Commerce) (Colombia)
SOE	state-owned enterprise
TDLC	Tribunal de Defensa de la Libre Competencia (Competition Court) (Chile)

TFP   total factor productivity
TFPQ   physical (output-based) total factor productivity
TFPR   revenue-based total factor productivity
TPSEP   Trans-Pacific Strategic Economic Partnership Agreement
WTO   World Trade Organization

1

Competition, Innovation, and Productivity in Latin America and the Caribbean

Productivity Trends in Latin America and the Caribbean

The Latin America and the Caribbean region has not succeeded in converging toward the income level of the United States. For well over a century, the region's average income per capita has stagnated at about 25 percent of this benchmark. Given the region's ample factor endowments in land, labor, and capital, output per worker should be about 60 percent of the US level (Restuccia 2011). For a few decades in the twentieth century, the region outperformed emerging peers, thanks to factor accumulation, mainly fixed capital and skilled labor.[1] However, since the 1980s, output per worker relative to the United States has steadily declined (figure 1.1). Underlying this trend is an inability to attain productivity convergence. Total factor productivity (TFP)—which measures efficiency in the use of factor endowments and other resources—is the key driver of long-term growth, for instance, through innovation (box 1.1).[2]

Figure 1.1 Productivity in Latin America has been on a declining trend since the 1980s

Percent

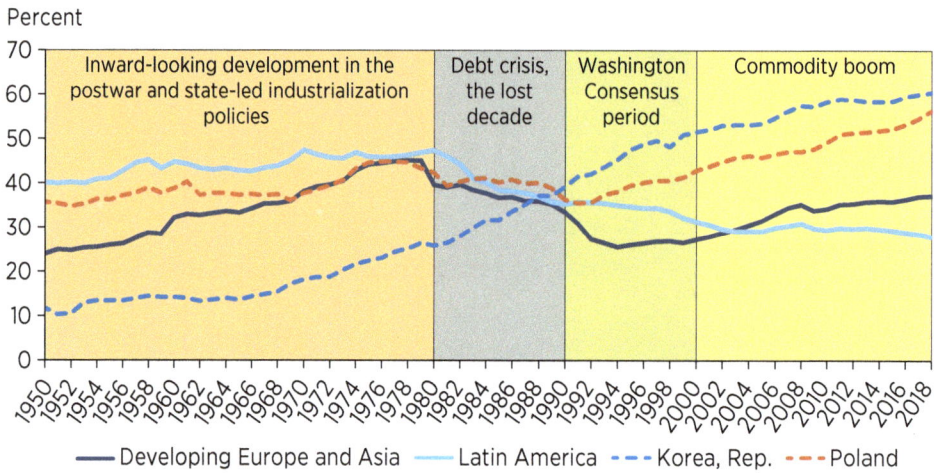

Source: Total Economy Database, Conference Board, New York, https://www .conference-board.org/data/economydatabase/.

Note: The figure shows the output per worker relative to the United States from 1950 to 2018. Regional groupings follow the original source.

Box 1.1

Total factor productivity and its determinants

In the literature on economic growth, productivity is calculated as the amount of output that can be produced with one unit of each of the factors of production (physical and human capital) and other resources. Labor productivity is the output that can be produced with one unit of labor. The more output a firm is able to produce using the same volume of resources, the higher the firm's productivity (or efficiency).

Total factor productivity (TFP) is a measure of the productivity of all factors of production. It accounts for growth that cannot be explained by growth in observable production factors, such as labor and capital. Therefore, TFP reflects unobservable factors that can boost growth, such as managerial skills, advanced technology, innovation, knowledge spillovers, and other externalities associated with infrastructure investment and human capital accumulation. For example, a firm in which a manager employs several workers who use machines to produce tortillas might raise productivity by improving internal processes, such as by acquiring a more rapid rolling pin for tortilla making, reducing corn flour waste by upgrading

box continued next page

Box 1.1

Total factor productivity and its determinants *(continued)*

the relevant machinery, or changing shifts to give workers the opportunity to apply their skills more efficiently. With greater productivity, the firm can produce more tortillas per day while relying on the same workers, hours, and amounts of flour and other ingredients.

Figure B1.1.1 presents the components of productivity growth.[a] There are three main channels through which productivity may grow: the within-firm or innovation channel, which refers to the increase in the capabilities of each firm; the between-firm or allocation channel, which focuses on the allocation of resources and market share to more productive firms; and the net entry, churning, or selection channel, which reflects the exit and entry of firms. Although distinct, these channels are not independent. Any policy or institution that misallocates factors may generate additional effects through the innovation and selection channels as well.

Figure B1.1.1   The components of productivity growth

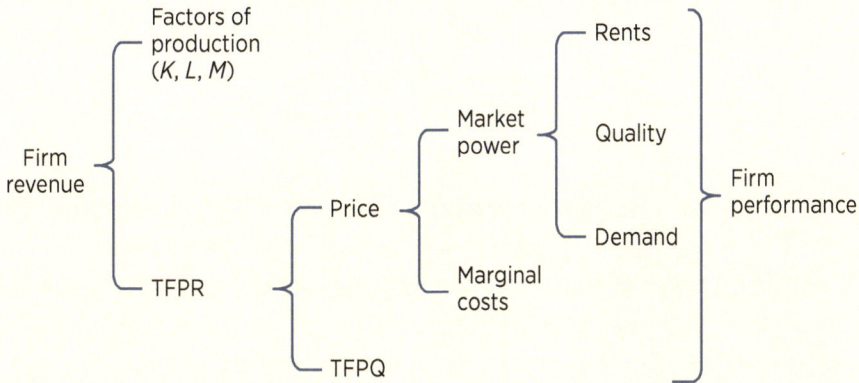

Source: Cusolito and Maloney 2018.

Note: K = capital; L = labor; M = materials; TFP = total factor productivity; TFPQ = physical (output-based) total factor productivity; TFPR = revenue-based total factor productivity.

In addition to illustrating the various factors that affect productivity growth, figure B1.1.1 distinguishes between the measurement of revenue-based total factor productivity (TFPR) and the measurement of physical (output-based) total factor productivity (TFPQ), which is stripped of price effects. In the absence of direct price data, chapters 2 and 3 of this report

box continued next page

Box 1.1

Total factor productivity and its determinants *(continued)*

use TFPR and endogenously measured market power (markups) to estimate the effects on TFPQ. Chapter 4 uses price data for Chile to estimate TFPQ.

Sources: Analysis based on Cusolito and Maloney 2018; Melitz and Polanec 2015; Restuccia 2011; Restuccia and Rogerson 2017; Syverson 2011.

a. Productivity Project (dashboard), World Bank, Washington, DC, https://www .worldbank.org/en/topic/competitiveness/brief/the-world-bank-productivity -project.

The empirical evidence presented in this report supports the case that a long history of weak competition is a critical factor behind the region's anemic productivity growth. Barriers to the functioning of the creative destruction process—impediments that slow entry and exit, reduce incentives for innovation, or interfere with the efficient allocation of factors of production—are responsible for most of this lag in TFP. This report examines the market power and technological differences that act along these channels and are equally important.

This chapter presents stylized facts on the strength of competitive pressures in the region, showing that weak competition slows the process of creative destruction, resulting in low productivity growth. This adverse result may stem from market failures or government-induced distortions, such as bad policies or regulations. Stylized facts on markets are presented in the next section. Government distortions are investigated in the subsequent section. The last section concludes with a discussion of the barriers to competition and innovation.

Growth and Creative Destruction in Latin America and the Caribbean

Long-term growth is an open-ended process of economic rejuvenation and creative destruction, as Joseph Schumpeter posited in *Capitalism, Socialism, and Democracy* (Schumpeter 1942, 1947). New products supplant the old, and innovation replaces traditional ways. The result is greater productivity and, ultimately, a better quality of life:

> [the] kind of competition which counts [is] the competition from the new commodity, the new technology, the new source of supply, the new type of organization …. competition which commands a decisive cost or quality advantage, and which strikes not at the margins of the profits and the outputs of the existing firms but at their foundations and their very lives. (Schumpeter 1947, 84)

This sort of competition is the "powerful lever that in the long run expands output and brings down prices" Schumpeter (1947, 84).

Competitive pressure fuels this process in three broad ways. First, it ensures that factors of production are reallocated to the most productive firms. Second, it allows new and more productive firms to enter the market and induces weak firms to exit (churning). Third, it leads incumbent firms to seek to escape competition by making tough decisions, using resources more intelligently, and addressing evolving market needs. Competitive pressures incentivize firms to take risks, to upgrade by adopting new processes, technologies, and managerial techniques or inventing their own (Aghion, Akcigit, and Howitt 2015; Aghion and Howitt 1990; Syverson 2011). Several studies have found that firms in more competitive markets are more efficient. For example, in the ready-mix concrete industry, innovation and other internal changes drive firms' responses to greater competition (Backus 2020). The result is that firms innovate to produce new or better products or offer products at lower prices, which ultimately translates into greater productivity growth and higher standards of living.

However, not all firms raise their productivity by favoring competition. Firms that are farther from the technological frontier or lack the resources or capability to innovate may withdraw products from the market or even cease operations. Competition may discourage innovation if it erodes the rents that firms seek from research and development (R&D), a view that dates to Schumpeter. Moreover, the process of adapting to competition is not easy. Firms need access to managerial skills, financing, and human capital, as well as an internal culture of change. For example, when the emergence of new technologies and competition began to accelerate at the turn of the twenty-first century, the absence of entrepreneurial capability in Latin America led to lost industries (Maloney and Zambrano 2022). In an inversion of the standard view, this situation led to the establishment of rent-seeking structures.[3] Incumbent firms with weak capabilities had an incentive to lobby for protection from competitive pressures.

Governments have a vital role in making the process of creative destruction as productive and beneficial as possible for a nation's long-term growth and welfare. By removing artificially created market barriers and preventing the appearance of new ones, competition policy can clear space for fresh growth, expansion into new markets, movement of resources among firms, and greater overall allocative efficiency. Governments and regulators need to work carefully to resolve trade-offs and ensure that complementary policies are adopted to allow the creative destruction process to operate to its greatest potential. An economy in which creative destruction functions well exhibits substantial dynamism by churning (the growth of productive firms and the exit of less productive ones) and a high rate of innovation as firms compete for market share and survival by improving internal processes and products and pushing toward the domestic or global technology frontier (Aghion, Bloom, et al. 2005; Aghion, Blundell, et al. 2009; Aghion, Harris, et al. 2001).

Low Churning

Churning—the entry and exit of firms—is an important indicator that creative destruction is at work (Garcia-Macia, Hsieh, and Klenow 2018). In Chile, net entry contributed more than 60 percent of productivity growth in 1996–2006, suggesting that churning can be an important driver of productivity growth in the region. Entry is a product of entrepreneurial experimentation driven by the opportunities and capabilities of entrepreneurs and the operating or enabling environment, including the level of competition (Cusolito and Maloney 2018). New productive firms enter the market with fresh or better products enabled by more efficient production. They gain market share at the expense of incumbent firms that are unable to compete. However, if there are barriers to entry, fewer firms will step into the market and incumbents will not be challenged to improve. Stable market shares among incumbents tend to reflect low contestability in a market or significant barriers to entry and competition (Akcigit et al. 2021).

The Latin America and the Caribbean region exhibits less churning than many other regions. Turnover rates among large firms are low (figure 1.2). The same corporate names crowd the top of the list year after year. Entry rates are low, too, although not many firms are active (figure 1.3).[4] If new firms do enter the market, they are usually small and have little chance of success, only 5 or 6 percent in Peru, for instance (Gil Mena 2019). Only a few manage to succeed, such as MercadoLibre, a regional online retail company in Argentina that initially operated from a garage and now has thousands of employees (Bresler 2021).

Figure 1.2   Large firms are at the top longer

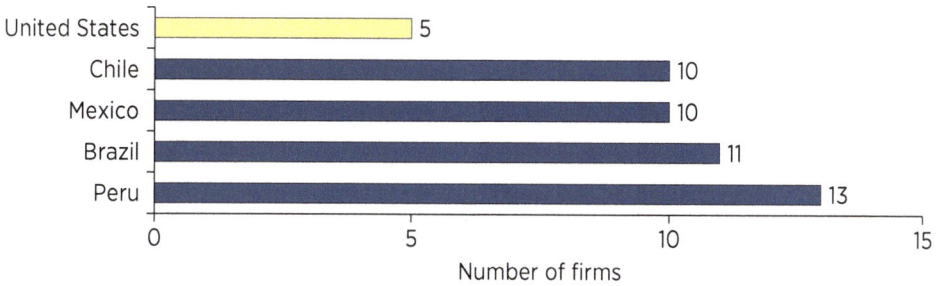

Country	Number of firms
United States	5
Chile	10
Mexico	10
Brazil	11
Peru	13

Number of firms

Source: World Bank estimates based on Orbis (database), Moody's, https://www
.moodys.com/web/en/us/capabilities/company-reference-data/orbis.html.

Note: The figure shows the number of firms appearing in the stock market top 10 in
2005, 2010, and 2019.

Figure 1.3   Entry rates are low, despite the low density of firms

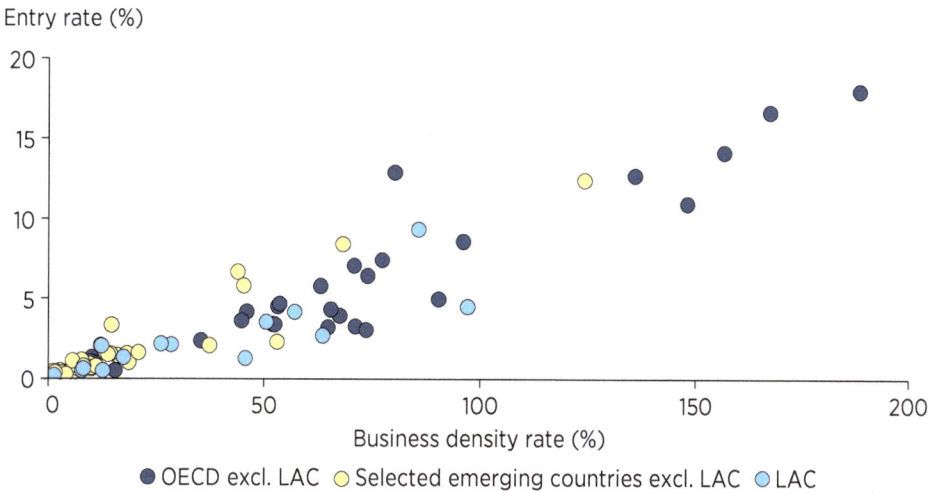

Entry rate (%)

● OECD excl. LAC ○ Selected emerging countries excl. LAC ○ LAC

Source: Entrepreneurship Database, World Bank, Washington, DC, http://www
.doingbusiness.org/en/data/exploretopics/entrepreneurship.

Note: The entry rate is the average annual number of new limited liability firms registered
per 1,000 working-age population in 2006–20. The business density rate is the average
annual total number of registered firms (at the end of each calendar day) with limited
liability per 1,000 working-age population in 2006–20. LAC = Latin America and the
Caribbean; OECD = Organisation for Economic Co-operation and Development.

Regulatory barriers to entry are high in the region. On average, it takes more than 60 days to obtain an operating license, compared to about 15 days in South Asia (figure 1.4). Would-be entrepreneurs face excessively complex regulations—for instance, the need to visit multiple government agencies to obtain a single license—and high permit fees. Such barriers translate into high costs. Thus, barriers in El Salvador are equivalent to a 50 percent tax on entry (Fattal Jaef 2022). In 2019, the cost of opening a business in the region was equivalent to 35 percent of income per capita, compared to 4.3 percent in Europe and Central Asia and 12.5 percent in South Asia.[5] The number of days needed to obtain an operating license in the region was double the world average, and average entry costs in Latin America were the second highest in the world.

Figure 1.4   Too many days to obtain a business license

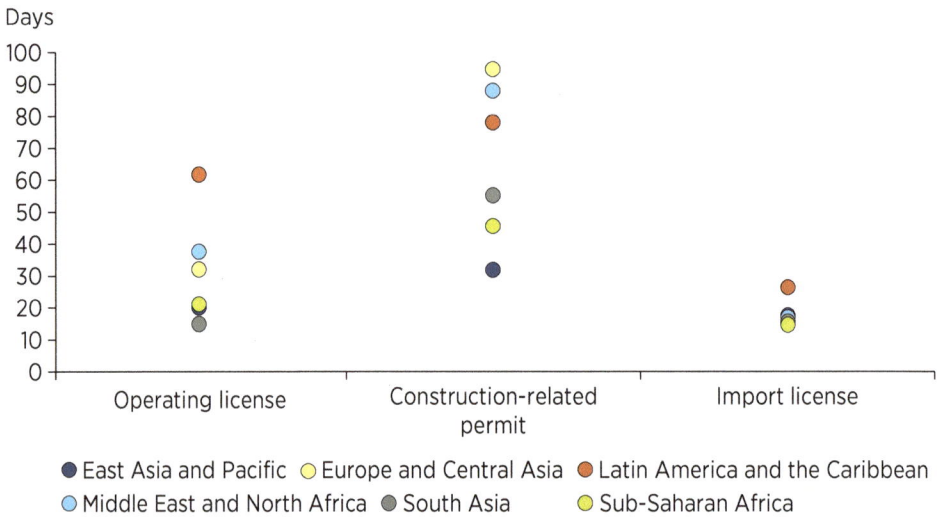

● East Asia and Pacific   ○ Europe and Central Asia   ● Latin America and the Caribbean
○ Middle East and North Africa   ● South Asia   ○ Sub-Saharan Africa

Source: World Bank Enterprise Surveys (dashboard), World Bank, Washington, DC, https://www.enterprisesurveys.org/en/enterprisesurveys.

Note: The figure shows the number of days to obtain a business license. Regional averages of indicators are computed by taking a simple average of the economy-level point estimates. For each economy, only the latest available year of survey data is used in this computation. Only surveys posted since 2014 and adhering to the Enterprise Surveys Global Methodology are used to compute these averages.

Figure 1.5   Barriers to domestic and foreign entry are pervasive

Index

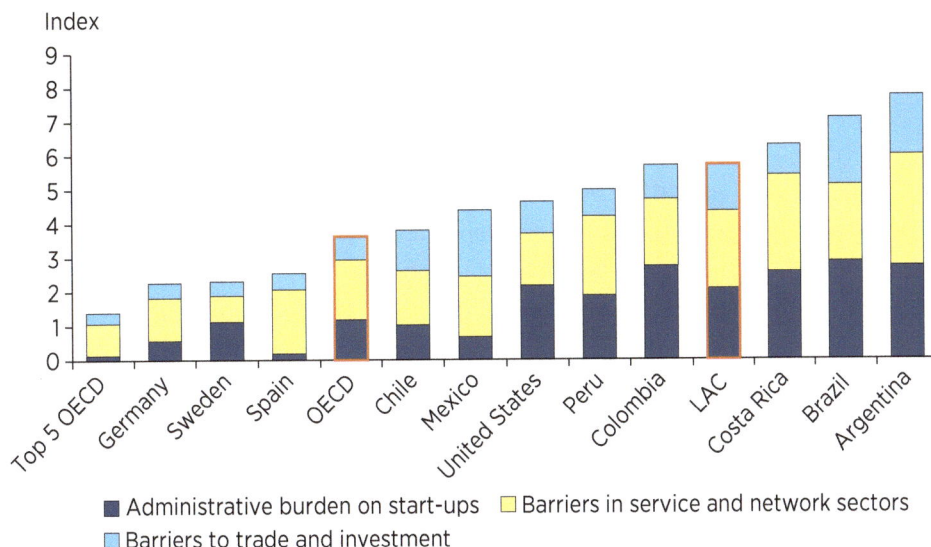

■ Administrative burden on start-ups   □ Barriers in service and network sectors
□ Barriers to trade and investment

Sources: OECD–World Bank Group Product Market Regulation database, 2018–20 (dashboard), Data Catalogue, World Bank, Washington, DC, https://prosperitydata360 .worldbank.org/en/dataset/OECDWBG+PMR; PMR Indicators (Indicators of Product Market Regulation) (dashboard), OECD, Paris, https://www.oecd.org/en/topics/sub -issues/product-market-regulation.html.

Note: The figure shows the barriers to domestic and foreign entry in 2018. On the index, 0 = best practice. The countries included in LAC are Argentina, Brazil, Chile, Colombia, Costa Rica, Mexico, and Peru. LAC = Latin America and the Caribbean; OECD = Organisation for Economic Co-operation and Development.

Figure 1.5 shows that barriers are higher in Latin America than among the Organisation for Economic Co-operation and Development (OECD) countries. It highlights the particularly high barriers in network sectors (refer to chapters 3 and 4 of this report). Overall, these data reflect a market that is generally unfriendly to newcomers.

Large Rents

Local firms are perceived as having greater market dominance in the region's countries than in peer countries. A small number of firms dominate a large number of markets (figures 1.2 and 1.6). Business density—the number of firms registered per 1,000 population—is also low. In a typical manufacturing sector in the region, a dominant firm has a market share of 20 to 60 percent (Eslava, Meléndez, and Urdaneta 2021). Although concentration may be beneficial in some markets, average markups—the difference between the cost and selling price of a product—have been historically high and, until recently, higher than the markups in other regions (figure 1.7).[6] In Mexico, before the competition reforms in 2013, América Móvil held more than 70 percent of the telecommunications market, with profit margins double the average of telecom firms in OECD countries (OECD 2012). The top 500 firms in Peru are more profitable in relative terms than the top 500 firms on the US Forbes list (Alarco, Castillo, and Leiva 2019). They are not more productive or innovative, however, suggesting that the profits are rents enabled by greater market dominance (Crespi, Fernández-Arias, and Stein 2014; Vargas 2022).

Figure 1.6 Perceptions of market dominance are more pervasive in the region, relative to peers

Index

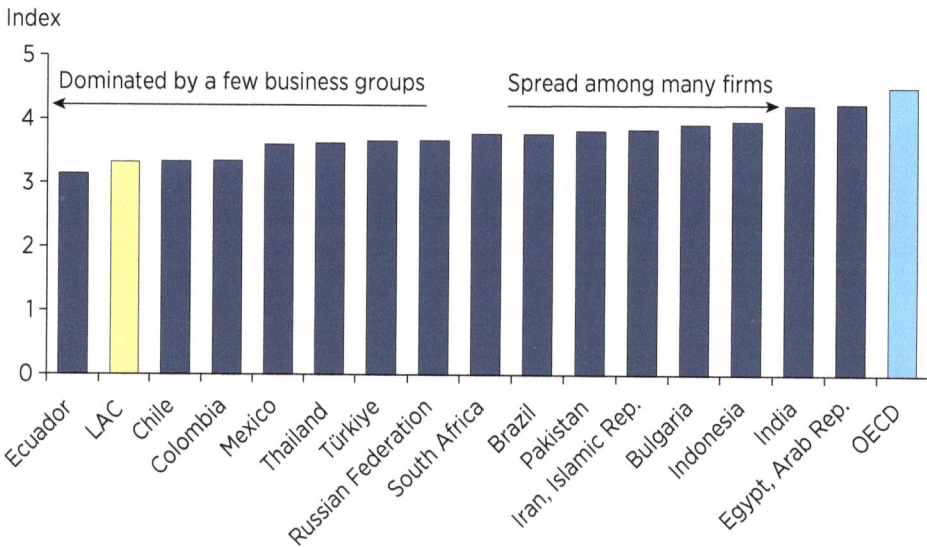

Source: Schwab 2019.

Note: The figure shows the perceptions of market dominance in 2019. The market dominance index reflects the responses to the survey question "In your country, how do you characterize corporate activity?" 1 = dominated by a few business groups; 7 = spread among many firms. LAC = Latin America and the Caribbean; OECD = Organisation for Economic Co-operation and Development.

Figure 1.7   Markups are historically high

Markup (%)

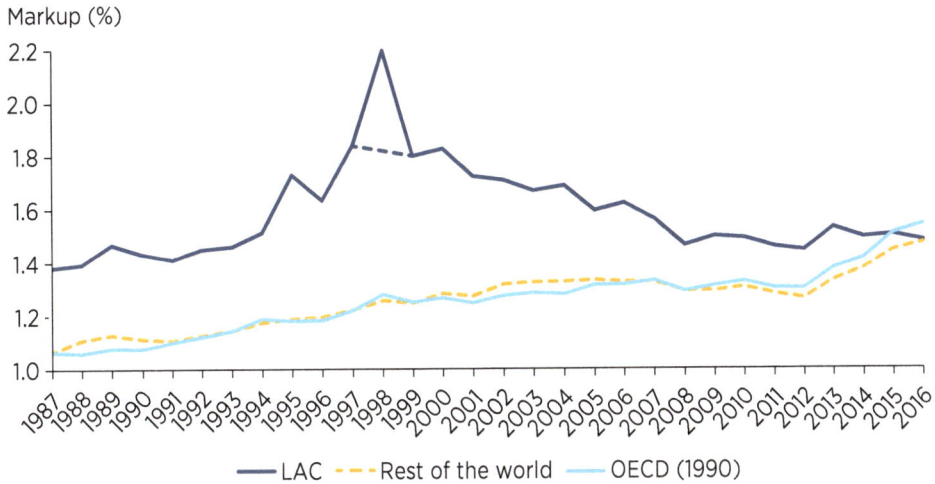

Source: Eslava, Meléndez, and Urdaneta 2021 using estimates from De Loecker and Eeckhout 2018.

Note: Average markups by year are estimated as the year fixed effects from a linear regression on the average markup by country, with year and country-level fixed effects. OECD (1990) corresponds to countries that belonged to the OECD in 1990. The rest of the world corresponds to all countries in the sample that are not part of LAC. LAC = Latin America and the Caribbean; OECD = Organisation for Economic Co-operation and Development.

High rents captured by large dominant firms lead to significant economic costs and consumer welfare losses, and are a drag on innovation (box 1.2).[7] This is the typical state of affairs in the region, where long-standing, politically influential monopolies are found in many markets.[8] They dominate through entrenched power and political connections rather than innovation (Acemoglu and Robinson 2019; Campos et al. 2021; Philippon 2019). They find that thwarting competition is less costly than innovating (Akcigit, Baslandze, and Lotti 2023; Egan 2010; Faccio 2006). Other factors solidify their standing, including the special privileges of state-owned enterprises (SOEs) or those deriving from import substitution policies (World Bank 2023). Regulatory restrictions on the number of operating licenses also curtail entry (Miralles, Dauda, and Zipitria 2021). In some sectors, network effects may reinforce dominance if standardization and compatibility are important to productivity, such as in software technologies (Gilbert 2022).

Box 1.2

What are cartels, and what do they do to survive?

Incumbent firms that might otherwise be rivals may coordinate their activities to gain market power, which, in turn, enables them to set prices and control entry into their favored market segments. A group of firms engaged in such behavior is a cartel. Cartels are agreements among competitors to fix prices, share markets, or rig bids.

The most widely recognized impact of cartels is higher prices for consumers. Hundreds of cases prosecuted in Latin America and the Caribbean have shown that, for prolonged periods, the prices of basic goods remain up to 50 percent higher under cartels than they would be otherwise, and sometimes 100 percent higher.

Collusive firms do more than overcharge consumers. A cartel may create entry barriers and use other anticompetitive practices to protect its price markups. Although such arrangements are sometimes unstable, some cartels endure for decades, slowing the process of creative destruction.

Most important, cartels weaken the incentives for efficiency. They may impede labor productivity growth by as much as 30 percentage points relative to industries without cartels. Analysis by Bridgman, Qi, and Schmitz (2009) of a 40-year cartel in US sugar manufacturing suggests that sectoral output declined by 22 percent more than it would have without the cartel. Systematic cartel activity can curb productivity growth economywide. Nickell (1996) shows this effect empirically for the United Kingdom, and Petit, Kemp, and van Sinderen (2015) do so for the Netherlands. Following Adam Smith ([1776] 1937), Van Reenen (2011) proposes managerial quality as the main driver of these impacts.

Cartels are not the only obstacle to competition in less developed economies, but they are especially harmful to poor households. A World Bank (2021) analysis of cartels in Latin America and the Caribbean, based on the World Bank cartels database, finds that 65 cartels have been identified and investigated across nine countries in the region. The largest numbers of cases in which cartels had a negative effect on the markets for basic consumption products, such as sugar, toilet paper, wheat, poultry, milk, and medicines, were in Brazil (10), Colombia (11), and Mexico (15). Cartels in the region have typically increased prices by 5 to 20 percent, but anticompetitive

box continued next page

Box 1.2

What are cartels, and what do they do to survive? *(continued)*

agreements (cartels) raised consumer prices by 100 percent in at least 4 percent of the cases. World Bank (2016) research in South Africa suggests that public resources spent on anticartel enforcement may be as much as 38 times more effective than cash transfers in reducing poverty, because cartels capture a significant share of the cash transfers targeted to eligible households.

The involvement of cartels in government procurement constrains the supply of public goods and services; in some cases, cartels may even distort the market for government bonds. Between 1980 and 2020, at least one cartel of every four in the region was established among firms participating in government procurement processes, with taxpayers bearing the burden of overcharges. In Peru, 31 providers of hemodialysis services rigged the public health administration's bidding process by abstaining from participating in public tenders to increase reference prices for subsequent tenders. In 2010–12, this scheme led to overcharges of approximately US$10 million per tender. Licetti and Goodwin (2015) report that, in 2014, Peru sanctioned a cartel among engineering firms involving US$50 million in contracts for expansion of the public highway network. In Mexico in 2010–13, seven banks entered into at least 142 agreements to manipulate the price of the Mexican sovereign bond market by limiting the sales and acquisitions of bonds. This scheme resulted in losses on the market of more than US$1.4 billion. In Colombia, an anticompetitive agreement that favored a particular group of firms in the concession process for the construction of a major highway (Ruta del Sol II) cost the government and, ultimately, taxpayers at least US$11 million in overcharges.

Stigler (1964) argues that many firms encounter incentives not to form cartels. However, the potential profits derived from covertly working together may overwhelm these incentives. Levenstein and Suslow (2006) analyze cartel operations and find that the distribution of duration is bimodal. Thus, although the average life of a cartel across a range of studies is about 5 years, many break up in less than a year.

box continued next page

Box 1.2

What are cartels, and what do they do to survive? (continued)

Evidence suggests that cartels succeed to varying degrees in increasing prices and profits. They may also affect other nonprice variables, including advertising, innovation, investment, barriers to entry, and concentration. The most important of these are innovation and investment. Amid a collusion scenario, efforts to increase productivity or outpace the competition are futile or would crack the foundations of the collusion.

Cartels break up occasionally because of cheating by participants, but the biggest challenges cartels face are changing economic conditions and the entry of other competitors despite the cartel's efforts. Cartels that develop organizational structures to respond to these changing conditions are more likely to survive. Sophisticated cartels are able to monitor the operations of individual members to deter cheating and intervene to raise the barriers to entry.

Sources: Analysis based on Connor 2020; OECD 2014; World Bank 2021; and the studies cited.

In their day-to-day operations, dominant firms often seek to safeguard their high markups. Collusion with other incumbents and abuses of market dominance may create artificially high entry barriers that keep new competitors out. If other firms with the potential to become leaders are locked out of a market in this way, industrywide productivity suffers (box 1.2). Lackluster antitrust enforcement can also enable high markups (Gutiérrez and Philippon 2018).

The average number of cartels detected in the region has been increasing,[9] and, since the 1980s, about 35 percent of them have been in manufacturing. Transportation and wholesale and retail trade account for 15 percent each (figure 1.8). In manufacturing, cartels are particularly common in meat processing in Brazil, Chile, and Panama and in the production of basic chemicals in Argentina, Brazil, Colombia, Panama, and Peru. In pharmaceuticals (both wholesale and retail), cartels have been discovered in Brazil, Chile, El Salvador, and Honduras. In transportation, Chile imposed a US$95 million fine on six shipping lines for colluding in tender processes to provide maritime transportation to manufacturers and consignees of imported cars. Mexico sanctioned seven shipping lines for making nine agreements to split up the car transportation market (Begazo et al. 2018).

Figure 1.8   Cartels distort virtually every sector of the economy in Latin America and the Caribbean

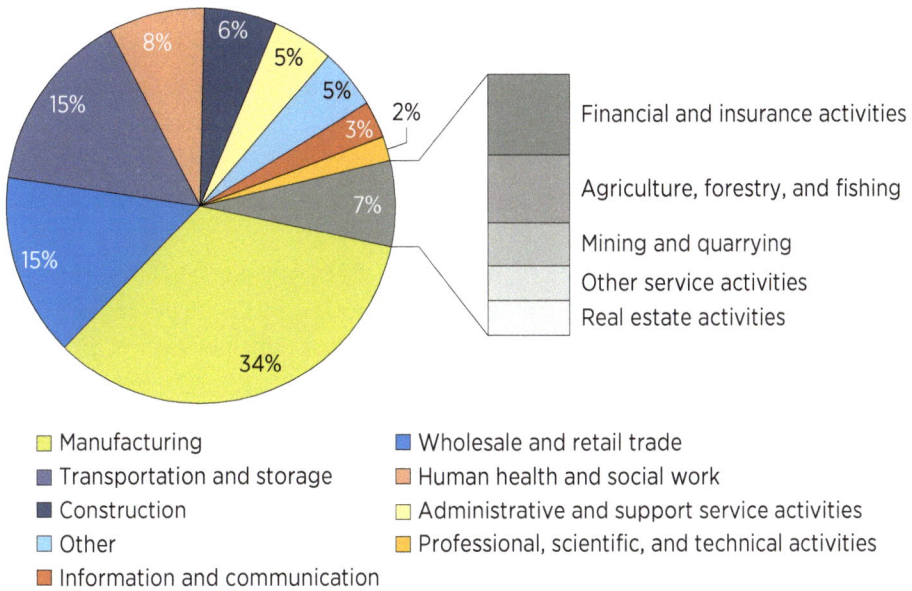

Manufacturing 34%, Wholesale and retail trade 15%, Transportation and storage 15%, Construction 8%, Other 6%, Administrative and support service activities 5%, Professional, scientific, and technical activities 5%, Information and communication 3%, Human health and social work 2%, 7%

Financial and insurance activities
Agriculture, forestry, and fishing
Mining and quarrying
Other service activities
Real estate activities

- □ Manufacturing
- ■ Transportation and storage
- ■ Construction
- □ Other
- ■ Information and communication
- ■ Wholesale and retail trade
- ■ Human health and social work
- □ Administrative and support service activities
- ■ Professional, scientific, and technical activities

Source: World Bank 2021.

Note: The figure shows cartels prosecuted in Latin America and the Caribbean, by sector, 1980–2020.

Significant Barriers to Expansion

The Latin America and the Caribbean region has many small firms that, together, employ a large share of workers. Approximately 70 percent of workers are active in businesses with fewer than 10 employees, compared to 23 percent in the United States (Eslava et al. 2023). The number of microfirms is also much higher in Latin America and the Caribbean. In Colombia and Mexico, almost 90 percent of establishments are microfirms, compared to 50 percent in the United States (Eslava 2018; Eslava, Haltiwanger, and Pinzón 2019).[10] In the region, 96 percent of establishments have five or fewer employees, compared to 81 percent in high-income countries (Klapper and Randall 2012). The presence of so many microfirms that employ such a large share of workers puts a drag on productivity through the allocation channel, but mostly it indicates a lack of growth and distortions in the formal sector (Fattal Jaef 2022; Perry et al. 2007).

Small and medium enterprises are developing at a slow pace in the region. In high-income countries, 20 percent of firms employ six or more workers; more than 10 percent do so in Europe and Central Asia; however, in Latin America and the Caribbean, the share is only 4 percent (Lederman et al. 2014). Only 11 percent of these enterprises in the region are rapidly growing young firms with productivity, R&D, and innovation levels on par with the levels of more mature firms. Among all small and medium enterprises in the region, 44 percent barely grow at all (Grazzi and Pietrobelli 2016). Medium enterprises, which should face fewer constraints relative to microfirms, also do not grow (Lederman et al. 2014; Tybout 2014). On average, a firm in the United States will triple in size by age 26 and grow sevenfold by age 40 (Hsieh and Klenow 2014) (figure 1.9). Plants grow much more slowly in Latin America and the Caribbean. In Uruguay, hardly any firms show growth in size by age 26; in Mexico, the size only doubles by age 40 (Hsieh and Klenow 2014). Even rapidly growing young firms typically do not achieve superstardom (that is, highly productive, rapidly growing firms) like Big Cola, which was once a small soda company in Peru's Cajamarca region. Through improvements in internal processes and product innovations, Big Cola became an international player that challenged Coca-Cola in developing Asia (Eslava, Haltiwanger, and Pinzón 2019).

Figure 1.9   Firms grow more slowly

Average employment index

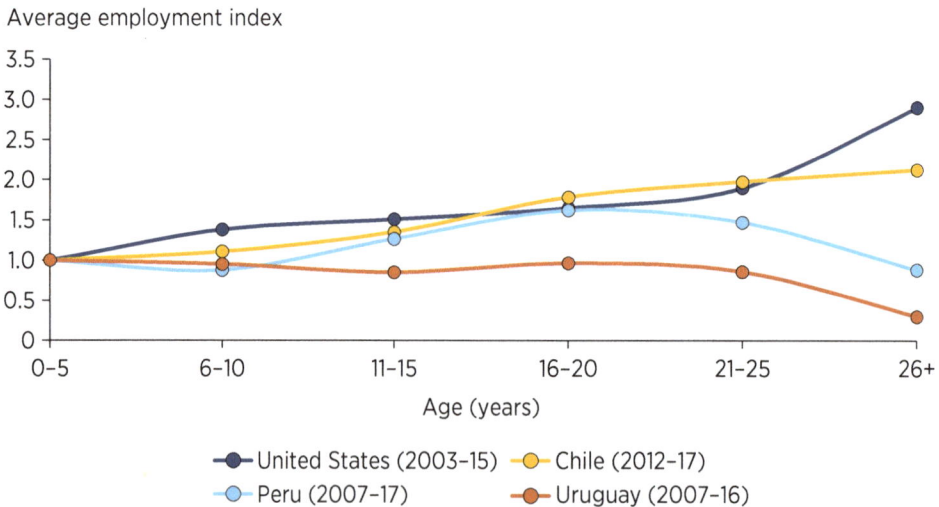

Sources: Chile, Peru, and Uruguay: World Bank Enterprise Surveys, https://www
.enterprisesurveys.org/en/enterprisesurveys; United States: Aghion et al. 2018.

Note: On the index, 1 represents the average employment for firms 0–5 years of age.
National surveys may bias the exit rate estimates because they reflect real exits or
firms not included in the sample. These biases decline with firm size because national
statistical offices attempt to include the full universe of large firms in the sample.

The slow growth in the medium-size segment indicates that there are barriers to the creative destruction process that hold back the growth of productive firms and the exit of unproductive firms. If the creative destruction process works well, newcomers tend to expand quickly, become the main contributors to job creation, and are more likely to pursue knowledge-intensive activities (Ayyagari, Demirgüç-Kunt, and Maksimovic 2014; Haltiwanger, Jarmin, and Miranda 2013; OECD 2017). As a result, a typical surviving firm should become more productive as it grows along the life cycle. Therefore, every firm should eventually reach an equilibrium size, which depends on cost structure and industry effects (Hopenhayn 1992; Jovanovic 1982). This is what happens in much of the world, but it is rare in Latin America and the Caribbean (figure 1.10). If firms in the region grow, productivity improvements seem not to be the main reason (Aghion et al. 2001; Ding and Niu 2019; OECD 2021). The relationship between firm size and productivity is mostly negative or zero among manufacturing firms in the region, compared to the positive relationship in the United States.

Figure 1.10 Big manufacturing firms are not as productive

Change in TFP (%)

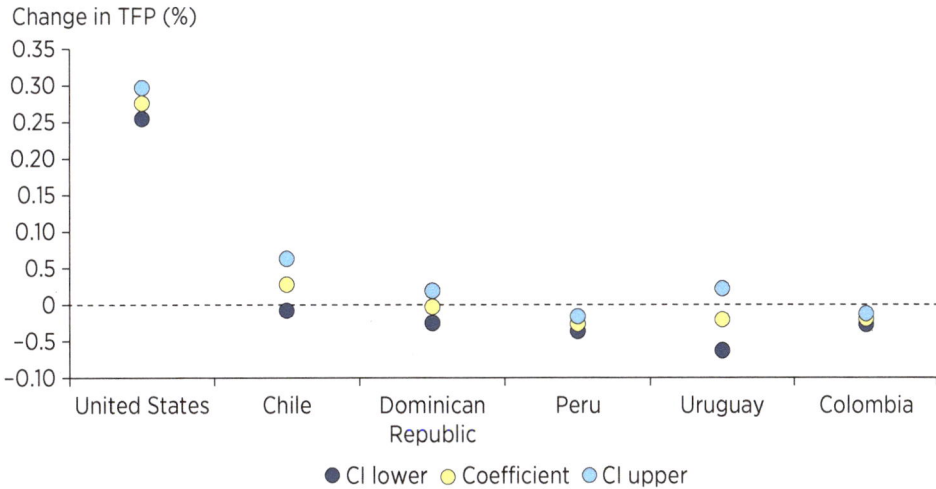

● CI lower ○ Coefficient ○ CI upper

Source: Calculations using databases on manufacturing firms.

Note: The figure shows the percent change in TFP of manufacturing firms with a 1 percent increase in the number of employees. Data for Peru and Colombia are from 2007–17; Chile, 2012–17; Uruguay, 2007–16; the Dominican Republic, 2015–19; and the United States, 1987–2019. Firm productivity is estimated by assuming a Cobb-Douglas production function and following the methodology of Ackerberg, Caves, and Frazer (2015). The US numbers are based on aggregate information on manufacturing at the three-digit level from the US Bureau of Labor Statistics. In a robustness check, the regression coefficients for Chile and Peru remained near zero in a smaller sample including only large firms. CI lower = lower confidence interval band value; CI upper = upper value; TFP = total factor productivity.

The data presented in this section also show that even productive firms in the region are unable to reach optimal size. Significant barriers to firm expansion are found in the underlying cost structures, managerial and organizational capabilities, or access to financing for investment or R&D (Audretsch et al. 2018; Cirera and Maloney 2017; OECD 2019). Firms in the region may lack the fundamental ability to shift direction and expand to new markets. Increasing their product quality may be difficult because of entry barriers that curtail competition (refer to chapter 3 of this report).

Low Innovation Effort

The region's innovation rate is low year after year (figures 1.11 and 1.12). Firms introduce new products less often, hold fewer patents, and use less sophisticated managerial practices than in other regions (Lederman et al. 2014). Compared to firms in OECD countries, firms in the region tend to invest less in R&D and rely more on non-R&D activities for innovation (Crespi et al. 2022; Phelps 2013). Some countries—Chile, Brazil, and Argentina—are better than others at innovating. However, they engage mostly in catch-up innovation, the introduction of products or processes that have been established elsewhere but are new to the firm. Even that procedure should be more widely adopted (figure 1.13).

Figure 1.11 Limited innovation adds little to productivity

Contribution to TFPR growth (%)

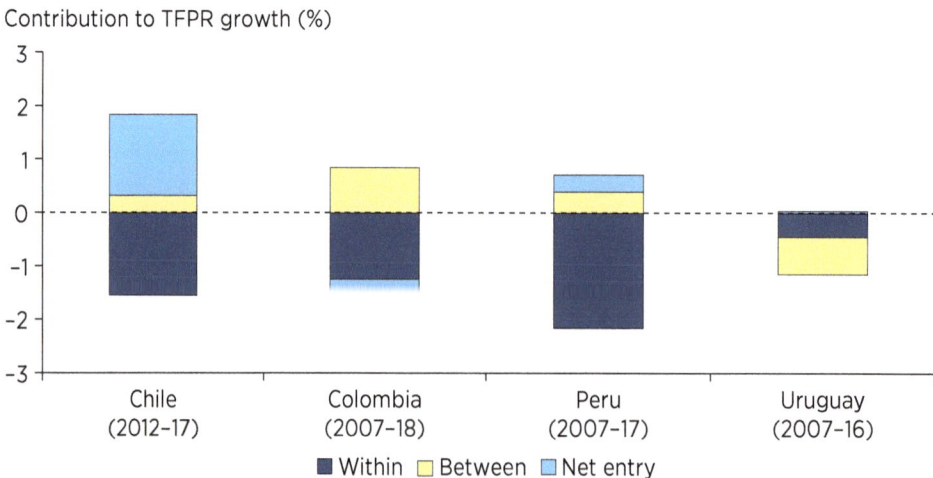

Source: World Bank staff estimates based on the methodology of Melitz and Polanec (2015).

Note: The figure shows the TFPR growth of manufacturing firms, by productivity margin. The estimates are calculated assuming a trans-log production function and approximating human capital by wages. Therefore, labor is accounted for by wage compensation. Similar results are obtained by assuming a Cobb-Douglas production function and using only the number of employees as labor. Limited innovation is reflected in the decline in the "within" productivity margin contribution. TFPR = revenue-based total factor productivity.

Figure 1.12 Few global patent applications are in the LAC region, despite population comparable to Europe and North America

Share of world population (%)

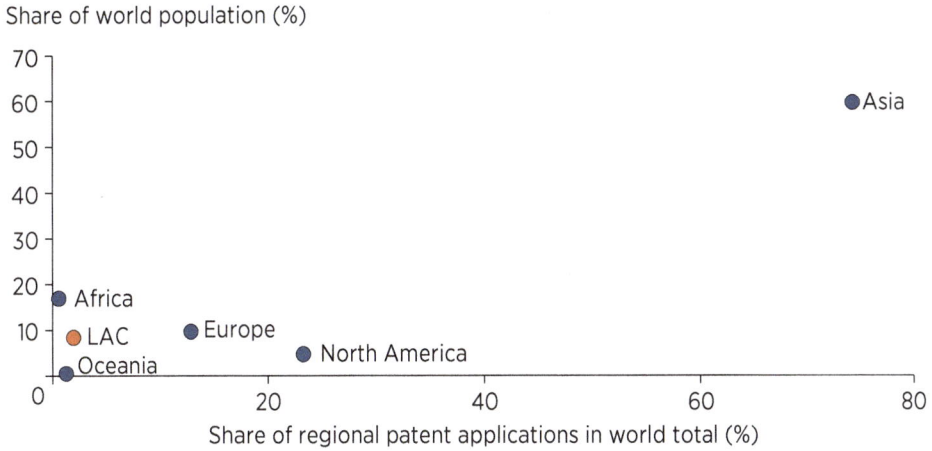

Share of regional patent applications in world total (%)

Sources: Regional patent applications: World Intellectual Property Indicators, 2020; population shares: United Nations Population Division data for 2019.

Note: The figure shows the share of patent applications relative to the share of world population in 2019. Regional groupings follow the original sources. LAC = Latin America and the Caribbean.

Figure 1.13 Latin America and the Caribbean has few product innovating firms

Share of firms (%)

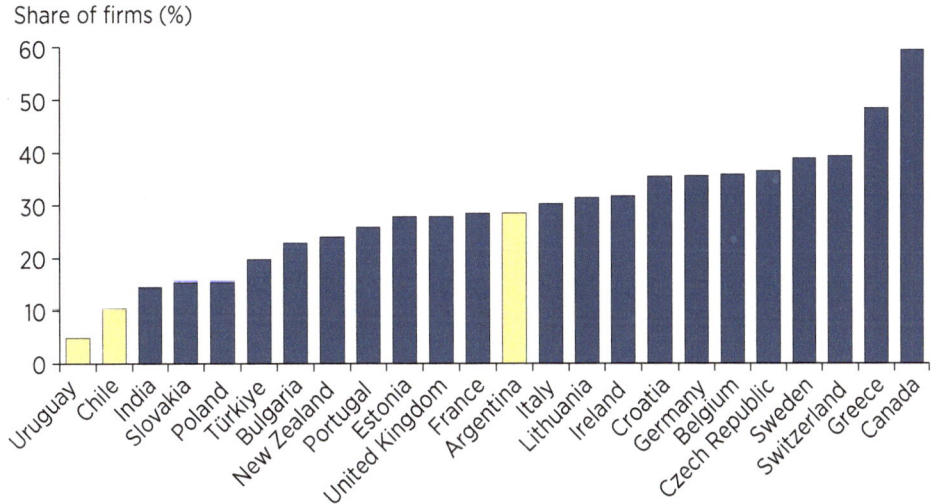

Source: Organisation for Economic Co-operation and Development Innovation Dataset, 2021, using national innovation surveys and Eurostat.

Note: The figure shows the share of firms that innovate on products in 2018–19. Yellow bars denote countries in Latin America and the Caribbean.

Firms in the region report a low incidence of intellectual property rights claims and low patenting activity relative to the OECD average. Only 14 percent of firms in the region applied for rights in 2008–10, suggesting that much of the innovation in the region consists of using technologies developed elsewhere (Cheng 2022; Cirera and Maloney 2017).

Innovation displays an inverted U-shaped relationship with the degree of competition and depends on firm size (figure 1.14). Two basic forces are behind the relationship. Schumpeter (1942) argues that imperfectly competitive markets promote innovation because they provide higher returns to innovation. Arrow (1962) finds that a monopolist who is protected from competition has less incentive to innovate than a firm in a competitive industry. In a seminal series of studies, Aghion et al. (2001) show that these two effects coexist and depend on the incumbents' distance from the technology or productivity frontier. Thus, under competitive pressure, capable incumbents innovate and escape competition. Low-productivity incumbents that are far from the frontier may find that profits are so low that they will not or cannot upgrade and are forced to exit.

Figure 1.14 There is an inverted U-shaped relationship between innovation and competition

Share of firms (%)

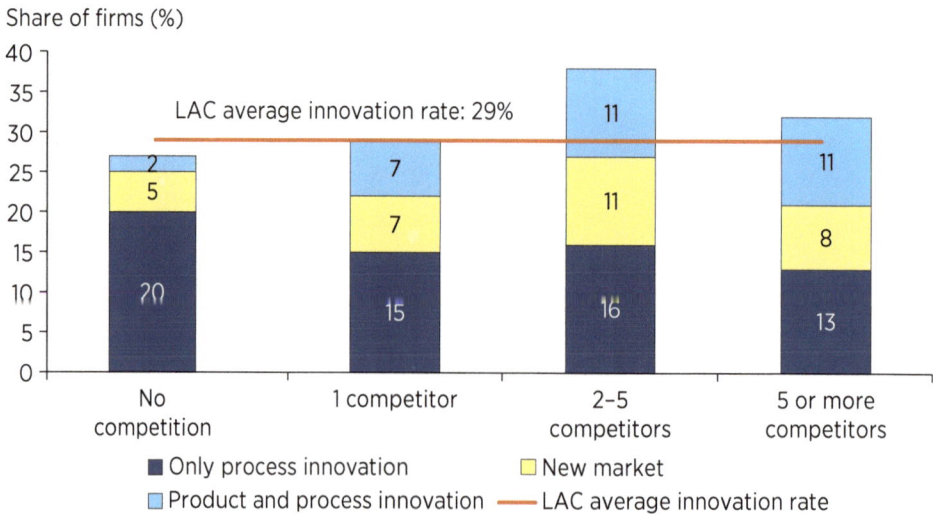

Sources: Crespi, Fernández-Arias, and Stein 2014; World Bank Enterprise Surveys, 2010, https://www.enterprisesurveys.org/en/enterprisesurveys.

Note: The figure depicts the innovation rate by the number of competitors and type of innovation. LAC = Latin America and the Caribbean.

Chapters 2, 3, and 4 of this report examine this complementarity to demonstrate empirically the crucial link between productivity growth and incumbent capacity to innovate under competitive pressure. The entry of new, capable firms or the threat of such entry motivates incumbents to innovate rather than try to capture the market and enjoy hefty markups (Akcigit, Baslandze, and Lotti 2023). Some newcomers may be more capable than the old, established incumbents. The process or product innovation rate in the region is lower among old firms than among dynamic young firms that enter a market with a new product or aim to export (figure 1.15).[11]

Figure 1.15 Old firms innovate less than dynamic young firms

Share of firms (%)

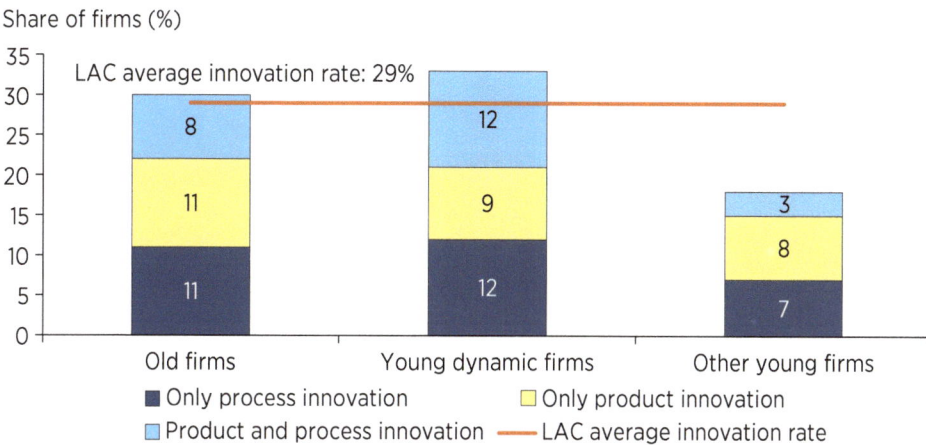

Sources: Crespi, Fernández-Arias, and Stein 2014; World Bank Enterprise Surveys, 2010, https://www.enterprisesurveys.org/en/enterprisesurveys.

Note: The figure depicts the innovation rate by the age of firm and type of innovation. LAC = Latin America and the Caribbean.

Several factors help to explain why the rate of innovation is low in the region overall. First, the share of small firms that do not innovate is large. Second, small, young firms face significant growth constraints. For example, access to finance, investment in R&D, and adoption of technology may be challenging, especially in manufacturing, which often requires large-scale investment in machinery (Audretsch et al. 2018; OECD 2019). Third, the managerial capabilities and entrepreneurship among firms in the region—vital indicators of innovation capacity—compare poorly with those in other regions (Bloom and Van Reenen 2010; Cirera and Maloney 2017). Firms may have limited incentives to use existing technology to increase productivity. Returns to innovation might be low partly because of market structure (Goñi and Maloney 2014). If firms enjoy protection through market dominance or political influence, they may have less incentive to introduce productivity-enhancing innovations (Eslava, Meléndez, and Urdaneta 2021; Grazzi and Pietrobelli 2016; Paus, Robinson, and Tregenna 2022).

Work at the World Bank by Iacovone, Pereira López, and Schiffbauer (2016) shows that Mexican firms that possessed information technology used it to increase productivity only if they faced competitive pressure (figure 1.16). Similar to Bloom, Draca, and Van Reenen (2016), who establish that import shocks have led to higher R&D and other forms of innovation in Europe, Iacovone, Pereira López, and Schiffbauer (2016) find that import competition accelerates the creative destruction process by incentivizing incumbents to pursue organizational changes that make more effective use of computer technologies (refer to chapter 4 of this report, on leading firms in Chile).

Figure 1.16 Firms start using computers to increase productivity if they are under competitive pressure

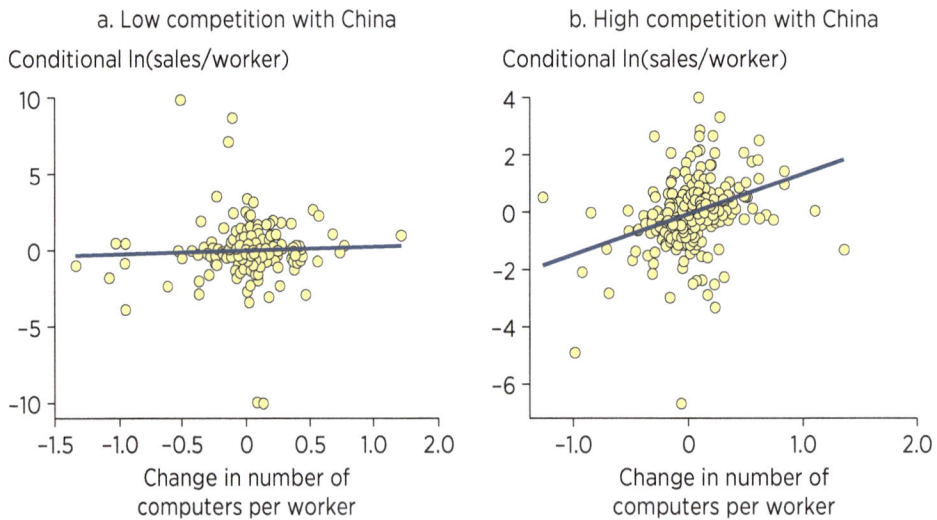

Source: Iacovone, Pereira López, and Schiffbauer 2016.

Note: The figures show the productivity benefits from the use of computers by the level of competition with China. Each dot represents a firm.

Policy and Regulatory Distortions Hamper Competition in the Region

Whereas some regulations directly aim to promote free and fair competition, others may inadvertently block competition. For instance, factor market regulation or size-dependent policies have specific social objectives but may distort incentives for firm growth. The high cost of firing employees may preclude hiring new workers, and incentives to stay small to pay lower taxes may propel firms into the informal sector (Levy 2018). This effect occurs in industrialized countries, too. The lack of competition may often be traced back to policy choices that are influenced by lobbying (Philippon 2020). Firms' political connections increase their market power and reward them with regulatory favors (Akcigit, Baslandze, and Lotti 2023).

Although some governments in the region score well on paper on competition policy, haphazard enforcement can mean that it results in little support for productivity. Both competition policy and ex ante regulation influence the environment in which firms enter, operate, and exit markets and condition their ability to innovate and grow. Some regulations encourage productivity by removing barriers to entry and exit. Others set quality standards that incentivize within-firm upgrading. Regulations may also add heavy burdens, hindering firm growth and blocking the allocation of resources to more productive uses.

Public ownership in the region also heightens anticompetitive distortions (Miralles, Dauda, and Zipitria 2021). Overall, countries in the region trail other upper-middle-income countries in the size and importance of SOEs. But state enterprises remain significant players, particularly in Argentina, Costa Rica, and Brazil (figure 1.17). Some participate in markets in which a public sector presence is rare in other parts of the world. SOEs have a marked presence in gas production, the refining of petroleum products, and other extractive industries.[12] Sectors in the region with unusual SOE participation include shipbuilding and the repair of ships, production of aircraft and spacecraft, and gambling.[13] A decomposition of the drivers of restrictiveness confirms that the governance and scope of SOEs are the most problematic drivers in the region, except in Costa Rica, where government involvement in networks is the key concern.

Figure 1.17 State enterprises remain significant players in several countries

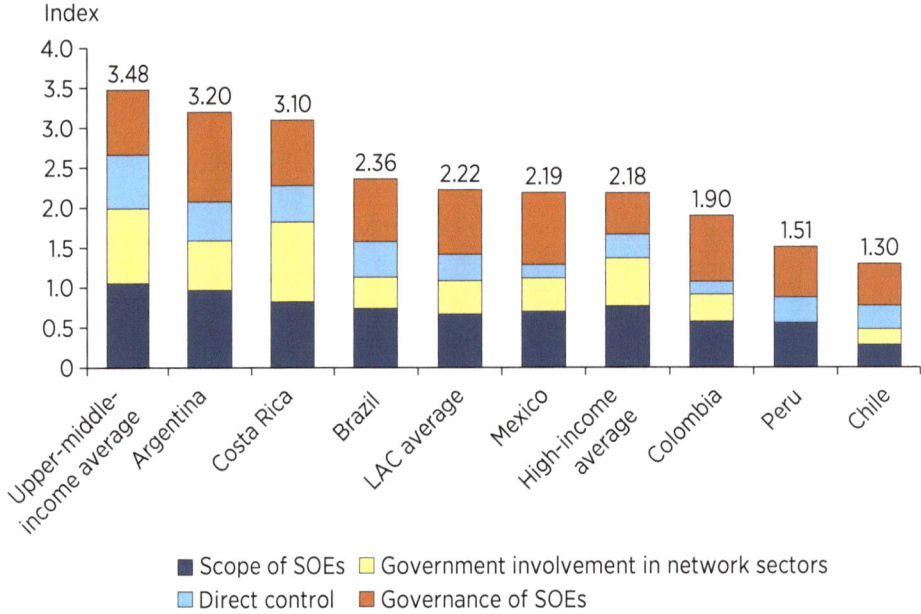

Source: OECD–World Bank Group Product Market Regulation Database (dashboard), Data Catalogue, World Bank, Washington, DC, https://prosperitydata360.worldbank .org/en/dataset/OECDWBG+PMR; PMR Indicators (Indicators of Product Market Regulation) (dashboard), OECD, Paris, https://www.oecd.org/en/topics/sub-issues /product-market-regulation.html.

Note: The figure shows the decomposition of the product market regulation index of public ownership in 2018–20. LAC = Latin America and the Caribbean; OECD = Organisation for Economic Co-operation and Development; SOEs = state-owned enterprises.

The market presence of SOEs is not as large in the region as in other middle-income regions. Nonetheless, SOEs are a concern because some operate with special advantages in markets where private initiative is available. Product market regulation data confirm that Argentina, Chile, Costa Rica, and Mexico host SOEs that are not incorporated as limited liability firms. Some of these SOEs are not subject to private law except in Costa Rica. Many SOEs deliver both commercial and noncommercial services, but only Mexican SOEs in selected sectors are required to separate their commercial and noncommercial activities. This separation is critical to identifying and separating the costs and revenues of commercial and noncommercial activities. Limited regulatory neutrality affects Argentina, Brazil, and Mexico, in which SOEs are exempted from the application of certain regulations applicable to private sector operators. Meanwhile, SOEs in Costa Rica benefit from exemptions in the application of the Competition Law.[14] Moreover, except in Brazil and Peru, SOEs in the region have access to financing at better terms than the private sector. In Argentina, Colombia, and Costa Rica, SOEs also have access to other privileges.[15]

Figure 1.18 Rules that protect vested interests restrict competition the most

Index

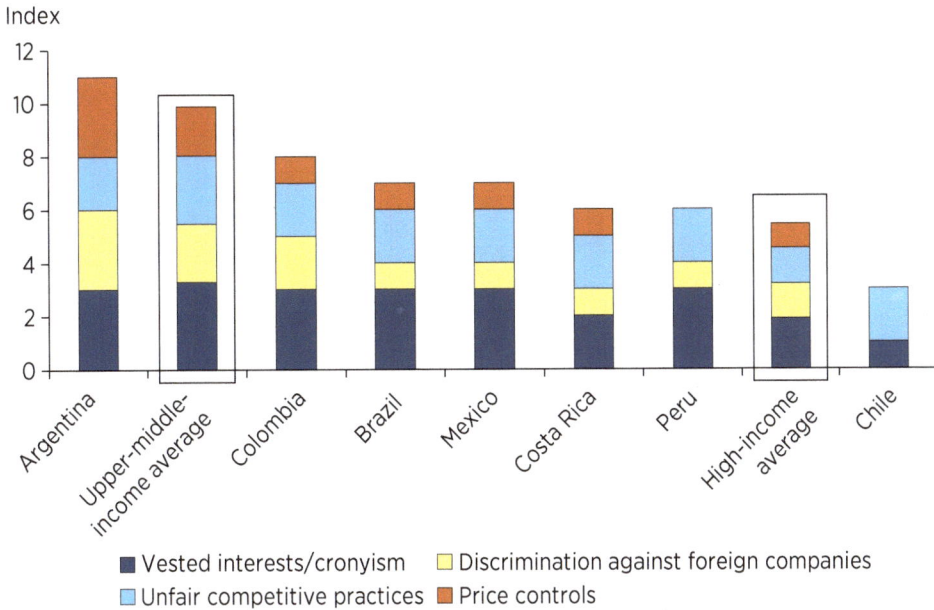

Source: Miralles, Dauda, and Zipitria 2021; calculations based on data from the EIU Risk Tracker, January 2021.

Note: The figure shows the perceived business risks in 2018–20. The EIU Risk Tracker is a perception indicator. The graph shows an aggregation of four indicators, each scored on a scale from 0 (very little risk) to 4 (very high risk). EIU = Economist Intelligence Unit.

A common impediment to growth in the region is rules that protect vested interests and thereby raise barriers to market entry (figure 1.18). Restrictive regulations on network activity, such as in information and communication technology, transportation, and energy, create bottlenecks that hamper the rest of the economy. Formal regulatory barriers to trade and investment add to the distortions (box 1.3). Although regulations restricting competition also exist in the high-income countries of the OECD, the regulations in the region are almost twice as restrictive as the regulations among the top performers in the OECD (figure 1.19) (Arnold, Nicoletti, and Scarpetta 2008; Nicoletti and Scarpetta 2003).

Figure 1.19 Regulations are much more restrictive of competition in LAC countries than in OECD countries

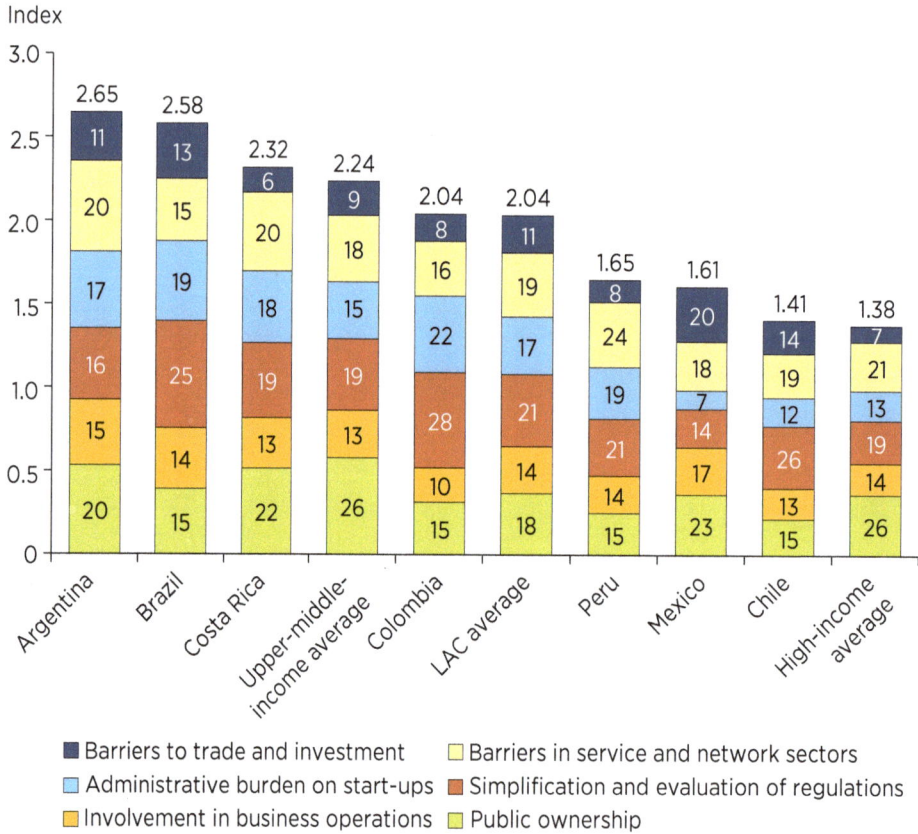

Sources: Miralles, Dauda, and Zipitria 2021; OECD–World Bank Group Product Market Regulation Database (dashboard), Data Catalogue, World Bank, Washington, DC, https://prosperitydata360.worldbank.org/en/dataset/OECDWBG+PMR; PMR Indicators (Indicators of Product Market Regulation) (dashboard), OECD, Paris, https://www.oecd.org/en/topics/sub-issues/product-market-regulation.html.

Note: Data cover the years 2018–20. Higher product market regulation index values are more restrictive on competition. LAC = Latin America and the Caribbean; OECD = Organisation for Economic Co-operation and Development.

Box 1.3

How competition-related distortions undermine productivity growth in the region

Caliendo, Parro, and Tsyvinski (2022) find that, relative to external frictions that affect transactions across countries, domestic distortions that affect transactions across sectors within a country have a much larger impact on gross domestic product (figure B1.3.1). This is because inputs in the market have a vital impact on growth. Both the intensity and the combination of inputs are important. A reduction in distortions affects the economy through input-output links, reduces prices, and leads to denser production networks. A small change in one industry may thus cause large structural shifts in many other industries.

Figure B1.3.1   Elasticity of GDP to domestic versus external distortions, Dominican Republic, 2016

GDP elasticity

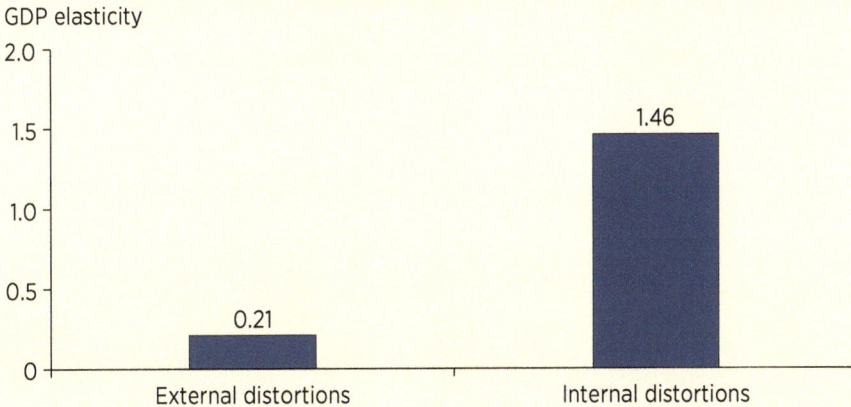

Source: Parro and Zentner 2019.
Note: GDP = gross domestic product.

Such intermediate input dynamic effects highlight the importance of the focus on core industries, as discussed by Acemoglu and Azar (2020), Baqaee and Farhi (2020), and Jones (2011). There is ample evidence of this effect. New input combinations in the production process account for 40–64 percent of average total factor productivity (TFP) growth in the United States. A 1 percent reduction in distortions in the telecommunications

box continued next page

Box 1.3

How competition-related distortions undermine productivity growth in the region *(continued)*

sector in the Dominican Republic may increase gross domestic product by 0.21 percent (figure B1.3.2). In Mexico, eliminating sectoral distortions would result in a 15 percent increase in value added in the agriculture sector. Eliminating labor wedges and monopolistic markups could yield an aggregate value-added increase of 7 percent in Brazil and 15 percent in Mexico. Focusing on eliminating distortions in the top 10 industries might yield output improvements of 10 percent in Mexico and 5 percent in Brazil, according to Leal (2017).

Figure B1.3.2   Elasticity of GDP to internal sectoral distortions, Dominican Republic, 2016

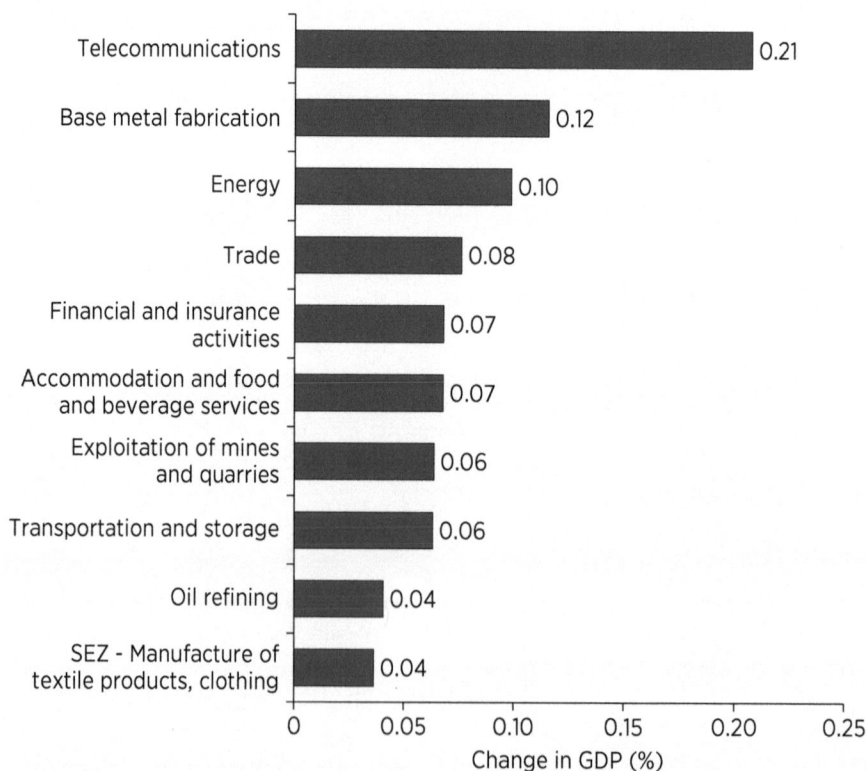

Sector	Change in GDP (%)
Telecommunications	0.21
Base metal fabrication	0.12
Energy	0.10
Trade	0.08
Financial and insurance activities	0.07
Accommodation and food and beverage services	0.07
Exploitation of mines and quarries	0.06
Transportation and storage	0.06
Oil refining	0.04
SEZ - Manufacture of textile products, clothing	0.04

Source: Parro and Zentner 2019.

Note: GDP = gross domestic product; SEZ = special economic zone.

box continued next page

Box 1.3

How competition-related distortions undermine productivity growth in the region *(continued)*

Colombia offers additional evidence of the significant growth benefits of reducing distortions. There, Eslava and Haltiwanger (2021) find that the welfare effect of eliminating dispersion in input prices and markups is twice as large as the effect of eliminating all other distortions, explaining 7 of 17 percentage points of the negative contribution of distortions to sales growth. If distortions are large in the service sector (for example, in business services), manufacturing might not receive the inputs needed for productivity growth or might receive them only at high prices. The benefits depend on market structure and the distortions in input-output links. For instance, World Bank (2015) concludes that, in Bolivia, Chile, Ecuador, and Peru, eliminating distortions in services would bring much higher overall productivity gains than removing distortions in manufacturing. Meanwhile, Fattal Jaef (2022) finds that, the elimination of competition-related distortions, such as entry barriers and idiosyncratic misallocation, may be associated with productivity benefits of up to 50 percent. The greatest benefits may be reaped in low-income countries. For example, El Salvador might increase TFP by 28 percent, while Chile and Peru could raise TFP by 18 percent (figure B1.3.3). This means that reforms supporting competition are even more important among countries such as El Salvador than they would be in most of the countries studied in this report.

box continued next page

Box 1.3

How competition-related distortions undermine productivity growth in the region *(continued)*

Figure B1.3.3 Total factor productivity gains from the removal of all distortions

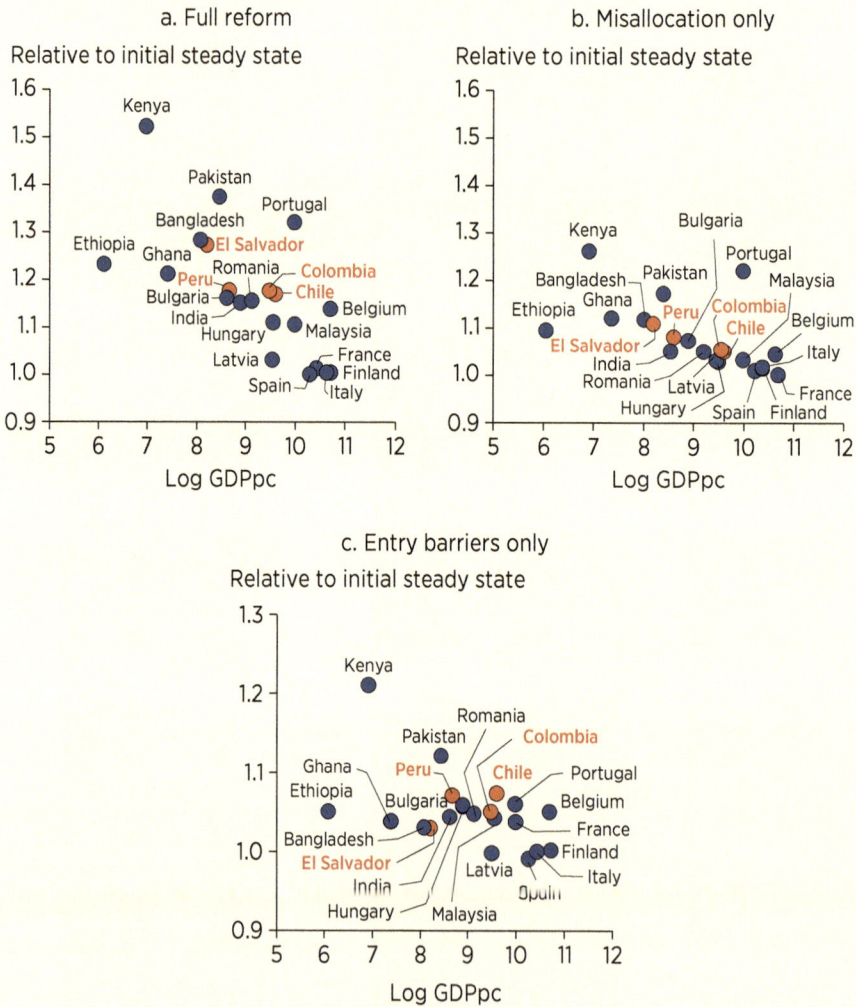

a. Full reform
Relative to initial steady state

Log GDPpc

b. Misallocation only
Relative to initial steady state

Log GDPpc

c. Entry barriers only
Relative to initial steady state

Log GDPpc

Source: Fattal Jaef 2022.

Note: Red dots denote Latin America and the Caribbean countries. The y-axis depicts the TFP without distortions as a share of the TFP in the case of distortions (100 percent). The data are from the following years: Bangladesh, 2012; Chile, 2023; Colombia, 2016; El Salvador, 2004; Ethiopia, 2011; Ghana, 2003; India, 2004–05; Kenya, 2010; Malaysia, 2015; Pakistan, 2005; Peru, 2008; and Belgium, Bulgaria, Finland, France, Hungary, Italy, Latvia, Portugal, Romania, and Spain, 2014. GDPpc = per capita gross domestic product; TFP = total factor productivity.

Source: Bhagwati 1969 and the studies cited.

Weak Enforcement of Antitrust Law

Competition authorities in some countries in the region have become more autonomous and now operate as specialized bodies with strengthened sanctioning capacity. However, in many countries, these agencies have tended to remain small and underresourced for the huge job they face (figures 1.20 and 1.21). International best practice has yet to be adopted fully across the region. Mexico recognized competition principles in its 1917 Constitution and adopted an antimonopoly law in 1934, but authorities there operated without sufficient funding until 1993, when an independent body was established to investigate anticompetitive behavior. Overall, reforms of competition law have lagged behind other reform programs, such as macro stabilization. Although detecting and punishing violations of competition law are difficult and resource consuming, the potential benefits are large.

Overall, entry barriers are associated with a reduced number of firms in an economy, larger average firm size, and lower average productivity. Idiosyncratic distortions are closely linked to competition (refer to chapter 2 of this report). Their effects interact with the effects of entry barriers. If an entry barrier occurs in an economy with already substantial idiosyncratic distortions, the average starting size of a firm is smaller than in an economy that lacks these distortions.

Figure 1.20   Competition authorities are understaffed

Number of staff per 1 million population

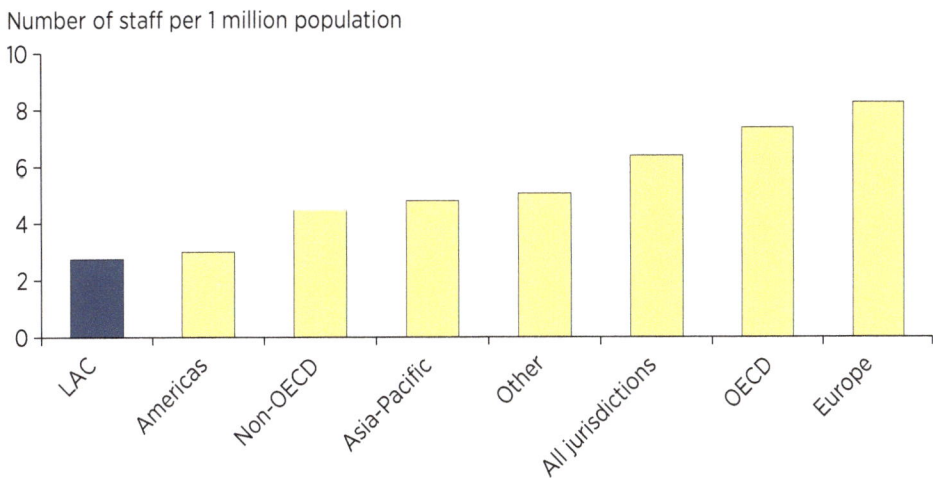

Source: Araujo and Meester 2023 based on OECD 2020.

Note: The figure shows the number of competition authority staff per 1 million population in 2015–19. Regions are named following the original data source. LAC = Latin America and the Caribbean; OECD = Organisation for Economic Co-operation and Development.

Figure 1.21   Competition authorities are underbudgeted

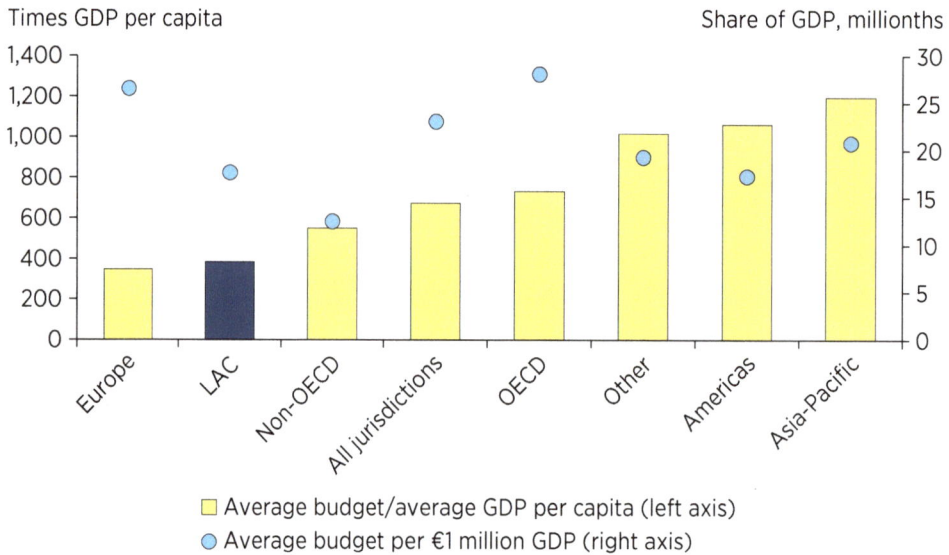

Source: Araujo and Meester 2023 based on OECD 2020.

Note: The figure shows the average 2015 competition authority budget by region, expressed in GDP per capita terms (left axis) and in euros per 1 million euros of GDP. Regions are named following the original data source. GDP = gross domestic product; LAC = Latin America and the Caribbean; OECD = Organisation for Economic Co-operation and Development.

Conclusion: The Region Has Been Plagued by Pervasive Barriers to Competition

The stylized facts presented in this chapter reveal a landscape of weak competitive pressures reflected in low entry rates, historically high markups, significant barriers to expansion, and low effort on innovation. The region also exhibits many policy and regulatory barriers to competition, including restrictive product market regulations, weak enforcement of antitrust law, and limited capacity among competition authorities. These barriers to competition dampen the creative destruction process, contributing to stagnant productivity growth in most of the region. They also restrain factor reallocation toward the most productive firms and sectors, and impede innovation and quality upgrading, which are at the core of productivity growth (box 1.4).

Box 1.4

Innovation and quality upgrading

The characteristics of an incumbent firm matter if competitive pressures increase. Whether an incumbent firm can survive competition depends on its capacity to innovate or upgrade quality to provide markets with better products. However, the steps a firm takes to innovate differ by the firm's development level or the economy and market conditions. At the early stages of development, innovation mostly involves improving internal operations or processes, followed by the adoption of existing technologies new to the firm. Only at the late stages of progress toward upper-middle-income status of the economy do firms begin to create new knowledge, which is reflected in the rise of international patents.

Verhoogen (2021) summarizes the process of upgrading undertaken by a firm as follows: (1) *learning*, defined as an accumulation of capabilities; (2) *quality upgrading*, defined as the output-weighted average quality of the goods produced; (3) *technology adoption*, defined as the adoption of a technique not previously used; and (4) *innovation*, defined as product expansion or the production of a good not previously produced. Although each of these may occur simultaneously, they are distinct. As Verhoogen (2021) suggests, a firm may be able to achieve quality upgrading without increasing learning. He proposes that upgrading is not optimal if the costs outweigh the benefits. It is dependent on the output demand and input supply facing the firm.

A key concept in upgrading is a firm's ability to adjust. Firms that are unable to adjust to competition lose profits and may eventually exit the market. A working assumption is that firms have a profit-maximizing objective function; in cases in which firms do not maximize profit, the various constraints in input and output markets encountered by firms need to be understood. The ability to adjust (or entrepreneurial ability) is often linked to managerial skill and focus, and agency issues or organizational matters. More effective management is correlated with higher productivity and adequate rewards for workers for innovation and technology adoption. Another important characteristic is the learning process both within and across firms. Learning may occur if knowledge is shared among employees and firms through learning by doing and because of the mobility of workers among firms.

box continued next page

Box 1.4

Innovation and quality upgrading *(continued)*

The growth response to competitive pressure depends on where upgrading takes place. Innovations in input markets may lower the cost of intermediate inputs for output products and generate higher markups for output firms without necessarily fostering greater productivity in output markets (that is, there is little benefit for the consumer). Some evidence suggests that upgrading may have counterintuitive results in productivity and competition if the intangibles become more important. De Ridder (2024) shows that intangibles, such as information technology, reduce marginal costs but raise fixed costs, thereby giving firms with low adoption costs a competitive edge (because of scale effects). This advantage deters entry, reduces incentives to perform quality upgrades, and, in essence, raises the market power of some while reducing market dynamism through, for example, declining worker reallocation and entry rates. This result seems to be consistent with the superstar hypothesis of Autor et al. (2020), whereby globalization and technological change propel the sales of the most productive firms.

Low-productivity firms, or laggards, may not survive competition. Leaders, or high-productivity firms, may survive competition because they are able to do so. Their size, turnover, and experience allow the latter to adapt by upgrading, which may involve upgrading quality (if the demand exists) at higher marginal costs or innovating. If incumbent firms do not survive the competition in one market, they may reallocate to another market through innovation.[a]

Sources: Aghion et al. 2004; Atkin et al. 2017; Bandiera et al. 2020; Bertrand and Schoar 2003; Blaum, Lelarge, and Peters 2019; Cai and Wang 2022; Cheng 2022; Criscuolo et al. 2021; Hardy and McCasland 2021; Irwin and Klenow 1994; Jiang et al. 2018; Kugler and Verhoogen 2012; Poole 2013; Van Biesebroeck 2005; and the studies cited.

a. Xu and Gong (2017) discuss the impact of resource allocations to research and development in the United States because of competition from China, and Cantoni, Dittmar, and Yuchtman (2018) discuss the effects of competition in religious institutions over resource reallocations.

The next chapters present empirical evidence on the ways in which policies, in both their design and implementation, can make competition more intense, creating incentives for incumbent innovation and productivity growth. Chapter 2 focuses on the elimination of local entry and expansion barriers that hamper productivity growth, and the success of the reforms that led to this outcome. Chapter 3 examines the positive impacts of the enforcement of competition laws in the region on reducing anticompetitive behavior and increasing innovation and productivity among incumbents. Chapter 4 explores international trade for examples of the importance of the distance to the frontier for innovation in an environment of competitive pressure. Chapter 5 summarizes the policy lessons and highlights the importance of the competition and innovation nexus. Chapter 6 is the conclusion.

Notes

1. This growth was led by commodity exports in 1900–36 and state-led industrialization and import substitution in 1936–37.
2. Cole et al. (2005) and Restuccia and Rogerson (2008). Innovation in this report is understood broadly and includes creating new technologies, adopting new managerial capabilities, imitating existing technologies new to a firm, or simply adjusting internal processes (box 1.1).
3. Murphy, Shleifer, and Vishny (1991) discuss the standard view.
4. The analysis in this section covers only formal sector firms.
5. The data are for 2019 and represent the total cost for five married men or women entrepreneurs to complete the procedures to incorporate and operate a business. The cost is calculated as a percentage of income per capita. Only incorporation costs are counted, which excludes value added taxes and bribes. Refer to B-Ready (Business Ready): Doing Business Legacy (dashboard), World Bank, Washington, DC, https://www.worldbank.org/en/programs/business-enabling-environment/doing -business-legacy.
6. The OECD average markup hides a much higher US markup.
7. Drawing on data from the US Census of Manufactures, Edmond, Midrigan, and Xu (2023) find that the removal of markup distortions can increase the welfare of the representative consumer by up to 25 percent. Refer to ASM (Annual Survey of Manufactures) (dashboard), US Census Bureau, US Department of Commerce, Suitland, MD, https://www.census.gov/programs-surveys/asm.html.
8. Also known as zombies, these low-productivity firms would otherwise have exited (Stein and Tommasi 2008). Andrews, Adalet McGowan, and Millot (2017) discuss the survival of zombies and ways that restructuring policies may heighten productivity.
9. This average reflects the per country average, averaged across years (World Bank 2021).
10. Refer also to Economic Censuses 2019 (dashboard), Instituto Nacional de Estadistica y Geografia (National Institute of Statistics and Geography Mexico), Aguascalientes, Mexico, https://en.www.inegi.org.mx/programas/ce/2019/.
11. Firms are old if they were created more than 10 years ago. Crespi, Fernández-Arias, and Stein (2014) define dynamic young firms as those that were founded based on new products, have created more employment since their foundation than the median firm in the country, or sell their production in foreign markets.

12. State participation in gas production in the region includes YPF in Argentina (51.0 percent state ownership), Empresa Nacional de Petróleo in Chile (full state ownership), Ecopetrol SA in Colombia (88.5 percent state ownership), Petrobras in Brazil (50.3 percent state ownership), and PEMEX (an SOE) in Mexico. Petroperú in Peru and RECOPE in Costa Rica, both fully owned by the state, manufacture refined petroleum products.

13. Shipping: EMGEPRON in Brazil, Astilleros y Maestranzas de la Armada in Chile, and SIMA (Servicios Industriales de la Marina) in Peru. Aircraft production: Fábrica Argentina de Aviones "Brig. San Martín" SA in Argentina, Embraer in Brazil, and Empresa Nacional de Aeronáutica de Chile in Chile. Gambling: Casino de Mar del Plata in Argentina, Caixa Econômica Federal in Brazil, Polla Chilena de Beneficencia in Chile, Junta de Protección Social in Costa Rica, and Lotería Nacional para la Asistencia Pública in Mexico.

14. The exemptions were established by Law 7472, article 9, 1994.

15. Other favorable treatment includes the granting of specific economic advantages over competing private firms, such as (1) direct financial subsidies, (2) debt write-offs, (3) a more favorable tax regime, (4) exemptions from certain taxes, and (5) eligibility for benefits in-kind, such as land use or rights of way at a price below the price available to private sector competitors in like circumstances.

References

Acemoglu, Daron, and Pablo D. Azar. 2020. "Endogenous Production Networks." *Econometrica* 88 (1): 33–82.

Acemoglu, Daron, and James A. Robinson. 2019. *The Narrow Corridor: States, Societies, and the Fate of Liberty*. New York: Penguin Press.

Ackerberg, Daniel A., Kevin Caves, and Garth Frazer. 2015. "Identification Properties of Recent Production Function Estimators." *Econometrica* 83 (6): 2411–51.

Aghion, Philippe, Ufuk Akcigit, and Peter Howitt. 2015. "The Schumpeterian Growth Paradigm." *Annual Review of Economics* 7: 557–75.

Aghion, Philippe, Antonin Bergeaud, Matthieu Lequien, and Marc J. Melitz. 2018. "The Impact of Exports on Innovation: Theory and Evidence." Working Paper WP 678, Banque de France, Paris.

Aghion, Philippe, Nicholas Bloom, Richard Blundell, Rachel Griffith, and Peter Howitt. 2005. "Competition and Innovation: An Inverted-U Relationship." *Quarterly Journal of Economics* 120 (2): 701–28.

Aghion, Philippe, Richard Blundell, Rachel Griffith, Peter Howett, and Susanne Prantl. 2004. "Entry and Productivity Growth: Evidence from Microlevel Panel Data." *Journal of the European Economic Association* 2 (2–3): 265–76.

Aghion, Philippe, Richard Blundell, Rachel Griffith, Peter Howitt, and Susanne Prantl. 2009. "The Effects of Entry on Incumbent Innovation and Productivity." *Review of Economics and Statistics* 91 (1): 20–32.

Aghion, Philippe, Christopher Harris, Peter Howitt, and John Vickers. 2001. "Competition, Imitation, and Growth with Step-by-Step Innovation." *Review of Economic Studies* 68 (3): 467–92.

Aghion, Philippe, and Peter Howitt. 1990. "A Model of Growth through Creative Destruction." NBER Working Paper 3223, National Bureau of Economic Research, Cambridge, MA. http://www.nber.org/papers/w3223.

Akcigit, Ufuk, Salomé Baslandze, and Francesca Lotti. 2023. "Connecting to Power: Political Connections, Innovation, and Firm Dynamics." *Econometrica* 91 (2): 529–64.

Akcigit, Ufuk, Wenjie Chen, Federico J. Díez, Romain Duval, Philipp Engler, Jiayue Fan, Chiara Maggi, Marina Mendes Tavares, Daniel A. Schwarz, Ippei Shibata, and Carolina Villegas-Sánchez. 2021. "Rising Corporate Market Power: Emerging Policy Issues." IMF Staff Discussion Note SDN/21/01, International Monetary Fund, Washington, DC.

Alarco, Germán, César Castillo, and Favio Leiva. 2019. *Riqueza y Desigualdad en el Perú: Visión Panorámica*. Lima, Peru: Oxfam America. https://www.lboro.ac.uk/media /wwwlboroacuk/content/library/downloads/advicesheets/Chicago%20notes%20 and%20bibliography%20(footnotes)%20style.pdf.

Andrews, Dan, Müge Adalet McGowan, and Valentine Millot. 2017. "Confronting the Zombies: Policies for Productivity Revival." OECD Economic Policy Paper 21, Organisation for Economic Co-operation and Development, Paris.

Araujo, Sonia, and Wouter Meester. 2023. *Competition Authorities in LAC: Resources and Activity. An International Benchmark*. Washington, DC: World Bank and Organisation for Economic Co-operation and Development.

Arnold, Jens Matthias, Giuseppe Nicoletti, and Stefano Scarpetta. 2008. "Regulation, Allocative Efficiency, and Productivity in OECD Countries: Industry and Firm-Level Evidence." OECD Economics Department Working Paper 616, Organisation for Economic Co-operation and Development, Paris. https://doi.org/10.1787 /241447806226.

Arrow, Kenneth J. 1962. "The Economic Implications of Learning by Doing." *Review of Economic Studies* 29 (3): 155–73.

Atkin, David Guy, Azam Chaudhry, Shamyla Chaudry, Amit K. Khandelwal, and Eric A. Verhoogen. 2017. "Organizational Barriers to Technology Adoption: Evidence from Soccer-Ball Producers in Pakistan." *Quarterly Journal of Economics* 132 (3): 1101–64.

Audretsch, David B., Marian Hafenstein, Alexander S. Kritikos, and Alexander Schiersch. 2018. "Firm Size and Innovation in the Service Sector." IZA Discussion Paper DP 12035, Institute of Labor Economics, Bonn, Germany.

Autor, David H., David Dorn, Lawrence F. Katz, Christina Patterson, and John Michael Van Reenen. 2020. "The Fall of the Labor Share and the Rise of Superstar Firms." *Quarterly Journal of Economics* 135 (2): 645–709.

Ayyagari, Meghana, Asli Demirgüç-Kunt, and Vojislav Maksimovic. 2014. "Who Creates Jobs in Developing Countries?" *Small Business Economics* 43 (1): 75–99.

Backus, Matthew. 2020. "Why Is Productivity Correlated with Competition?" *Econometrica* 88 (6): 2415–44.

Bandiera, Oriana, Andrea Prat, Stephen Hansen, and Raffaella Sadun. 2020. "CEO Behavior and Firm Performance." *Journal of Political Economy* 128 (4): 1325–69.

Baqaee, David Rezza, and Emmanuel Farhi. 2020. "Productivity and Misallocation in General Equilibrium." *Quarterly Journal of Economics* 135 (1): 105–63.

Begazo, Gomez, Priscilla Tania, Tanja K. Goodwin, Mesa Gramegna, and Fatima Soulange. 2018. "Promoting Open and Competitive Markets in Road Freight and Logistics Services: The World Bank Group's Markets and Competition Policy Assessment Tool Applied in Peru, the Philippines, and Vietnam." Working Paper, World Bank, Washington, DC.

Bertrand, Marianne, and Antoinette Schoar. 2003. "Managing with Style: The Effect of Managers on Firm Policies." *Quarterly Journal of Economics* 118 (4): 1169–208.

Bhagwati, Jagdish N. 1969. "The Generalized Theory of Distortions and Welfare." Department of Economics Working Paper 39, Massachusetts Institute of Technology, Cambridge, MA.

Blaum, Joaquin, Claire Lelarge, and Michael Peters. 2019. "Firm Size, Quality Bias, and Import Demand." *Journal of International Economics* 120: 59–83.

Bloom, Nicholas, Mirko Draca, and John Michael Van Reenen. 2016. "Trade Induced Technical Change? The Impact of Chinese Imports on Innovation, IT, and Productivity." *Review of Economic Studies* 83 (1): 87–117.

Bloom, Nicholas, and John Michael Van Reenen. 2010. "Why Do Management Practices Differ across Firms and Countries?" *Journal of Economic Perspectives* 24 (1): 203–24.

Bresler, Tomas. 2021. "How Mercadolibre Became the Biggest Company in Latin America." *Assignment: Platform Variety* (blog), March 3, 2021. https://d3.harvard.edu/platform -digit/submission/how-mercadolibre-became-the-biggest-company-in-latin-america/.

Bridgman, Benjamin, Shi Qi, and James A. Schmitz, Jr. 2009. "The Economic Performance of Cartels: Evidence from the New Deal U.S. Sugar Manufacturing Cartel 1934–74." Research Department Staff Report 437, Federal Reserve Bank of Minneapolis, Minneapolis, MN.

Cai, Jing, and Shing-Yi Wang. 2022. "Improving Management through Worker Evaluations: Evidence from Auto Manufacturing." *Quarterly Journal of Economics* 137 (4): 2459–97.

Caliendo, Lorenzo, Fernando Parro, and Aleh Tsyvinski. 2022. "Distortions and the Structure of the World Economy." *American Economic Journal: Macroeconomics* 14 (4): 274–308.

Campos, Nicolás, Eduardo Engel, Ronald D. Fischer, and Alexander Galetovic. 2021. "The Ways of Corruption in Infrastructure: Lessons from the Odebrecht Case." *Journal of Economic Perspectives* 35 (2): 171–90.

Cantoni, Davide, Jeremiah Dittmar, and Noam Yuchtman. 2018. "Religious Competition and Reallocation: The Political Economy of Secularization in the Protestant Reformation." *Quarterly Journal of Economics* 133 (4): 2037–96.

Cheng, Thomas K. 2022. *Competition and Innovation Policy Nexus in Developing Countries.* Washington, DC: World Bank.

Cirera, Xavier, and William F. Maloney. 2017. *The Innovation Paradox: Developing-Country Capabilities and the Unrealized Promise of Technological Catch-Up.* Washington, DC: World Bank.

Cole, Harold L., Lee E. Ohanian, Alvaro Riascos, and James A. Schmitz, Jr. 2005. "Latin America in the Rearview Mirror." *Journal of Monetary Economics* 52 (1): 69–107.

Connor, John M. 2020. "Private International Cartels (PIC) Full Data 2019 Edition." Version 2.0, Purdue University Research Repository, West Lafayette, IN. https://purr.purdue .edu/publications/2732/2.

Crespi, Gustavo A., Eduardo Fernández-Arias, and Ernesto Stein, eds. 2014. *Rethinking Productive Development: Sound Policies and Institutions for Economic Transformation.* New York: Palgrave Macmillan.

Crespi, Gustavo A., Charlotte Guillard, Mónica Salazar, and Fernando Vargas. 2022. "Harmonized Latin American Innovation Surveys Database (LAIS): Firm-Level Microdata for the Study of Innovation." IDB Technical Note IDB-TN-2418, Competitiveness, Technology, and Innovation Division, Inter-American Development Bank, Washington, DC. https://publications.iadb.org/en/harmonized-latin-american -innovation-surveys-database-lais-firm-level-microdata-study-innovation-0.

Criscuolo, Chiara, Peter Gal, Timo Leidecker, and Giuseppe Nicoletti. 2021. "The Human Side of Productivity: Uncovering the Role of Skills and Diversity for Firm Productivity." OECD Productivity Working Paper 29, Organisation for Economic Co-operation and Development, Paris.

Cusolito, Ana Paula, and William F. Maloney. 2018. *Productivity Revisited: Shifting Paradigms in Analysis and Policy.* Washington, DC: World Bank.

De Loecker, Jan K., and Jan Eeckhout. 2018. "Global Market Power." NBER Working Paper 24768, National Bureau of Economic Research, Cambridge, MA.

De Ridder, Maarten. 2024. "Market Power and Innovation in the Intangible Economy." *American Economic Review* 114 (1): 199–251.

Ding, Chengri, and Yi Niu. 2019. "Market Size, Competition, and Firm Productivity for Manufacturing in China." *Regional Science and Urban Economics* 74: 81–98.

Edmond, Chris, Virgiliu Midrigan, and Daniel Yi Xu. 2023. "How Costly Are Markups?" *Journal of Political Economy* 131 (7): 1619–75.

Egan, Patrick J. W. 2010. "Hard Bargains: The Impact of Multinational Corporations on Economic Reform in Latin America." *Latin American Politics and Society* 52 (1): 1–32.

Eslava, Marcela. 2018. "Anatomy of Productivity in Latin America." In *RED 2018, Institutions for Productivity: Towards a Better Business Environment*, edited by Development Bank of Latin America, 51–92. Report on Economic Development 1410. Bogotá, Colombia: Development Bank of Latin America.

Eslava, Marcela, and John C. Haltiwanger. 2021. "The Life-Cycle Growth of Plants: The Role of Productivity, Demand, and Wedges." NBER Working Paper 27184 rev., National Bureau of Economic Research, Cambridge, MA.

Eslava, Marcela, John C. Haltiwanger, and Álvaro Pinzón. 2019. "Job Creation in Colombia vs the U.S.: 'Up or Out Dynamics' Meets 'the Life Cycle of Plants.'" NBER Working Paper 25550, National Bureau of Economic Research, Cambridge, MA.

Eslava, Marcela, Marcela Meléndez, Laura Daniela Tenjo, and Nicolas Urdaneta. 2023. "Business Size, Development, and Inequality in Latin America: A Tale of One Tail." Policy Research Working Paper 10584, World Bank, Washington, DC.

Eslava, Marcela, Marcela Meléndez, and Nicolás Urdaneta. 2021. "Market Concentration, Market Fragmentation, and Inequality in Latin America." UNDP LAC Working Paper 11, Latin America and Caribbean Region, United Nations Development Programme, New York.

Faccio, Mara. 2006. "Politically Connected Firms." *American Economic Review* 96 (1): 369–86.

Fattal Jaef, Roberto N. 2022. "Formal Sector Distortions, Entry Barriers, and the Informal Economy: A Quantitative Exploration." In *Hidden Potential: Rethinking Informality in South Asia*, edited by Maurizio Bussolo and Siddarth Sharma, 41–60. South Asia Development Forum Series. Washington, DC: World Bank. https://doi.org/10.1596/978-1-4648-1834-9_ch2.

Garcia-Macia, Daniel, Chang-Tai Hsieh, and Peter J. Klenow. 2018. "How Destructive Is Innovation?" NBER Working Paper 22953, National Bureau of Economic Research, Cambridge, MA. http://www.nber.org/papers/w22953.

Gil Mena, Fiorella. 2019. "Menos del 10% de emprendimientos peruanos llegan a tener éxito, ¿cómo no ser parte del fracaso?" [Fewer Than 10% of Peruvian Ventures Are Successful: How Not to Become Involved in the Fiasco]. *Tu Dinero* (blog), January 17, 2019. https://gestion.pe/tu-dinero/10-emprendimientos-peruanos-llegan-exito-parte-fracaso-255933-noticia/?ref=gesr.

Gilbert, Richard J. 2022. *Innovation Matters: Competition Policy for the High-Technology Economy*. Cambridge, MA: MIT Press. https://mitpress.mit.edu/9780262545792/innovation-matters/.

Goñi, Edwin, and William F. Maloney. 2014. "Why Don't Poor Countries Do R&D?" Documento CEDE 2014–23, Center for Economic Development Studies, Department of Economics, Universidad de Los Andes, Bogotá, Colombia. https://repositorio.uniandes.edu.co/server/api/core/bitstreams/be35fec2-fbde-4c82-9996-51d2ee0311c5/content

Grazzi, Matteo, and Carlo Pietrobelli, eds. 2016. *Firm Innovation and Productivity in Latin America and the Caribbean: The Engine of Economic Development*. Washington, DC: Inter-American Development Bank; New York: Palgrave Macmillan. https://publications.iadb.org/publications/english/viewer/Firm-Innovation-and-Productivity-in-Latin-America-and-the-Caribbean-The-Engine-of-Economic-Development.pdf.

Gutiérrez, Germán, and Thomas Philippon. 2018. "How European Markets Became Free: A Study of Institutional Drift." NBER Working Paper 24700, National Bureau of Economic Research, Cambridge, MA.

Haltiwanger, John C., Ron S. Jarmin, and Javier Miranda. 2013. "Who Creates Jobs? Small versus Large versus Young." *Review of Economics and Statistics* 95 (2): 347–61.

Hardy, Morgan, and Jamie McCasland. 2021. "It Takes Two: Experimental Evidence on the Determinants of Technology Diffusion." *Journal of Development Economics* 149: 102600.

Hopenhayn, Hugo A. 1992. "Entry, Exit, and Firm Dynamics in Long Run Equilibrium." *Econometrica* 60 (5): 1127–50.

Hsieh, Chang-Tai, and Peter J. Klenow. 2014. "The Life Cycle of Plants in India and Mexico." *Quarterly Journal of Economics* 129 (3): 1035–84.

Iacovone, Leonardo, Mariana De La Paz Pereira López, and Marc Tobias Schiffbauer. 2016. "Competition Makes IT Better: Evidence on When Firms Use IT More Effectively." Policy Research Working Paper 7638, World Bank, Washington, DC.

Irwin, Douglas A., and Peter J. Klenow. 1994. "Learning-by-Doing Spillovers in the Semiconductor Industry." *Journal of Political Economy* 102 (6): 1200–27.

Jiang, Kun, Wolfgang Keller, Larry D. Qiu, and William Ridley. 2018. "International Joint Ventures and Internal Technology Transfer vs. External Technology Spillovers: Evidence from China." NBER Working Paper 24455, National Bureau of Economic Research, Cambridge, MA.

Jones, Charles I. 2011. "Intermediate Goods and Weak Links in the Theory of Economic Development." *American Economic Journal: Macroeconomics* 3 (2): 1–28.

Jovanovic, Boyan. 1982. "Selection and the Evolution of Industry." *Econometrica* 50 (3): 649–70.

Klapper, Leora F., and Douglas Randall. 2012. "Trends in New Firm Creation through the Crisis and into Recovery." *All About Finance* (blog), October 23, 2012. https://blogs .worldbank.org/allaboutfinance/trends-in-new-firm-creation-through-the -crisis-and-into-recovery.

Kugler, Maurice David, and Eric A. Verhoogen. 2012. "Prices, Plant Size, and Product Quality." *Review of Economic Studies* 79 (1): 307–39.

Leal, Julio. 2017. "Input-Output Linkages and Sector-Specific Distortions in the Latin American Development Problem." CAF Working Paper 2017/24, Development Bank of Latin America, Caracas, República Bolivariana de Venezuela. https://scioteca.caf.com /bitstream/handle/123456789/1113/Leal_nov2017.pdf?sequence=1&isAllowed=y.

Lederman, Daniel, Julián Messina, Samuel Pienknagura, and Jamele Rigolini. 2014. *Latin American Entrepreneurs: Many Firms but Little Innovation*. World Bank Latin American and Caribbean Studies Series. Washington, DC: World Bank.

Levenstein, Margaret C., and Valerie Y. Suslow. 2006. "What Determines Cartel Success?" *Journal of Economic Literature* 44 (1): 43–95.

Levy, Santiago. 2018. *Under-Rewarded Efforts: The Elusive Quest for Prosperity in Mexico.* Washington, DC: Inter-American Development Bank.

Licetti, Martha Martínez, and Tanya K. Goodwin. 2015. "Bad News for Cartels, Good News for the Poor in Latin America." *Private Sector Development Blog*, October 23, 2015. https://blogs.worldbank.org/en/psd/bad-news-cartels-good-news-poor-latin -america-0#:~:text=An%20enginee.

Maloney, William F., and Andrés Zambrano. 2022. "Learning to Learn: Experimentation, Entrepreneurial Capital, and Development." Documento CEDE 2, Center for Economic Development Studies, Department of Economics, Universidad de Los Andes, Bogotá, Colombia.

Melitz, Marc J., and Saso Polanec. 2015. "Dynamic Olley-Pakes Productivity Decomposition with Entry and Exit." *RAND Journal of Economics* 46 (2): 362–75.

Miralles, Graciela, Seidu Dauda, and Leandro Zipitria. 2021. *Barriers to Competition in Product Market Regulation: New Insights on Latin American Countries*. Washington, DC: World Bank.

Murphy, Kevin M., Andrei Shleifer, and Robert W. Vishny. 1991. "The Allocation of Talent: Implications for Growth." *Quarterly Journal of Economics* 106 (2): 503–30.

Nickell, Stephen J. 1996. "Competition and Corporate Performance." *Journal of Political Economy* 104 (4): 724–46.

Nicoletti, Giuseppe, and Stefano Scarpetta. 2003. "Regulation, Productivity, and Growth: OECD Evidence." *Economic Policy* 18 (36): 9–72.

OECD (Organisation for Economic Co-operation and Development). 2012. *OECD Review of Telecommunication Policy and Regulation in Mexico*. Paris: OECD.

OECD (Organisation for Economic Co-operation and Development). 2014. *Factsheet on How Competition Policy Affects Macro-Economic Outcomes*. Paris: OECD.

OECD (Organisation for Economic Co-operation and Development). 2017. *Business Dynamics and Productivity*. Paris: OECD.

OECD (Organisation for Economic Co-operation and Development). 2019. *Equity Market Development in Latin America: Enhancing Access to Corporate Finance*. Paris: OECD.

OECD (Organisation for Economic Co-operation and Development). 2020. *Competition Trends 2020*. Paris: OECD.

OECD (Organisation for Economic Co-operation and Development). 2021. *OECD Compendium of Productivity Indicators 2021*. Paris: OECD.

Parro, Francisco, and Joaquin Zentner. 2019. "Domestic and External Trade in the Dominican Republic: Diagnosis, Challenges, and Opportunities." Technical Note IDB-TN-01829, Inter-American Development Bank, Washington, DC.

Paus, Eva, Michael Robinson, and Fiona Tregenna. 2022. "Firm Innovation in Africa and Latin America: Heterogeneity and Country Context." *Industrial and Corporate Change* 31 (2): 338–57.

Perry, Guillermo E., William F. Maloney, Omar S. Arias, Pablo Fajnzylber, Andrew D. Mason, and Jaime Saavedra-Chanduví. 2007. *Informality: Exit and Exclusion*. World Bank Latin American and Caribbean Studies Series. Washington, DC: World Bank.

Petit, Lilian T. D., Ron G. M. Kemp, and Jarig van Sinderen. 2015. "Cartels and Productivity Growth: An Empirical Investigation of the Impact of Cartels on Productivity in the Netherlands." *Journal of Competition Law and Economics* 11 (2): 501–25.

Phelps, Edmund S. 2013. *Mass Flourishing: How Grassroots Innovation Created Jobs, Challenge, and Change*. Princeton, NJ: Princeton University Press.

Philippon, Thomas. 2019. *The Great Reversal: How America Gave Up on Free Markets*. Cambridge, MA: Belknap Press.

Philippon, Thomas. 2020. "On Fintech and Financial Inclusion." BIS Working Paper 841, Monetary and Economic Department, Bank for International Settlements, Basel, Switzerland.

Poole, Jennifer P. 2013. "Knowledge Transfers from Multinational to Domestic Firms: Evidence from Worker Mobility." *Review of Economics and Statistics* 95 (2): 393–406.

Restuccia, Diego. 2011. "The Latin American Development Problem." Working Paper 432, Department of Economics, University of Toronto, Canada. https://www.economics .utoronto.ca/workingPapers/tecipa-432.pdf.

Restuccia, Diego, and Richard Rogerson. 2008. "Policy Distortions and Aggregate Productivity with Heterogeneous Establishments." *Review of Economic Dynamics* 11 (4): 707–20.

Restuccia, Diego, and Richard Rogerson. 2017. "The Causes and Costs of Misallocation." *Journal of Economic Perspectives* 31 (3): 151–74.

Schumpeter, Joseph Alois. 1942. *Capitalism, Socialism, and Democracy*. New York: Harper and Brothers.

Schumpeter, Joseph Alois. 1947. *Capitalism, Socialism, and Democracy*. 2nd ed. New York: Harper and Brothers.

Schwab, Klaus, ed. 2019. *Insight Report: The Global Competitiveness Report 2019*. Geneva: World Economic Forum.

Smith, Adam. (1776) 1937. *An Inquiry into the Nature and Causes of the Wealth of Nations*. Book 2. Modern Library Series Reprint. New York: Random House.

Stein, Ernesto, and Mariano Tommasi, eds. 2008. *Policymaking in Latin America: How Politics Shapes Policies*. With Pablo T. Spiller and Carlos Scartascini. Cambridge, MA: David Rockefeller Center for Latin American Studies, Harvard University; Washington, DC: Inter-American Development Bank.

Stigler, George J. 1964. "A Theory of Oligopoly." *Journal of Political Economy* 72 (1): 44–61.

Syverson, Chad. 2011. "What Determines Productivity?" *Journal of Economic Literature* 49 (2): 326–65.

Tybout, James R. 2014. "The Missing Middle: Correspondence." *Journal of Economic Perspectives* 28 (4): 235–36.

Van Biesebroeck, Johannes. 2005. "Firm Size Matters: Growth and Productivity Growth in African Manufacturing." *Economic Development and Cultural Change* 53 (3): 545–83.

Van Reenen, John Michael. 2011. "Big Ideas: How Competition Improves Management and Productivity." *CentrePiece* 16 (1): 10–13.

Vargas, Fernando. 2022. "How Do Firms Innovate in Latin America? Identification of Innovation Strategies and Their Main Adoption Determinants." IDB Technical Note IDB-TN-2450, Institutions for Development Sector, Competitiveness, Technology, and Innovation Division, Inter-American Development Bank, Washington, DC. https://doi.org/10.18235/0004211.

Verhoogen, Eric A. 2021. "Firm-Level Upgrading in Developing Countries." NBER Working Paper 29461, National Bureau of Economic Research, Cambridge, MA.

World Bank. 2015. *Peru: Building on Success, Boosting Productivity for Faster Growth*. Washington, DC: World Bank. https://documents1.worldbank.org/curated/en/600921467995400041/pdf/Peru-Building-on-success-boosting-productivity-for-faster-growth.pdf.

World Bank. 2016. "Promoting Faster Growth and Poverty Alleviation through Competition." South Africa Economic Update 8, World Bank, Washington, DC.

World Bank. 2021. *Fixing Markets, Not Prices: Policy Options to Tackle Economic Cartels in Latin America and the Caribbean*. Washington, DC: World Bank.

World Bank. 2023. *The Business of the State*. Washington, DC: World Bank.

Xu, Rui, and Kaiji Gong. 2017. "Does Import Competition Induce R&D Reallocation? Evidence from the U.S." IMF Working Paper WP/17/253, International Monetary Fund, Washington, DC.

2

Removing Barriers to Entry and Expansion

Introduction

Entry barriers take many forms and differ in how they affect markets. Natural or structural barriers are entry barriers resulting from industry characteristics, such as economies of scale (when average production costs decrease as the quantity produced increases) or network effects (when the number of consumers using a product or service affects the value of the product or service among other consumers). *Strategic barriers* are barriers that incumbent firms in a market raise intentionally to deter entry and protect market share. There are also often *exogenous barriers* resulting from government policies or regulations restricting entry. Tariffs and operating licenses are examples.

This chapter first presents stylized facts and key concepts related to barriers to entry and expansion in the Latin America and the Caribbean region. Next, the chapter focuses on the impact of removing local entry barriers on productivity growth, drawing on firm-level evidence from Peru, following Schiffbauer, Sampi, and Coronado (2022). The following section describes the harmfulness of expansion barriers for existing firms. The chapter then shows that productivity gains in the information and communication technology (ICT) sector, resulting from removing entry barriers, create positive economywide spillovers. The next section discusses how regulatory improvements can lead to quality upgrades, following Arayavechkit, Jooste, and Urrutia Arrieta (2022).

Entry Barriers Harm Productivity

The ease or difficulty that firms encounter as they enter a market is a vital determinant of market competition. Entry barriers protect incumbents from the competitive forces represented by new entrants. Entry barriers reduce incumbents' incentives to innovate to escape competition or expand to a higher-quality market. The following are examples of entry barriers, by category.[1]

Endogenous or structural barriers reflect industry characteristics:

- *Economies of scale.* Under economies of scale, the per unit costs of output fall as output increases. Entry barriers can arise if the minimum efficient scale is at a large production capacity. If a firm enters with a production capacity below the minimum efficient scale, then the costs facing the entrant are larger than those facing an incumbent that has already reached scale. Thus, the larger the minimum efficient scale is relative to total industry capacity, the larger the cost for the entrant.

- *Input convertibility.* Certain types of inputs (such as capital and specific skills) cannot be easily redeployed to produce a different product or service. Tight labor markets or a shortage of skills in a geographic area imply high sunk costs that may deter entry. If a venture fails, the entrant must internalize a large cost.

- *Brand recognition and loyalty.* Consumers may be biased toward the products they already use and know. Firms may use anticompetitive practices to raise the costs of switching to new products or brands; thus, this barrier may be both endogenous and strategic.

- *Strategic barriers.* Incumbent firms in a market may intentionally raise strategic barriers to deter entry and protect market share. Some barriers may be both structural and strategic.

- *Access to distribution channels and infrastructure.* Incumbents may limit new entrants' integration with retailers or infrastructure, such as fiber optic networks and payment systems.

- *Strategic investments.* An incumbent may hinder entry by sending a misleading signal about its potential response to new entry, for example, by overinvesting in production capacity.

- *Predatory pricing and other exclusionary practices.* At the emergence of a threat of entry, a dominant incumbent may set its prices slightly below the minimum level at which entry would be attractive. Other abuses of dominance, such as selectivity in the choice of suppliers or a refusal to deal, constrain entry directly.

- *Explicit or implicit collusion agreements to raise entry barriers.* Collusion and cartel agreements may be used to establish collective predatory processes or send signals about the behavior to expect upon entry.

Exogenous or regulatory entry barriers include the following:

- *Licenses and other regulatory requirements.* Governments issue licenses to firms, permitting them to sell goods or services. Owners of proprietary technology grant licenses to firms, allowing them to use the technology. The cost and time spent obtaining a license may be a de facto entry barrier, especially for new firms. Licenses may also limit the number of market participants or otherwise directly restrict entry. Other regulatory requirements that may become barriers include standards, minimum size rules, and certain types of taxes.

- *Patents and other forms of property rights protection.* Unequal access to resources may generate a cost advantage favoring incumbents. Patents and concessions protect incumbents. High costs of access to technology are another resource entry barrier.

- *Access to factors of production.* Because of a lack of collateral or other reasons, new firms may have to pay high interest rates or may be unable to obtain credit. Lack of financing is one of the most binding constraints on firm growth, especially among small firms, and is often cited as a reason for the missing middle problem in developing countries.[2] Other de facto barriers may arise because of difficulties in hiring workers or obtaining inputs.

- *Market signals.* These can also be distorted in the presence of connected firms that receive preferential treatment from the government, new legislation, or internal changes in firms that may affect an industry.

These types of barriers may impede the entry of new firms and incumbents seeking to expand into new markets. The chapter also considers the effects of *barriers to expansion.*

Public ownership may also act as an entry barrier. New evidence from the World Bank's *Business of the State* global report indicates that doubling the government's market share in a given sector reduces entry by 5–30 percent and increases market concentration (World Bank 2023). The impact of public ownership on the countries in the region examined in this report seems to be more pronounced than its impact on other upper-middle-income countries (figure 2.1).

Improving market contestability by removing entry barriers may generate significant productivity gains. For example, dismantling the entry barriers erected by the sugar cartel in the United States increased the productivity of the affected firms by 35 percent relative to that of unaffected firms (McGowan 2014). In a cross-country analysis of 153 countries, Barseghyan (2008) finds that a rise in entry costs of 80 percent of income per capita reduced total factor productivity by 22 percent.

Figure 2.1   Doubling the state's share: The associated decline in entry or rise in concentration, selected countries

Estimated effect

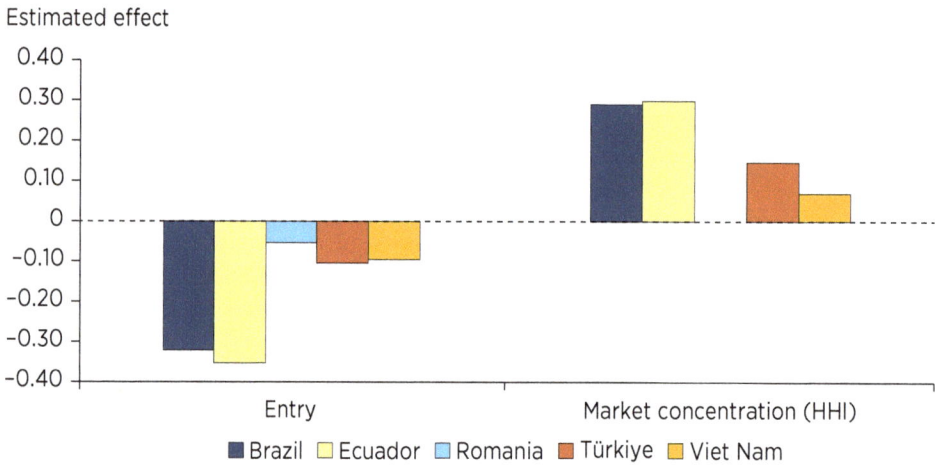

Source: World Bank 2023 based on country data and the World Bank Business of the State Database.

Note: The figure shows the coefficients from regressions at the two-digit sector level, controlling for sector size in the economy, the average age and size of firms in the sector, and sector and year dummies. Entry is based on the rate of entry of new firms in Romania and Türkiye and the share of revenues of young firms (younger than 5 years) in Brazil, Ecuador, and Viet Nam. All are statistically significant effects.

Incumbent innovation is important because it can help to advance firms to higher-quality markets. Removing barriers to expansion allows firms to move upward to escape competition, and it facilitates technology diffusion and generates direct productivity gains (Comin and Hobijn 2009). If they are allowed to persist, barriers to expansion heighten the effects of entry barriers and are more harmful because they hold back firms that have the capability to innovate (Aghion et al. 2009).

Empirical evidence on the economic costs of entry barriers in the region is limited. However, several global empirical studies suggest that they may be substantial. Fattal Jaef (2022) builds and calibrates a simple model to demonstrate the productivity gains derived from the elimination of input-output distortions. Eliminating the distortions created by entry barriers may raise aggregate productivity by up to 20 percent in the least developed economies. Similar effects have been documented in developed countries.

For instance, new barriers soon appeared when the Bersani Law of 1998 in Italy delegated entry regulations in the retail market to local municipalities, which led to an 8 percent increase in price margins and a 3 percent reduction in productivity among incumbent firms (Schivardi and Viviano 2011).

There may also be an interaction between entry and quality. For example, an analysis of a massive reform in Portugal showed that, after the simplification of entry, new entrants were less capable and productive than the industry average and were less likely to survive. Because of their greater capacity, large, more productive firms were not affected by the original entry barriers (Branstetter et al. 2010). This chapter looks into this pattern in a case study of Peru's ICT sector.

Ending Local Barriers to Entry Fuels Productivity Growth

Few studies estimate the link between productivity and greater competition after the removal of exogenous entry barriers in Latin America and the Caribbean. A critical exception is a study by Schiffbauer, Sampi, and Coronado (2022), who offer a pioneering analysis of a reform to address local sector-specific barriers to firm entry in Peru. The country's national competition agency, the National Institute for the Defense of Competition and the Protection of Intellectual Property (Indecopi), spearheaded the reform in 2013.[3] The authors show that giving a national competition authority a mandate to remove bureaucratic barriers or to oversee the implementation of local regulations may generate substantial benefits for a country's overall economic performance.

Business-related functions, such as issuing operating permits, defining local technical standards, and conducting inspections, have been decentralized to local public officials in Peru since 2013. As a result, each of the country's more than 1,800 municipalities has evolved its own code of business regulations, the Texto Unico de Procedimientos Administrativos. In principle, all the procedures in the codes are aligned with national legislation. In practice, this alignment has often been ignored. Licetti et al. (2015) estimate that in 2013 almost a third of the municipalities did not comply with the national legal framework for issuing operating licenses to firms. Several municipalities refused to issue licenses or construction permits to new firms. The municipality of Chilca, for example, refused, without providing a reason, even to receive the applications of certain firms seeking permits for the construction of a new building. All over the country, would-be entrants faced significant barriers. In Lima, for example, more than half of the time and costs of opening a business were consumed in overcoming barriers, such as the licensing and technical requirements imposed by municipalities (figure 2.2).

The government of Peru undertook a reform of Indecopi's mandate in 2013. For the first time, the agency obtained broad powers to dismantle local, sector-specific regulatory barriers to entry. Under the new framework, sanctions were imposed on municipalities that set up several common barriers, such as requiring additional local procedures before issuing a license. Indecopi was also allowed to perform ex officio investigations, publicly declare a local regulation illegal, and initiate a fast-track sanctioning procedure, including against individual local officials. As a result, the number of rulings against entry barriers in municipalities rose dramatically after 2013. Backed by fines that had increased by 400 percent, Indecopi swept away local regulatory barriers through direct enforcement or preemptive actions by local governments. Mayors and other officials faced personal fines that were as high as the equivalent of US$27,500. Municipalities thus had strong incentives to remove regulations that had been declared illegal.

Figure 2.2   Local regulatory barriers are still high in Peru

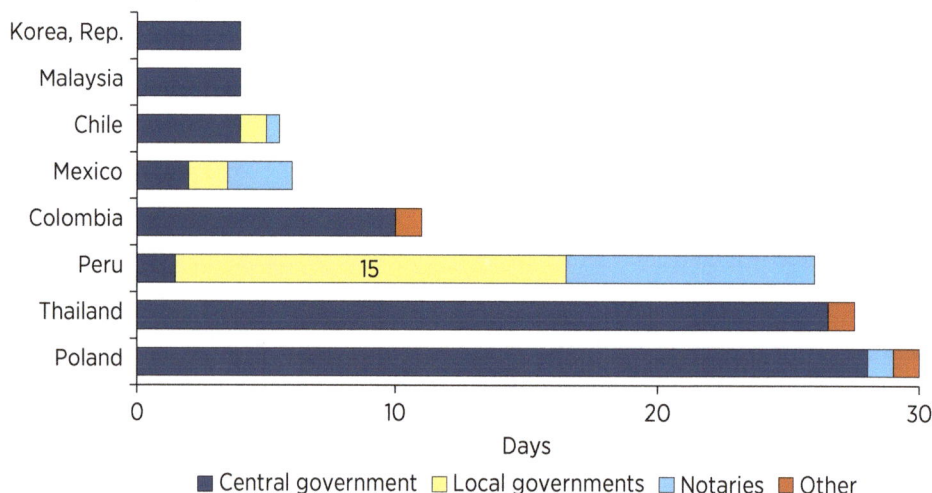

Source: B-Ready (Business Ready): Doing Business Legacy (dashboard), World Bank, Washington, DC, https://www.worldbank.org/en/programs/business-enabling -environment/doing-business-legacy.

Note: The figure shows the number of days required to start a business by source of legal requirement in 2016.

The change in Indecopi's mandate was akin to a quasi-natural experiment, allowing quantification of the impact of more intense competition on firm productivity. Aiding this analysis was the fact that decisions by the competition authority to remove barriers to entry were independent of both local market conditions and the sector or firm characteristics of the affected municipalities. Map 2.1 shows the provinces for which firm-level data are available (panel a) and the provinces where bureaucratic barriers, classified as licensing, technical requirements, or entry fees, were eliminated (panel b).

Map 2.1   Elimination of entry barriers in Peru, by province, 2013–14

a. Formal firm-level data are available   b. Local entry barriers were eliminated

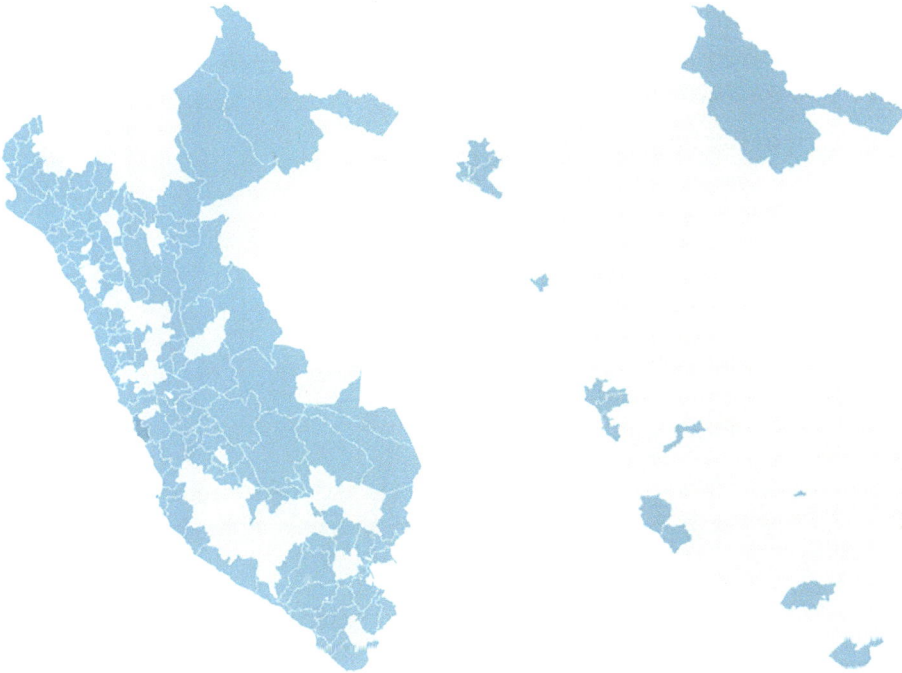

Sources: Based on data from the National Institute of Statistics and Informatics; National Institute for the Defense of Competition and the Protection of Intellectual Property.

Note: Peru consists of 26 first-level territorial units, 196 provinces, and more than 1,800 municipalities or districts. Panel a shows in blue the provinces with firm-level information available. Provinces without formal firm data lack major settlements and are in the Amazon Region in the northwest and the regions on the Andean Plateau in the center. Panel b shows in blue the provinces with formal firm-level data that also host municipalities that eliminated barriers to local market entry. Note that within each of these provinces, some municipalities eliminated local entry barriers while others did not.

The elimination of entry barriers was followed by a strong increase in firm productivity (figure 2.3). Firms operating in municipalities and sectors in which entry barriers were eliminated experienced a roughly 11 percent increase in revenue-based total factor productivity (TFPR). However, markups did not decline relative to comparable, same-sector firms that were not located in the reform municipalities. TFPR may rise because of increases in physical productivity or increases in the firm-specific prices associated with higher local product quality (which raises markups and offsets the decline in markups linked to lower local rents in sectors in reform municipalities). Therefore, the results suggest that physical (output-based) total factor productivity (TFPQ) also improved.

Figure 2.3   Competition policy reform reduced entry barriers and boosted productivity in Peru

Impact on firm productivity

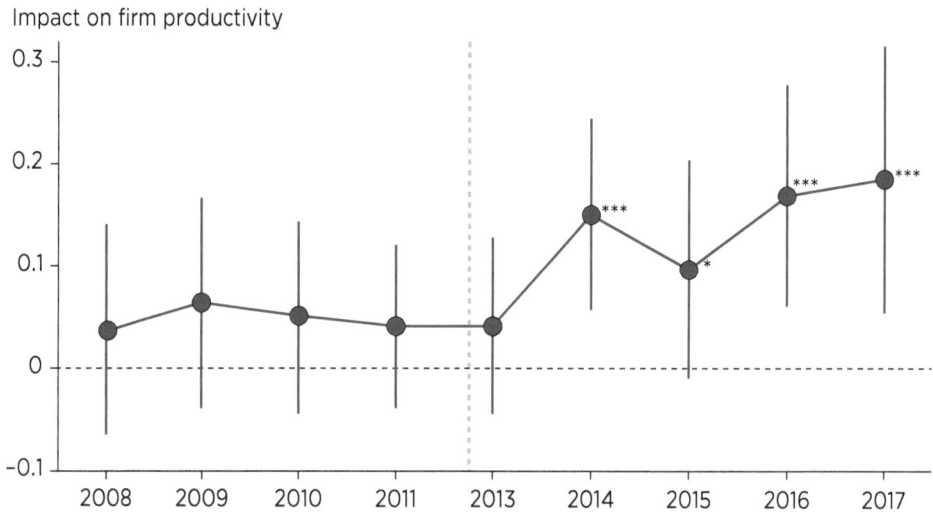

Source: Schiffbauer, Sampi, and Coronado 2022.

Note: The figure reflects the estimated impact of the competition policy reform each year relative to 2012, showing that firms operating in municipalities and sectors that eliminated entry barriers experienced a large rise in productivity relative to comparable firms in the same sector but not located in reform municipalities. The underlying estimation controls for firm, province-year, and sector-year fixed effects. The blue vertical lines show the 95 percent confidence intervals.

Significance level: * = 10 percent, *** = 1 percent.

Several robustness checks support a causal interpretation of this finding. First, the results are robust to different strategies for identifying the control group.[4] Second, treatment and control firms followed parallel productivity trends in the pre-reform years and did not anticipate the elimination of local entry barriers. This implies that the average productivities of the affected and unaffected firms were similar before the reform. Third, as expected, productivity growth was strongest when illegal licensing procedures (compared to technical requirements) were removed (figure 2.4), as these procedures had allowed local public officials to restrict the entry of competitors of local incumbents directly.

Firms operating in downstream sectors or in the same municipality also experienced productivity gains because of the reforms. The spillover effects from local reforms were strongest through value chain links, notably the links

Figure 2.4   Elimination of licensing and technical barriers had the greatest productivity impact

Percentage point increase over control group

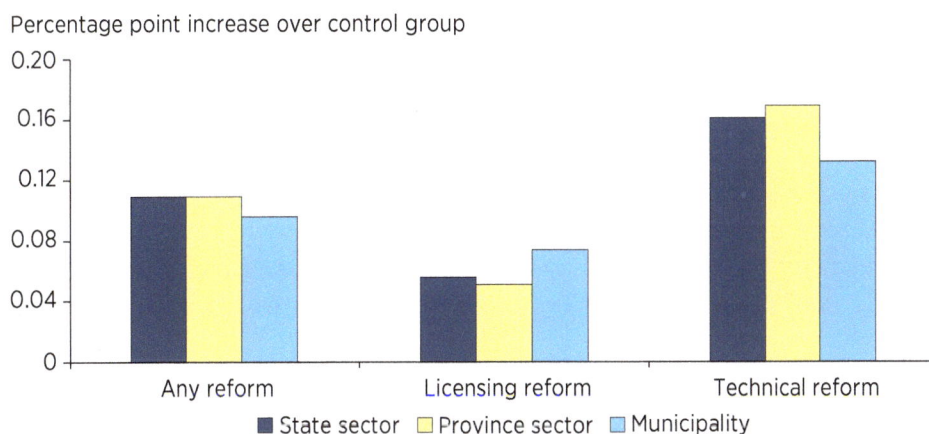

Source: Schiffbauer, Sampi, and Coronado 2022.

Note: The figure displays coefficients on the reform dummy in the regression of productivity of firms on reform in the sector or municipality, assuming a trans-log production function. The dark blue bars show productivity gains if the control group is defined by firms operating in the same sector and state as the reform municipality. The yellow bars show the control group, defined by firms in the same sector but only in the province of the reform municipality. The light blue bars show the control group defined by firms operating in the same reform municipality, regardless of the sector.

between firms in the affected sector or municipality and firms downstream in the same municipality. Many such examples involve transportation firms, which represent the majority of the sample analyzed by Schiffbauer, Sampi, and Coronado (2022), but geographic spillovers also occurred. For instance, the removal of barriers to the installation of antennas enabled internet and related telecom services to reach areas beyond the reforming municipalities, enhancing the productivity of firms outside the reform area. This last result highlights the importance of competition-enhancing reforms in network sectors, such as transportation and ICT, where the benefits may spread to the rest of the economy through value chain links.

Expansion Barriers for Existing Firms Can Be as Harmful as Entry Barriers for New Firms

Dispersion of markups within a market can reflect the market share of a small number of firms and their market power. Markup dispersion can reflect barriers to expansion or barriers to innovation by leading firms seeking to maintain market share. In a framework described by Peters (2020), innovation and productivity growth result from creative destruction through the entry of new firms, expansion of incumbents into new markets, or escape from the effects of competition that reflects a rise in innovation by incumbents.

Empirical evidence shows that, in markets with many small and old firms, barriers to expansion can be a binding constraint on productivity growth (Eslava et al. 2010). Eliminating these barriers can lead to productivity gains and a reduction in the number of firms, as incumbents leave one market to enter other markets.

Giuliano and Zaourak (2022) study the impact of barriers to expansion on productivity and markups in Chile, Peru, and Uruguay using the model from Peters (2020). In all three countries, greater dispersion in markups is associated with productivity losses before the reduction in expansion costs (figure 2.5). Although lower barriers to expansion are expected to yield productivity gains, they do so only if creative destruction through firm entry causes markups to fall as incumbents seek to escape competition.

Figure 2.5 Churning potential under lower expansion costs

Percent

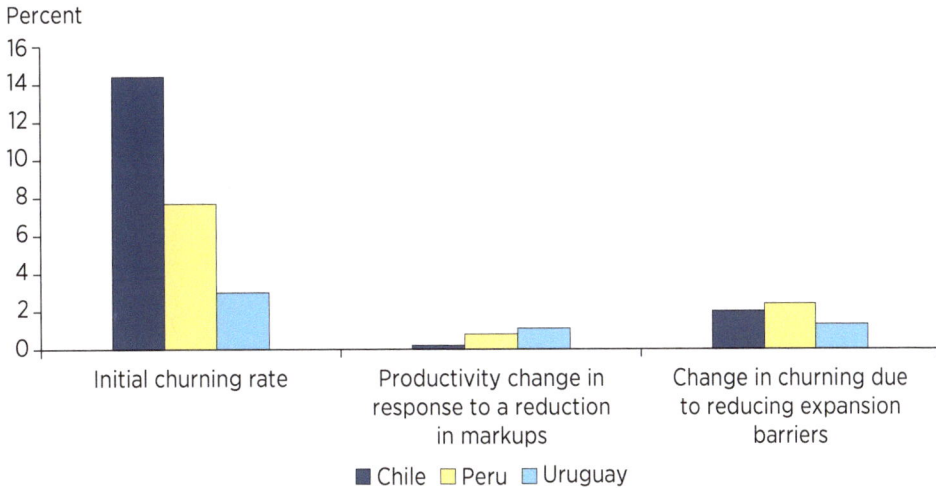

- Chile □ Peru □ Uruguay

Source: Giuliano and Zaourak 2022.

A reduction in barriers to expansion can lead to greater churning, whereby creative destruction dominates the effects of escaping competition, resulting in higher productivity gains. A simulation of a 5 percent reduction in barriers to expansion leads to reductions in both the output share of small firms (18 percent in Chile, 36 percent in Peru, and 6 percent in Uruguay) and the number of firms (25 percent in Chile and 50 percent in Peru) (figure 2.6). However, decreased dispersion of markups can improve the allocation of resources through a lower labor wedge.

If incumbents are unable to expand, there will be too many small and old firms, consistent with the evidence discussed in chapter 1 of this report. As a result, creative destruction will be crippled, and productivity growth will be slow.

The conclusion is that elimination of barriers to expansion—together with the end of entry barriers—will encourage churning in support of the creative destruction process. Even if the entry costs for new firms are low, high expansion costs could cause overall productivity to suffer because new firms tend to be small and exhibit low productivity.

Figure 2.6   Effects of reducing expansion costs by 5 percent on the number of firms and output

Change in number of firms (%)

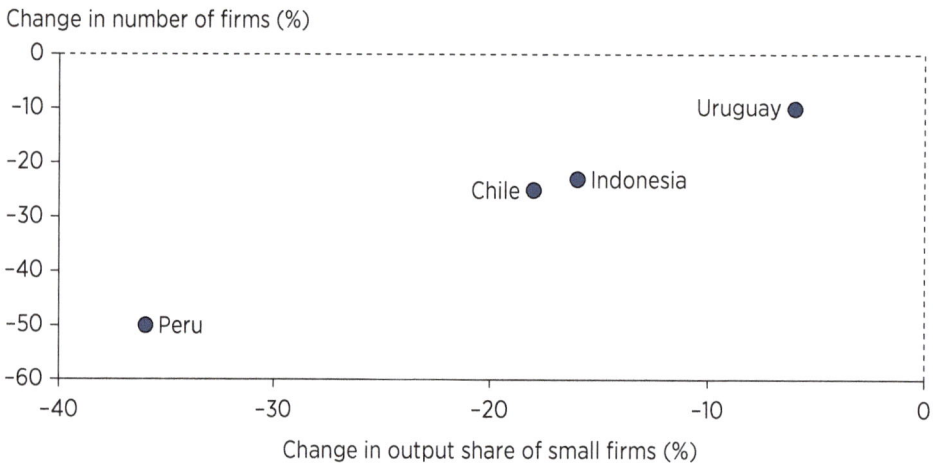

Change in output share of small firms (%)

Source: Giuliano and Zaourak 2022 for Chile, Peru, and Uruguay; Peters 2020 for Indonesia.

Productivity Gains from Removing ICT Entry Barriers Spill Over to Other Sectors

Greater productivity and competition in network sectors, such as ICT, can boost quality and reduce the prices of inputs for production in other sectors, thus helping to lift an entire national economy (Aghion et al. 2005, 2019; Bartelme and Gorodnichenko 2015). Conversely, if ICT firms wield strong market power, they can drive up costs in input markets, even when they make up just a fraction of the total firms in the country (4.1 percent in Peru, for example).

Market power in network sectors can also block new technologies and innovation in other sectors through value chain links. Increasing competition in network sectors can generate major gains. In their seminal paper, Parente and Prescott (1999) show that eliminating a factor supplier's monopoly on an input service can increase output by a factor of about three.

The network effects on some markets may favor monopoly power. This is the case if compatibility requirements increase quality and tend to coordinate consumer preferences around a single provider. Computer operating system software is an example (Gilbert 2022). It may be desirable for a single provider to supply essential services to ensure network efficiency and reliability, such as in the case of water and sewerage services, electric power generation, and railroads. In these areas, too much competition may lead to high social costs, for instance, if multiple providers build infrastructure that could have been shared (Posner 1968).

Thus, there is a need to strike a balance among regulation, competition, and standardization in industries characterized by network effects and desirable outcomes, such as productivity growth, coverage, and service quality. For example, improved entry regulations may generate a direct rise in industry quality. However, in a technologically complex sector, such as ICT, regulations aimed at fostering competition may have unintended consequences or create tacit trade-offs between competition and quality.[5]

ICT markets are often more highly concentrated in Latin America and the Caribbean than in other regions (Gillet 2011). Broadband, mobile, and fixed lines in the region all have high scores under the Herfindahl–Hirschman Index, which measures market concentration (OECD and IDB 2016). The Mexico-based firm América Móvil owns a substantial number of operators in the region and holds a large market share. Some governments are seeking to promote competition in ICT. For example, Peru has carried out major reforms to increase contestability and service quality (box 2.1).

High entry barriers may translate into market dominance and high markup dispersion. A reduction in entry barriers, for example, through competition-enhancing reforms, may lead to a rise in the entry of productive firms. Arayavechkit, Jooste, and Urrutia Arrieta (2022) calibrate a two-sector model (ICT and non-ICT) with several high- and low-productivity firms in Peru.[6] Theoretical modeling predicts that a reduction in entry barriers in ICT leads to the entry of more productive firms. In a simulation of the effects of Peru's various reforms and other market conditions, such as wage remuneration and the sales of firms, Arayavechkit, Jooste, and Urrutia Arrieta (2022) estimate that a 50 percent reduction in ICT entry costs would raise the economy's aggregate productivity by 0.9 percent (figure 2.7). Lower barriers to entry also appear to increase the share of ICT in the broader economy, spurring economywide productivity growth through value chain links (figure 2.8; box 2.2).

Box 2.1

Reforms and regulators in the ICT sector in Peru

The regulation of Peru's information and communication technology (ICT) sector, which includes telecommunications, infrastructure, hardware, and software, has undergone significant reforms since the market was opened to competition. These reforms supported an expansion of coverage and low prices, according to OBG (2019), and included various laws on the construction of the backbone network, infrastructure sharing, and operation of virtual network operators. This expansion has allowed operators that lack their own network infrastructure to enter markets based on the principles of nondiscrimination and free and fair competition. Other reforms helped to create a more dynamic ICT sector and reduced entry costs, such as assigning spectrum to entrants, the law sanctioning tie-in sales, and more active antitrust enforcement.

The Ministry of Transport and Communications defines and enforces policy with the goal of connecting economic players more effectively across the territory. Its functions include the design, coordination, and evaluation of regulations; granting of licenses; and allocation and supervision of spectrum assignments.

The Supervisory Body of Private Investment in Telecommunications is an autonomous public regulatory agency promoting market competition. It regulates tariffs and enforces competition law and technical norms in the sector. It conducts market evaluations and investigations based on third-party complaints or its own initiative. It hears and resolves disputes and imposes corrective measures.

The National Institute for the Defense of Competition and the Protection of Intellectual Property enforces competition law in all other sectors. It has the authority to evaluate and approve corporate mergers (or withhold approval) in any sector and to hear and rule on cases involving potential competition infringements in all sectors except telecommunications. Its role includes improving the relevant regulatory framework by removing unnecessary regulatory barriers and simplifying administrative procedures.

Source: Arayavechkit, Jooste, and Urrutia Arrieta 2022.

Figure 2.7   Productivity benefits of removing ICT entry barriers spill over to the economy

Productivity gain (%)

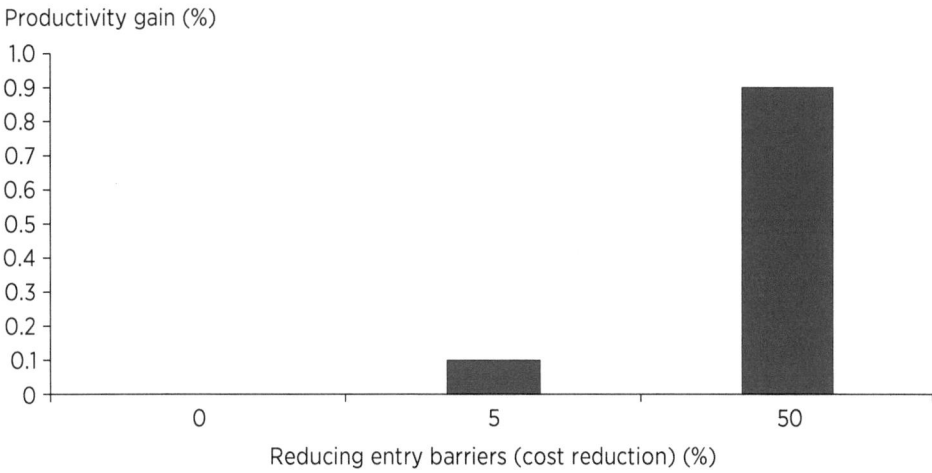

Reducing entry barriers (cost reduction) (%)

Source: Arayavechkit, Jooste, and Urrutia Arrieta 2022.

Note: Productivity of the economy is proxied by services and manufacturing as in the firm-level survey. Entry costs are fixed costs for permit fees, licenses, and bidding. ICT = information and communication technology.

Figure 2.8   The share of ICT firms in gross domestic product increases following a fall in entry costs

ICT market share (%)

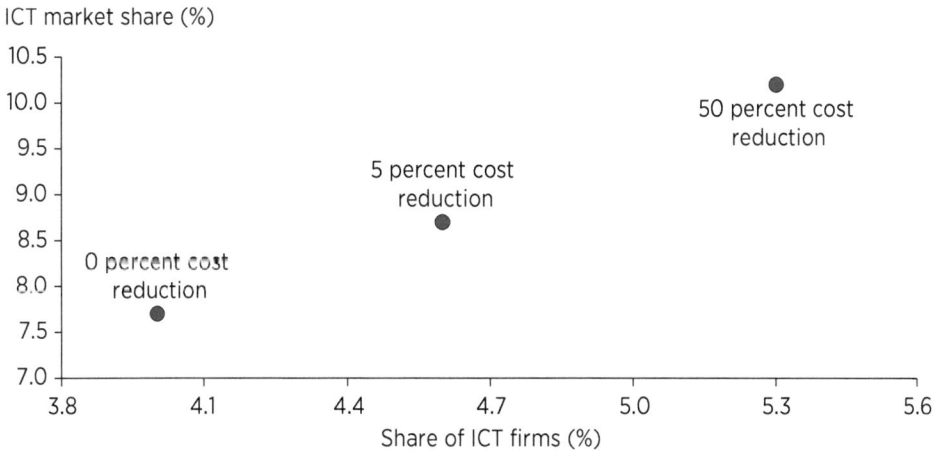

Share of ICT firms (%)

Source: Arayavechkit, Jooste, and Urrutia Arrieta 2022.

Note: The figure shows the effect of entry cost reductions on ICT firms' share of ICT sales and of total ICT firms. The economy is proxied by manufacturing and services. The total number of firms and total sales are proxies for the totals. ICT = information and communication technology.

Box 2.2

Forging competition in ICT and other input markets generates gains along the value chain

Quality upgrading is an important component of productivity growth under competitive pressure. However, such upgrading in output markets requires improvements throughout the entire complex of suppliers and downstream producers. For example, foreign direct investment exerts pressure on domestic suppliers to improve quality, and upgrading among downstream producers generates pressure on local suppliers to upgrade in a similar way. In India, a reduction of marginal costs in manufacturing generated higher markups, but these markups were followed by increased access to new and cheaper inputs that spurred innovation through new products. This process generated significant productivity gains, eventually accounting for a quarter of India's manufacturing growth.

If firms along the value chain miss out on access to technology and innovation infrastructure, upgrading or technology adoption in output markets cannot occur. Incumbents with high market shares can lobby for the protection of their industry, which may block technology transmission and reduce overall productivity. Varying impacts may occur related to the specific characteristics of firms. For instance, if some firms but not others have the capacity to use intangibles, such as software, to improve production processes, the advantage may turn into a de facto entry barrier affecting the other firms.

Information and communication technology (ICT) is an important input market. Like any network sector, it directly affects productivity through the production of goods and services and through spillover effects in the industries that use ICT. It fosters productivity by facilitating within-firm innovation that lowers the cost of information exchange. For instance, it allows individual firms to automate repetitive tasks or optimize factor utilization rates. It enhances consumer welfare by reducing inefficiencies in the delivery of goods and services and improves the quality of those goods and services.

Information technology upskills labor, makes workers more productive, and allows small firms to access external markets, thereby increasing competition and creating demand for skills. ICT also raises the stock of capital (such as wireless network towers and fiber optic cables) and

box continued next page

Box 2.2

Forging competition in ICT and other input markets generates gains along the value chain *(continued)*

enhances labor productivity through the learning opportunities opened by online platforms.

Therefore, poor regulation of ICT services may mean that there is suboptimal resource allocation in the upward value chain, hindering investment in services. It may harm the ability to translate ICT into productivity gains. Reduced productivity growth will ensue if sectors invest less in ICT because of regulatory hurdles.

More effective regulation is required in the region to obtain the best from ICT services and ensure the maximum potential of the huge infrastructure investment the region needs from governments and the private sector. A more competitive environment in ICT would channel more capital into infrastructure. A 10 percent increase in the competition framework index of the International Telecommunication Union would generate a nearly 7 percent rise in telecommunications capital investment and a drop of about 5 percent in the prices paid by end users.

Sources: Alam et al. 2008; Biagi 2013; Brynjolfsson and Hitt 2000; De Ridder 2024; Dedrick, Gurbaxani, and Kraemer 2003; Draca, Sadun, and Van Reenen 2006; Dutz, Almeida, and Packard 2018; Goldberg et al. 2010; ITU 2021; Javorcik 2004; Kugler and Verhoogen 2012; Parente and Prescott 1999; Patterson et al. 2020; Van Reenen 2010.

Well-Regulated Market Entry May Increase Quality

In the interaction between competition and quality, regulations may have conflicting effects through differing margins of productivity. For example, standardization and technological compatibility may facilitate quality upgrading and exports and are key to the smooth functioning of markets with network effects, such as digital platforms. But high standards can also preclude the entry of smaller or less capable firms, reinforcing monopolistic pressures in these markets (Gilbert 2022). Understanding the productivity effects of the policies would therefore be informative for policy makers.

This section distinguishes between two broad types of regulations: (1) *complexifying* regulations that encourage standardization and higher quality, and (2) *simplifying* regulations that reduce and streamline rules, thereby facilitating market entry (box 2.3).

Box 2.3

Trade-offs between entry and quality

Simplifying regulations aim at reducing administrative burdens, thereby drawing more entrants into the market. For example, in 2015, Peru approved a law that was designed to reduce red tape in the construction of telecom infrastructure. Before the law's enactment, firms needed to apply for special permits to undertake infrastructure work. They could proceed if they received no response within 30 days of the application. The new law provided for automatic approval. Infrastructure projects could be launched immediately under the assumption that the application would be green lighted.

The potential downside to these regulations is harm to productivity, especially immediately following their introduction. This situation can occur if firms that are newly able to enter the market have low productivity or were unable to enter earlier because they lacked the capacity to perform up to industry standards.

Complexifying regulations aim at upholding high standards and might make entry more difficult. They might include quality standards and administrative requirements, such as registration. However, standards can also facilitate quality upgrading. These regulations may generate improvements in innovation because they require firms to improve the quality of processes and products. They may initiate a race to the top in quality as firms strive to meet the new standards.

A draft law that would regulate application software for ride-hailing services, such as Uber, provides an example. The purpose is to ensure that

box continued next page

Box 2.3

Trade-offs between entry and quality *(continued)*

drivers have the required professional credentials. Although this requirement adds administrative hurdles and renders entry more complex, it also increases the quality of the services offered by boosting passenger security. The trade-off is that it may reduce the number of entrants and concentrate the market power of firms that do enter.

Sources: Arayavechkit, Jooste, and Urrutia Arrieta 2022; Gilbert 2022.

This section considers regulations established in Peru between 2007 and 2017 that affect the behavior of firms in the ICT sector. Using the Ackerberg, Caves, and Frazer (2015) methodology for productivity estimation, Arayavechkit, Jooste, and Urrutia Arrieta (2022) show that complexifying regulations result in higher productivity. In contrast, simplifying regulations have no effect on productivity. Increases in productivity in response to complexifying regulations are driven by firms at the top of the productivity distribution. They increase the productivity of firms among the top 5 percent in productivity. The more productive a firm is initially relative to its market peers, the greater the effort it makes in response to a change in ex ante regulations that raises industry standards.

Using the alternative Sampi, Jooste, and Vostroknutova (2021)[7] methodology for productivity estimation, both simplifying and complexifying regulations are found to increase the TFPR productivity of firms at the top of the productivity distribution (figure 2.9). For instance, simplifying regulations generate a 32 percent increase in TFPR among firms in the 95th percentile compared to those that were not subject to the regulations. In the case of complexifying regulations, the productivity of firms operating in the 95th percentile increases by 73 percent.

In response to simplifying regulations, which may reduce quality requirements or otherwise make entry easier, the average product quality, measured as in Khandelwal, Schott, and Wei (2013), decreases at the bottom of the productivity distribution (figure 2.10). This trend is consistent with simplification that eliminates an entry barrier facing low-productivity firms that may have trouble complying with quality regulations.

Figure 2.9   Entry regulations increase productivity in leading firms

Estimated change in TFPR (%)

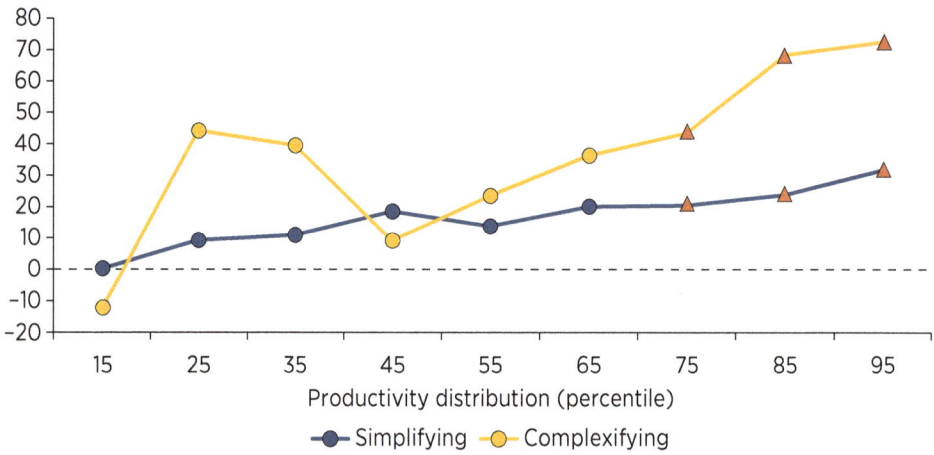

Productivity distribution (percentile)

—●— Simplifying   —○— Complexifying

Source: Arayavechkit, Jooste, and Urrutia Arrieta 2022.

Note: The figure shows the effect of entry regulations on TFPR of firms, relative to firms in unaffected markets, by productivity level. Red triangles indicate that estimates are statistically significant. TFPR = revenue-based total factor productivity.

Figure 2.10   Low-productivity firms reduce quality in response to simplifying entry regulations

Estimated change (%)

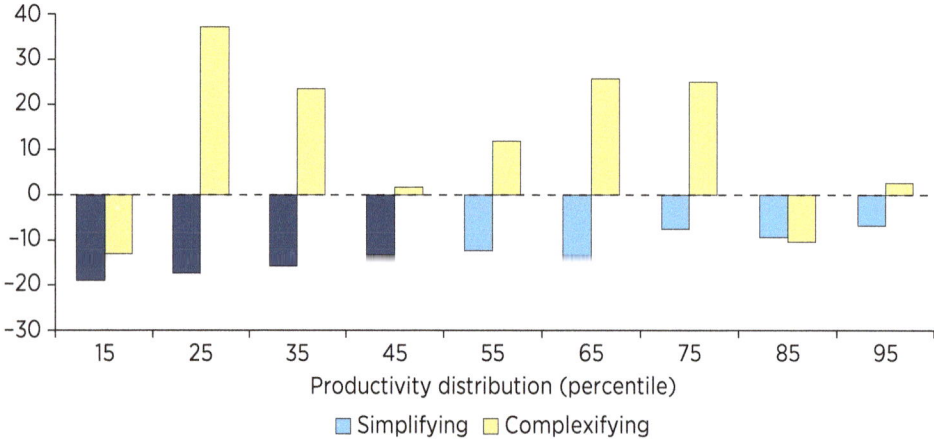

Productivity distribution (percentile)

☐ Simplifying   ☐ Complexifying

Source: Arayavechkit, Jooste, and Urrutia Arrieta 2022.

Note: The figure shows the effect of entry regulations on product quality of firms, relative to firms in unaffected markets, by productivity level. Dark blue bars indicate that estimates are statistically significant.

The effects on productivity (measured as in Sampi, Jooste, and Vostroknutova 2021) vary by firm age. Given the idea of cumulative innovations in Arrow (1962), older firms should be more capable of translating complex regulatory requirements into TFPR gains because they can use the new standards to increase quality. This appears to be the case (figure 2.11). However, the productivity of younger firms at the top of the productivity distribution also increases in response to simplifying regulations (figure 2.12). At the same time, markups rise significantly for older market leaders in response to complexifying regulations. The fact that only the experienced, more productive firms increase markups suggests that lowering entry barriers may not result in more competitive markets if it facilitates the entry of low-productivity firms.

Figure 2.11   Complexifying entry regulations favor older firms

Change in TFPR (%)

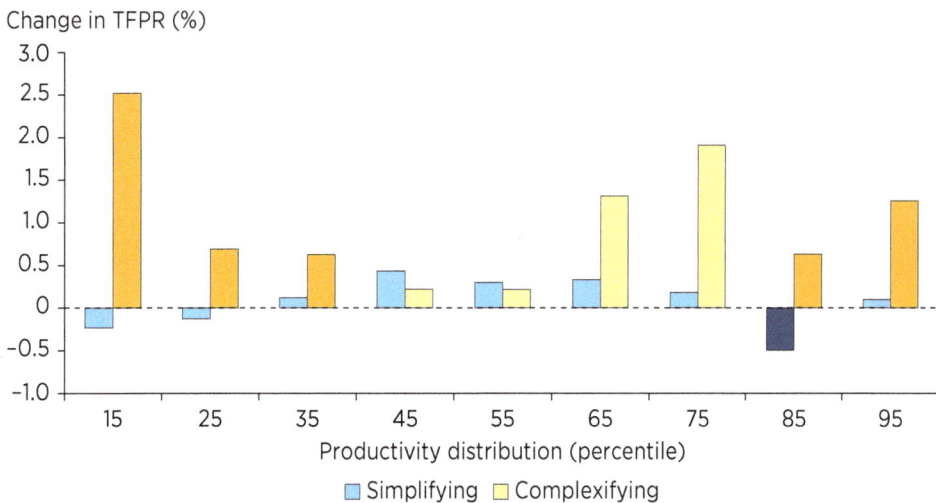

Productivity distribution (percentile)

□ Simplifying □ Complexifying

Source: Arayavechkit, Jooste, and Urrutia Arrieta 2022.

Note: The figure shows the effect of entry regulations on TFPR of older firms, relative to firms in unaffected markets, by productivity level. Dark blue and orange bars indicate statistically significant estimates. For a value on the y-axis, the corresponding % change in productivity = 100*(exp(y)−1). For example, for a 0.232 value, the % change = 100*(exp(0232)−1)), which equals 26 percent. TFPR = revenue-based total factor productivity.

Figure 2.12   Simplifying entry regulations favor younger firms

Change in TFPR (%)

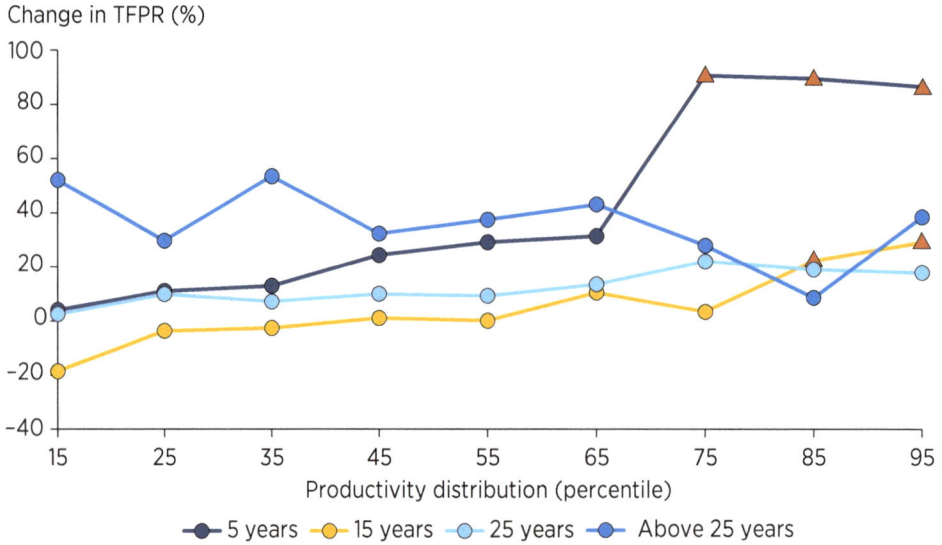

Source: Arayavechkit, Jooste, and Urrutia Arrieta 2022.

Note: The figure shows the effect of simplifying entry regulations on TFPR of firms, relative to firms in unaffected markets, by firm age and productivity level. Red triangles indicate statistically significant estimates. TFPR = revenue-based total factor productivity.

Box 2.4

Walmart's entry into Mexico transformed the country's upstream manufacturers

As in output markets, foreign entry in input markets can set firms apart by capability and transmit these effects along the value chain. Walmart's entry into Mexico's retail market provides an example. Made possible by the deregulation of foreign direct investment under the North American Free Trade Agreement, Walmart's arrival transformed not only Mexico's retail market but also the structure of upstream manufacturing industries.

Iacovone et al. (2015) highlight the links between retailers and manufacturers and develop a dynamic model of an upstream manufacturing industry in which firms of varying capabilities enter and

box continued next page

Box 2.4

Walmart's entry into Mexico transformed the country's upstream manufacturers *(continued)*

exit. In their model, incumbent firms decide how much to invest in quality-enhancing innovation and whether to sell their products through Walmex (as Walmart is known in Mexico) or a traditional retailer. Those who choose Walmex do so because the benefits of a larger customer base outweigh the costs of conforming to Walmex's standards in product quality and pricing.

Simulations of the model suggest that firms producing high-quality products should choose to sell their products through Walmex and increase their investments in innovation, while firms producing low-quality products should do the opposite or exit altogether. In this way, the appearance of Walmex should polarize Mexico's upstream industries, heightening differences in sales volume and product quality between large and small firms while reducing the total number of domestically produced varieties available to consumers. Industry-level innovation and consumer welfare should nonetheless increase because market shares would be reallocated to the stronger firms and because these firms would have invested more in innovation.

By factoring in geographic variations in the locations of Walmex stores and noting that suppliers of perishable goods are especially sensitive to the proximity of retailers, Iacovone et al. (2015) find that these predictions were accurate. Manufacturing survey data show that high-quality firms have sold more and become more productive in response to Walmex's presence in Mexico, whereas low-quality firms have lost ground in both dimensions. For the industry as a whole, reallocations of the associated market shares, adjustments in innovative effort, and exit patterns increased productivity and the rate of innovation.

Source: Based on Iacovone et al. 2015.

The results in this section are consistent with the findings of a study in Mexico (box 2.4). The study showed varying impacts across the productivity distribution and how these impacts are transmitted to the rest of the economy. In the case highlighted in box 2.4, Walmart's entry into the retail market in Mexico had a substantially more positive impact on large, higher-quality Mexican suppliers than on small, less innovative firms.

Conclusions

Barriers to entry and expansion are pervasive in the region and more restrictive than the Organisation for Economic Co-operation and Development average, taking a toll on incentives for entrepreneurship and innovation in Latin America and the Caribbean (refer to chapter 1 of this report). The evidence presented in this chapter confirms that these barriers hamper productivity growth, quality upgrading, and innovation along the value chain.

The empirical analysis of the Peruvian case conducted for this report shows that removing entry barriers at the local level speeds up productivity growth. The focus on the ICT sector sheds light on how regulatory entry barriers can generate negative spillovers in the rest of the economy. The analysis illustrates the importance of having a pro-competition regulatory framework to ensure that firms are challenged by competitive pressure. It also highlights the need to strengthen firms' capacity to innovate and increase quality in response to shocks.

Notes

1. The list and typology of barriers were constructed following Bain (1951); Dinh, Mavridis, and Nguyen (2010); Eswaran (1994); Gaskins (1971); OECD (2007); Peters (2020); Shepherd (1997); and Yip (1982).
2. Presbitero and Rabellotti (2016) discuss credit constraints that smaller firms face in the region.
3. The analysis is based on firm-level data from the National Survey of Economic Activity, which includes formal firms in the construction, hotels and restaurants, manufacturing, telecommunications, trade, transportation, and service sectors and covers 90 percent of total annual sales in Peru.
4. These strategies include selecting a different set of control groups of firms located in other regions and sectors, but with similar characteristics (size, sales, number of employees, and so on). These control groups are matched with the affected firms through a propensity score matching procedure. The online supplemental appendix in Schiffbauer, Sampi, and Coronado (2022) provides more details on the robustness exercises supporting these findings.
5. For instance, Kang (2023) reviews the literature on patents and investments in research and development in the United States and concludes that too much competition may sometimes damage risky frontier innovations. Although only a handful of countries in Latin America and the Caribbean can innovate at the global technological frontier and are therefore unlikely to face these issues, there may nonetheless be complementarities and trade-offs between competition and quality (Cheng 2022). Chapter 5 of this report discusses the nexus between innovation and competition policy.
6. The model parameters are calibrated using firm-level data from the Annual Economic Survey collected by the National Institute of Statistics and Information of Peru.

7. To avoid the identification problems raised by Bond et al. (2021) and Doraszelski and Jaumandreu (2021), Sampi, Jooste, and Vostroknutova (2021) use the quasi-maximum likelihood estimator to estimate the impact of regulatory enforcement on productivity. They modify the approach of Ackerberg, Caves, and Frazer (2015) to estimate productivity and markups simultaneously, to obtain the joint impact of a change in regulations.

References

Ackerberg, Daniel A., Kevin Caves, and Garth Frazer. 2015. "Identification Properties of Recent Production Function Estimators." *Econometrica* 83 (6): 2411–51.

Aghion, Philippe, Antonin Bergeaud, Timo Boppart, Peter J. Klenow, and Huiyu Li. 2019. "A Theory of Falling Growth and Rising Rents." NBER Working Paper 26448, National Bureau of Economic Research, Cambridge, MA.

Aghion, Philippe, Nicholas Bloom, Richard Blundell, Rachel Griffith, and Peter Howitt. 2005. "Competition and Innovation: An Inverted-U Relationship." *Quarterly Journal of Economics* 120 (2): 701–28.

Aghion, Philippe, Richard Blundell, Rachel Griffith, Peter Howitt, and Susanne Prantl. 2009. "The Effects of Entry on Incumbent Innovation and Productivity." *Review of Economics and Statistics* 91 (1): 20–32.

Alam, Asad, Paloma Anós Casero, Faruk Khan, and Charles Udomsaph. 2008. *Unleashing Prosperity: Productivity Growth in Eastern Europe and the Former Soviet Union.* Washington, DC: World Bank.

Arayavechkit, Tanida, Charl Jooste, and Ana Francisca Urrutia Arrieta. 2022. "How Regulation and Enforcement of Competition Affects ICT Productivity: Evidence from Matched Regulatory-Production Surveys in Peru's ICT Sector." Policy Research Working Paper 10151, World Bank, Washington, DC.

Arrow, Kenneth J. 1962. "The Economic Implications of Learning by Doing." *Review of Economic Studies* 29 (3): 155–73.

Bain, Joe S. 1951. "Relation of Profit Rate to Industry Concentration: American Manufacturing, 1936–1940." *Quarterly Journal of Economics* 65 (3): 293–324.

Barseghyan, Levon. 2008. "Entry Costs and Cross-Country Differences in Productivity and Output." *Journal of Economic Growth* 13 (2): 145–67.

Bartelme, Dominick, and Yuriy Gorodnichenko. 2015. "Linkages and Economic Development." NBER Working Paper 21251, National Bureau of Economic Research, Cambridge, MA.

Biagi, Federico. 2013 "ICT and Productivity: A Review of the Literature." Digital Economy Working Paper 2013/09, JRC Technical Report EUR 26216, Institute for Prospective Technological Studies, Joint Research Centre, European Commission, Luxembourg. http://ftp.jrc.es/EURdoc/JRC84470.pdf.

Bond, Steve, Arshia Hashemi, Greg Kaplan, and Piotr Zoch. 2021. "Some Unpleasant Markup Arithmetic: Production Function Elasticities and Their Estimation from Production Data." *Journal of Monetary Economics* 121: 1–14.

Branstetter, Lee G., Francisco Lima, Lowell J. Taylor, and Ana Venâncio. 2010. "Do Entry Regulations Deter Entrepreneurship and Job Creation? Evidence from Recent Reforms in Portugal." NBER Working Paper 16473, National Bureau of Economic Research, Cambridge, MA.

Brynjolfsson, Erik, and Lorin M. Hitt. 2000. "Beyond Computation: Information Technology, Organizational Transformation, and Business Performance." *Journal of Economic Perspectives* 14 (4): 23–48.

Cheng, Thomas K. 2022. "Competition and Innovation Policy Nexus in Developing Countries." World Bank, Washington, DC.

Comin, Diego A., and Bart Hobijn. 2009. "Lobbies and Technology Diffusion." *Review of Economics and Statistics* 91 (2): 229–44.

De Ridder, Maarten. 2024. "Market Power and Innovation in the Intangible Economy." *American Economic Review* 114 (1): 199–251.

Dedrick, Jason L., Vijay Gurbaxani, and Kenneth L. Kraemer. 2003. "Information Technology and Economic Performance: A Critical Review of the Empirical Evidence." *ACM Computing Surveys* 35 (1): 1–28.

Dinh, Hinh T., Dimitris A. Mavridis, and Hoa B. Nguyen. 2010. "The Binding Constraint on Firms' Growth in Developing Countries." Policy Research Working Paper 5485, World Bank, Washington, DC.

Doraszelski, Ulrich, and Jordi Jaumandreu. 2021. "Reexamining the De Loecker & Warzynski (2012) Method for Estimating Markups." CEPR Discussion Paper DP16027, Centre for Economic Policy Research, London.

Draca, Mirko, Raffaella Sadun, and John Michael Van Reenen. 2006. "Productivity and ICT: A Review of the Evidence." CEP Discussion Paper 749, Centre for Economic Performance, London School of Economics and Political Science, London.

Dutz, Mark A., Rita K. Almeida, and Truman G. Packard. 2018. *The Jobs of Tomorrow: Technology, Productivity, and Prosperity in Latin America and the Caribbean*. Directions in Development: Communication and Information Technologies Series. Washington, DC: World Bank.

Eslava, Marcela, John C. Haltiwanger, Adriana Kugler, and Maurice David Kugler. 2010. "Factor Adjustments after Deregulation: Panel Evidence from Colombian Plants." *Review of Economics and Statistics* 92 (2): 378–91.

Eswaran, Mukesh. 1994. "Licensees as Entry Barriers." *Canadian Journal of Economics* 27 (3): 673–88.

Fattal Jaef, Roberto N. 2022. "Formal Sector Distortions, Entry Barriers, and the Informal Economy: A Quantitative Exploration." In *Hidden Potential: Rethinking Informality in South Asia*, edited by Maurizio Bussolo and Siddarth Sharma, 41–60. South Asia Development Forum Series. Washington, DC: World Bank. https://doi.org/978-1-4648-1834-9_ch2.

Gaskins, Jr., Darius W. 1971. "Dynamic Limit Pricing: Optimal Pricing under Threat of Entry." *Journal of Economic Theory* 3 (3): 306–22.

Gilbert, Richard J. 2022. *Innovation Matters: Competition Policy for the High-Technology Economy*. Cambridge, MA: MIT Press.

Gillet, Joss. 2011. *Competition and Concentration: The Distribution of Market Power in the Global Cellular Industry*. London: GSMA Intelligence. https://data.gsmaintelligence.com/research/research/research-2011/competition-and-concentration-the-distribution-of-market-power-in-the-global-cellular-industry.

Giuliano, Fernando, and Gabriel Zaourak. 2022. "Entry Barriers, Churning, and Endogenous Markups in South America." Background paper for this report. World Bank, Washington, DC.

Goldberg, Pinelopi Koujianou, Amit Kumar Khandelwal, Nina Pavcnik, and Petia Topalova. 2010. "Imported Intermediate Inputs and Domestic Product Growth: Evidence from India." *Quarterly Journal of Economics* 125 (4): 1727–67.

Iacovone, Leonardo, Beata Smarzynska Javorcik, Wolfgang Keller, and James Tybout. 2015. "Supplier Responses to Walmart's Invasion in Mexico." *Journal of International Economics* 95 (1): 1–15.

ITU (International Telecommunication Union). 2021. *The Impact of Policies, Regulation, and Institutions on ICT Sector Performance*. Geneva: ITU.

Javorcik, Beata Smarzynska. 2004. "Does Foreign Direct Investment Increase the Productivity of Domestic Firms? In Search of Spillovers through Backward Linkages." *American Economic Review* 94 (3): 605–27.

Kang, Hyo. 2023. "How Does Price Competition Affect Innovation? Evidence from US Antitrust Cases." Research Paper, Marshall School of Business, University of Southern California, Los Angeles, CA.

Khandewal, Amit, Peter K. Schott, and Shang-Jin Wei. 2013. "Trade Liberalization and Institutional Reform: Evidence from Chinese Exporters." *American Economic Review* 103 (6): 2169–96.

Kugler, Maurice David, and Eric A. Verhoogen. 2012. "Prices, Plant Size, and Product Quality." *Review of Economic Studies* 79 (1): 307–39.

Licetti, Martha Martínez, Donato de Rosa, Tanya K. Goodwin, Congyan Tan, and Rachel Li Jiang. 2015. "Peru: Tackling Regulatory Barriers to Competition and Local Economy Development." World Bank, Lima, Peru.

McGowan, Danny. 2014. "Do Entry Barriers Reduce Productivity? Evidence from a Natural Experiment." *Economics Letters* 125 (1): 97–100.

OBG (Oxford Business Group). 2019. "Competition in Peru's ICT Sector Drives Down Costs and Expands Coverage in Rural Areas." OBG, London. https://oxfordbusinessgroup .com/reports/peru/2019-report/economy/making-connections-consumers -continue-to-benefit-from-market-competition-while-stakeholders-look-at-how -best-to-boost-service-to-rural-areas.

OECD (Organisation for Economic Co-operation and Development). 2007. "Competition and Barriers to Entry." Policy Brief, OECD Observer, OECD, Paris. https://www.oecd.org /competition/mergers/37921908.pdf.

OECD and IDB (Organisation for Economic Co-operation and Development and Inter-American Development Bank). 2016. *Broadband Policies for Latin America and the Caribbean: A Digital Economy Toolkit*. Paris: OECD.

Parente, Stephen L., and Edward C. Prescott. 1999. "Monopoly Rights: A Barrier to Riches." *American Economic Review* 89 (5): 1216–33.

Patterson, Iain, Ana Rincón-Aznar, Richard Sellner, Marion-Bianca Brandl, and Catherine Robinson. 2020. "Regulation of Services Industries and ICT Diffusion: Accounting for Upstream and Downstream Linkages." SERVICEGAP Discussion Paper DP23 rev., Institute for Advanced Studies, Vienna, Austria. https://irihs.ihs.ac.at/id/eprint/3256/1 /DP23_regulation_Paterson.pdf.

Peters, Michael. 2020. "Heterogeneous Markups, Growth, and Endogenous Misallocation." *Econometrica* 88 (5): 2037–73.

Posner, Richard A. 1968. "Natural Monopoly and Its Regulation." *Stanford Law Review* 21: 548–643.

Presbitero, Andrea F., and Roberta Rabellotti. 2016. "Credit Access in Latin American Enterprises." In *Firm Innovation and Productivity in Latin America and the Caribbean: The Engine of Economic Development*, edited by Matteo Grazzi and Carlo Pietrobelli, 245–83. Washington, DC: Inter-American Development Bank; New York: Palgrave Macmillan. https://doi.org/10.1057/978-1-349-58151-1_8.

Sampi, James Robert, Charl Jooste, and Ekaterina Vostroknutova. 2021. "Identification Properties for Estimating the Impact of Regulation on Markups and Productivity." Policy Research Working Paper 9523, World Bank, Washington, DC.

Schiffbauer, Marc Tobias, James Robert Sampi, and Javier Coronado. 2022. "Competition and Productivity: Evidence from Peruvian Municipalities." *Review of Economics and Statistics* 1–45.

Schivardi, Fabiano, and Eliana Viviano. 2011. "Entry Barriers in Retail Trade." *Economic Journal* 121 (551): 145–70.

Shepherd, William G. 1997. *The Economics of Industrial Organization: Analysis, Markets, Policies*. Upper Saddle River, NJ: Prentice-Hall International.

Van Reenen, John Michael. 2010. "Does Competition Raise Productivity through Improving Management Practices?" CEP Discussion Paper 1036, Centre for Economic Performance, London School of Economics and Political Science, London. http://cep .lse.ac.uk/pubs/download/dp1036.pdf.

World Bank. 2023. *The Business of the State*. Washington, DC: World Bank.

Yip, George S. 1982. *Barriers to Entry: A Corporate-Strategy Perspective*. Lexington, MA: Lexington Books.

3
Antitrust Enforcement

Introduction

Market power is highly advantageous for firms that possess it. To protect their market share, firms may engage in anticompetitive behavior. Major damage to the economy may result as entry and expansion barriers cripple the creative destruction process. The lack of contestability may reduce the incentive to innovate, especially in developing countries where innovations are mostly internal to firms and do not require rents from patenting (Aghion et al. 2005).[1]

Competition law makes anticompetitive behavior illegal. This chapter fills a critical gap in the empirical literature by evaluating the impact of competition policy—the institutions and norms that have been established to deter anticompetitive behavior among firms—on market- and firm-level productivity in a developing country setting. Most studies exploring the link between competition policy and productivity focus on industrialized countries (Aghion et al. 2022). The few studies that examine developing countries are limited in scope and coverage, especially on productivity outcomes.[2]

This chapter offers empirical evidence of the positive impact of antitrust enforcement on productivity. It shows that enforcement aids creative destruction because the greater market contestability that follows enforcement affects leading and lagging firms differently. The chapter also presents evidence that shows that ex officio initiatives raise productivity, highlighting the benefits of the independence of competition authorities. If cases are closed because of a lack of investigative capacity, the market outcomes may be negative, underlining the value of raising capacity. This is true of the often weak authority and funding of competition agencies in the

Latin America and the Caribbean region. Granting these agencies more funding, independence, and legal power may generate economic gains.

Novel Data Sets

To explore the relationship between competition policy and productivity, novel data sets on competition policy cases were constructed with the support of competition authorities in four countries (Chile, Colombia, Mexico, and Uruguay). The data sets contain detailed records on the alleged violations of competition law, the sectors and regions where these occurred, the sources of the complaints (from a competitor or ex officio—that is, initiated by the competition authority), the sanctions imposed, and key dates.

As reflected in these new data, conduct that triggers competition scrutiny is divided into (1) abuse of a dominant position, (2) collusion (including cartels), and (3) mergers and acquisitions that are likely to have a substantial market effect. This report focuses on the abuse of dominance and collusion and excludes bid rigging.[3] This approach partly arises because of data limitations. Cases of abuse of dominance and collusion account for the majority of cases investigated by competition authorities in the countries under study (figure 3.1). They are also broadly similar in mechanisms of implementation and impact on innovation and productivity. For example, firms that collude as a group tend to rely on the same tactics as single firms that abuse their dominant market position, for example, to block a competitor's entry.[4] In addition, the literature on antitrust law in developing countries prioritizes these two categories as a matter of policy (Fox et al. 2016; Gal et al. 2015). The data also allow a distinction across sectors and among the cases initiated by competition authorities or private sector complaints.

The institutional structure of competition authorities and how they initiate or investigate cases are important not only for understanding the policy conclusions but also for empirical analysis. Across the region, competition authorities have increasingly focused on sectors in which price changes have a large impact on the well-being of the poor, such as food processing and transportation (Begazo and Nyman 2016). This focus underpins the significance of the analysis in this chapter for poverty reduction.

Figure 3.1   Cases investigated by competition authorities, by type of alleged violation, selected countries

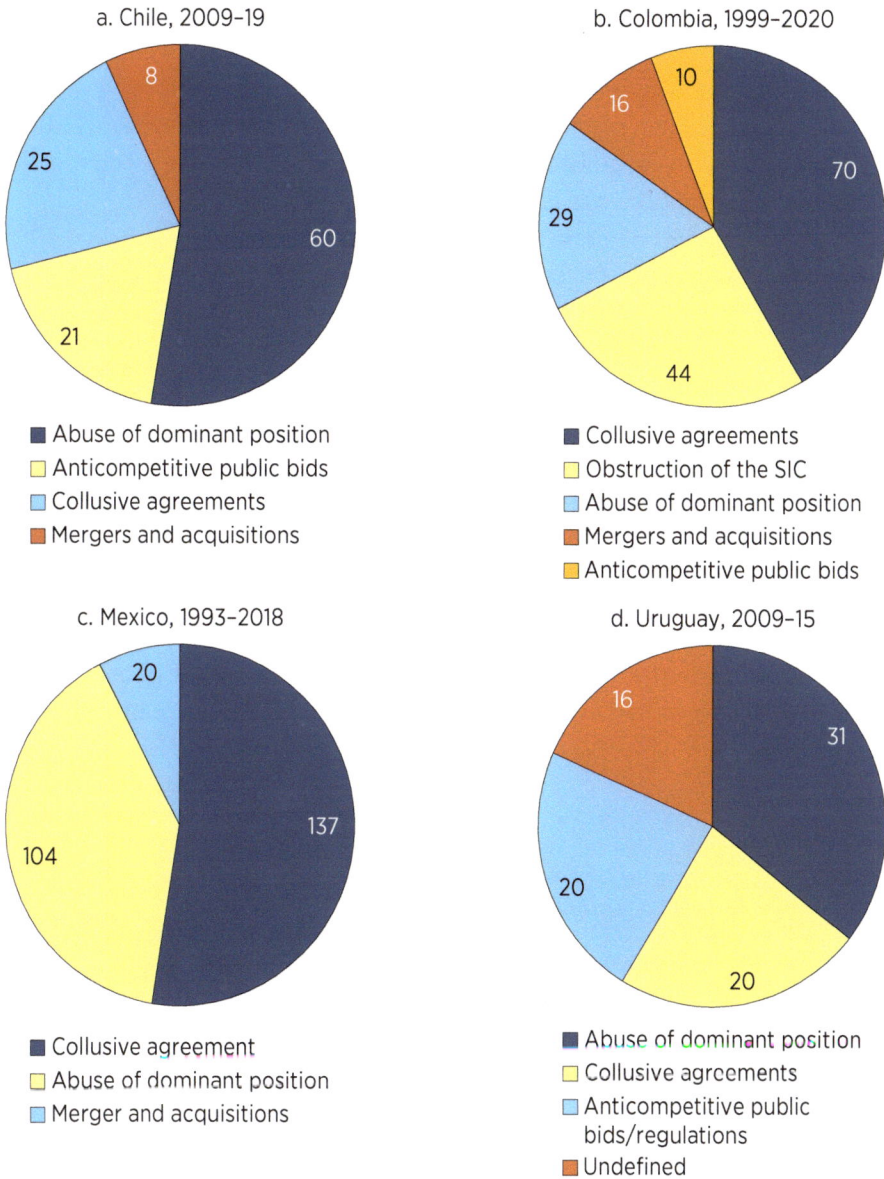

a. Chile, 2009–19

- ■ Abuse of dominant position
- ☐ Anticompetitive public bids
- ■ Collusive agreements
- ■ Mergers and acquisitions

b. Colombia, 1999–2020

- ■ Collusive agreements
- ☐ Obstruction of the SIC
- ■ Abuse of dominant position
- ■ Mergers and acquisitions
- ■ Anticompetitive public bids

c. Mexico, 1993–2018

- ■ Collusive agreement
- ☐ Abuse of dominant position
- ■ Merger and acquisitions

d. Uruguay, 2009–15

- ■ Abuse of dominant position
- ☐ Collusive agreements
- ■ Anticompetitive public bids/regulations
- ■ Undefined

Sources: Data collected from competition authorities in Chile (Fiscalía Nacional Económica [National Competition Authority]), Colombia (Superintendencia de Industria [Superintendence of Industry and Commerce]), Mexico (Comisión Federal de Competencia Económica [Federal Economic Competition Commission]), and Uruguay (Comisión de Promoción y Defensa de la Competencia [Commission for the Promotion and Protection of Competition]).

Note: For Mexico, alleged violations of mergers and acquisitions are noncompliance or violations of commitments to comply with approval for mergers and acquisitions. Sampi, Urrutia Arrieta, and Vostroknutova (2024) provide detailed data descriptions for Chile, Colombia, and Uruguay, and Reed et al. (2022) do so for Mexico. SIC = Superintendence of Industry and Commerce (Colombia).

Abuse of Dominance Is Associated with Barriers to Entry

Abuse of dominance occurs when a firm takes advantage of its dominant position to protect or increase its markups, for example, by limiting supply or directly influencing market entry and prices. These practices may include tying and bundling, unilateral refusal to deal, exclusive dealing, and predatory pricing. In many jurisdictions, punishing a firm for such practices requires demonstrating both that the firm has dominance and that the practice excludes rivals, thereby harming the market and consumers.

Abuse of dominance usually involves erecting entry barriers to protect the market share of the dominant firm. Such abuse is not unusual in network industries, given the presence of large incumbents, which are often former or current state-owned enterprises; the absence of import competition; and the strong emphasis on sales relative to production (figure 3.2, panel a). For instance, many cases have occurred in the information and communication technology (ICT) sector in Chile. One involved a telecom company that made its provision of fiber optic television conditional on subscription to its broadband internet services. In another case in Chile, mobile phone users were prevented from keeping their numbers if they migrated to competitors.

Figure 3.2   The majority of cases in Chile involve restricted entry in services and private complaints

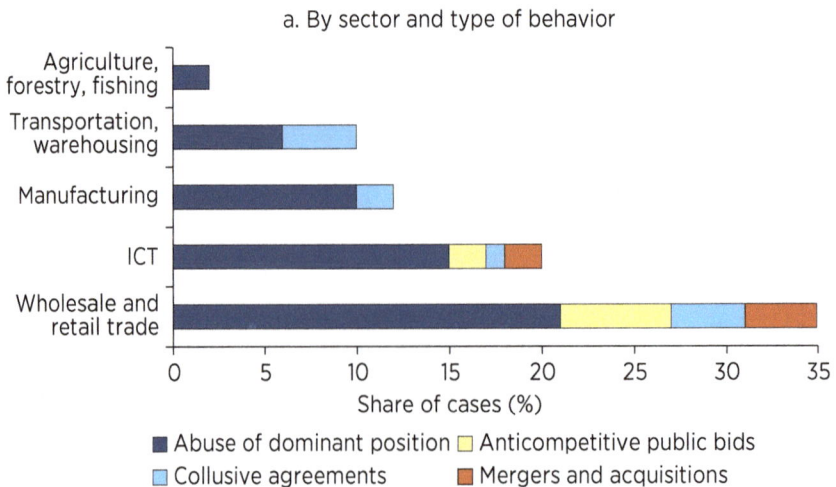

a. By sector and type of behavior

figure continued next page

Figure 3.2   The majority of cases in Chile involve restricted entry in services and private complaints *(continued)*

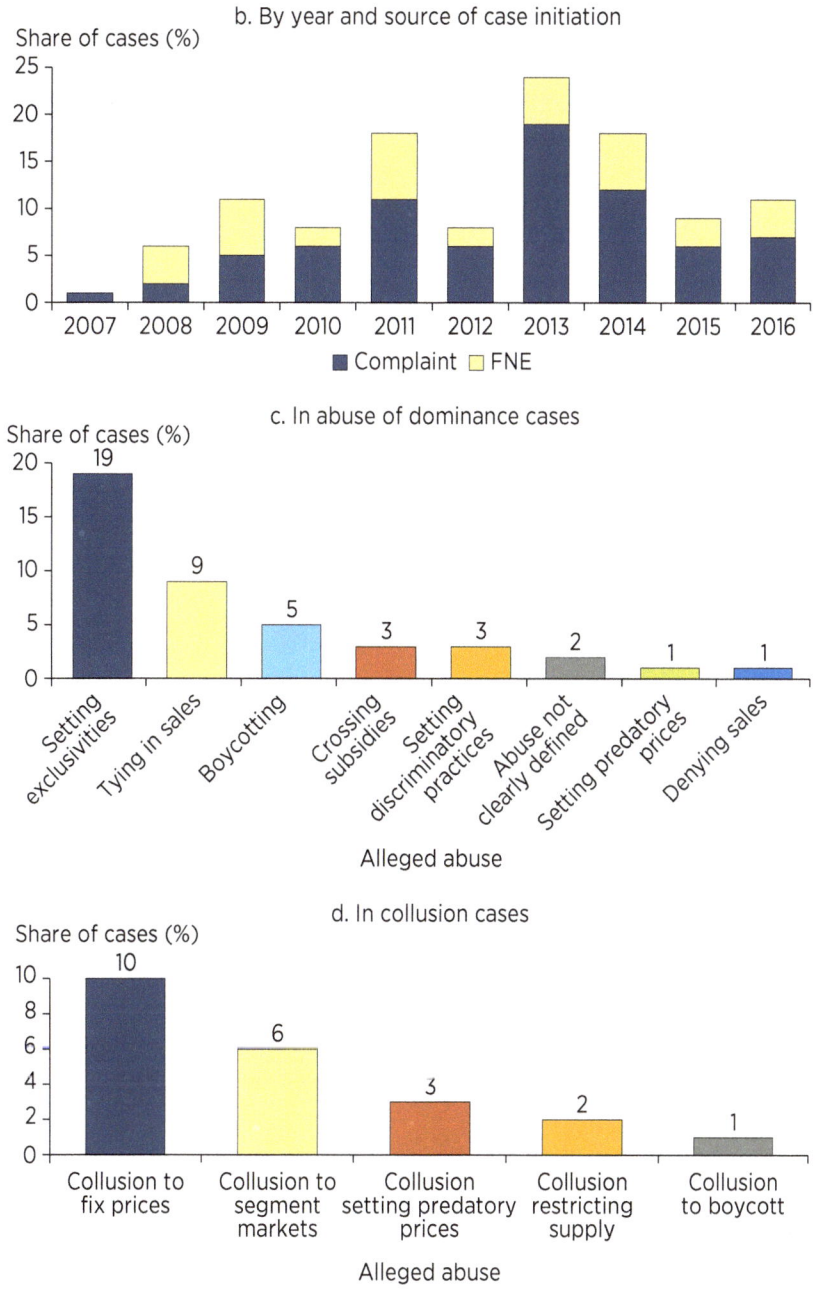

b. By year and source of case initiation

Share of cases (%)

■ Complaint ☐ FNE

c. In abuse of dominance cases

Share of cases (%)

Alleged abuse

d. In collusion cases

Share of cases (%)

Alleged abuse

Source: Sampi, Urrutia Arrieta, and Vostroknutova 2024.

Note: The figure illustrates data from 2009 to 2019 on regulatory enforcement drawn from the website of the Competition Court. In the empirical analysis, cases of abuse of dominance and collusion are pulled together. Refer to TDLC (Tribunal de Defensa de la Libre Competencia, Competition Court) (dashboard), TDLC, Santiago, Chile, https://www.tdlc.cl/. FNE = Fiscalía Nacional Económica (National Competition Authority in Chile); ICT = information and communication technology.

No sector of an economy is immune from abuse of dominance. In Chile, a foreign chemical producer supplying a domestic firm was pressured with limits to its access to input markets. The largest tobacco producer requested exclusive publicity for its brand at stores and bars, offering monetary incentives and credit facilities. A similar case involved a producer of matches that offered price discounts in exchange for exclusivity. In the Mexican state of Chiapas, a freight transportation firm was sanctioned for obstructing routes. Another case in Mexico involved the denial of sales by competing firms in the value chain for avocado exports to the United States.

Patterns of abuse may vary depending on the country. In Colombia, the most relevant investigations have involved activities in the health care sector and retail sale of food, beverages, and tobacco. In Uruguay, most cases have concerned health care and gambling. For instance, a pharmacy chain was accused of tying the sale of one product to the sale of another, a lottery firm was alleged to hinder the entry of new players, and a private school required uniforms from a specific supplier.

Cartels Keep Competitors Out and Raise Prices

Collusive practices involve two or more firms entering an agreement to gain or preserve market share or fix prices. In many countries in the region, these practices are illegal. Most of the cases that have been investigated have included agreements to fix prices or quantities, split up geographic markets, implement predatory prices, or limit market entry (box 1.2 in chapter 1 of this report).

Predatory pricing may involve a temporary price drop to prevent new entries.[5] For example, in Chile, a bus association facing new entry on one of its routes in the Maule Region boosted the frequency of buses on the route and reduced the transportation fee by two-thirds, from Ch$600 to Ch$200, well below the amount needed to cover variable costs. This strategy allegedly served to make entry a losing proposition for the competitor. In another case, the country's three largest poultry producers colluded to fix quotas, coordinate their supplies to the market, and protect their distribution systems, allowing them to set prices. Their collusion served as a de facto entry barrier because a new poultry producer entering the market would have to establish an alternative value chain for distribution to reach final consumers, in addition to creating production lines.

The prevalence of collusive practices has varied significantly across countries.

- In *Colombia*, investigations of collusive practices have been almost three times more frequent than investigations targeting abuses of dominance. About half of the collusive practices sanctioned in manufacturing were in the oils and fats industry. The highest monetary sanctions were imposed in the oligopolistic market for paper. In another case, two of the largest chocolate producers worked together to achieve a dominant position in the market and then pressured local producers of cacao, a key input, to accept a price that was well below the international market price. Meanwhile, an association of sugar producers colluded to monopolize the import of sugar from nearby countries by buying up excess supplies of sugar in those markets and rationing imports. Doing so created an obstacle to competition in the market and the supply of sugar products to other industries requiring sugar as a production input.

- In *Mexico*, about 80 percent of the collusion cases have involved price fixing. Market segmentation, supply restrictions, and coordination on public bids make up the rest of the collusion cases in the data set. Some internationally well-known examples include fixing the price of tortillas and discriminatory pricing that affected both consumers and competitors in cable television services.

- Most of the cases of collusion in *Uruguay* have occurred in food production. In a case that received extensive news coverage, poultry producers coordinated the timing of culling to manipulate supply and elevate prices. Other cases involved splitting the geographic market among tomato processing firms and tie-in sales arranged between two pharmaceutical firms.

Antitrust Enforcement Raises Sectorwide Productivity

Data on abuse of dominance and collusion cases in Chile, Colombia, Mexico, and Uruguay are combined with official firm-level surveys to estimate the impact of competition policy interventions on productivity growth.[6] This chapter discusses the results of this empirical work.

There are several important differences between the analysis of Mexico and the analysis of the other three countries. For Mexico, the analysis is carried out at the market level—that is, on a market defined as a specific sector in a specific region—and thus does not allow for observing effects on different types of firms or across the productivity distribution. However, in the case of Mexico, the chapter examines the effects of the sanctions imposed in antitrust cases and those closed without sanctions. Because of data limitations, this type of analysis was not possible for the cases of Chile, Colombia, or Uruguay. For the latter three countries, the analysis is carried out at both the market and firm levels to show the differential impacts across the productivity distribution and firm characteristics, such as size and age. Reed et al. (2022) and Sampi, Urrutia Arrieta, and Vostroknutova (2024) use several new methodologies and identification strategies. They study the impacts of competitive pressures enhanced by competition authority rulings on productivity and other firm-level outcomes, such as sales, marginal costs, and markups (box 3.1). These studies provide new empirical evidence on the impact of competition policy on productivity at the sector, market, and firm levels. The analysis can also flesh out how the decisions of the competition authority affect productivity.

Box 3.1

Empirical and identification strategies to clarify the impact of competition policy on productivity

Several methodologies and identification strategies are employed to understand empirically the impact of competition policy interventions on market- and firm-level productivity.

For Mexico, Reed et al. (2022) merge 261 investigations by the Federal Competition Commission of Mexico with plant-level microdata from the Mexican Economic Census from 1993 to 2018. The census is carried out by Mexico's national statistics authority, the Instituto Nacional de Estadística, Geografia e Informática [National Institute of Statistics, Geography and Informatics]. The cases studied are applicable at the national level. Region-level differentiation is not at the core of the identification strategy.

The commission discloses the relevant market for each investigation. The treated group is created by mapping each investigation to the relevant market according to a six-digit industry classification system.[a] The control group consists of all the other six-digit industries in the same three-digit sector as the treated group. The date of treatment is identified as the date of the commission's final decision to sanction the defendants or close the case.

box continued next page

Box 3.1

Empirical and identification strategies to clarify the impact of competition policy on productivity *(continued)*

This approach differs from that of Sampi, Urrutia Arrieta, and Vostroknutova (2024), who use only cases in which a punishment is applied. Given the scarce investigative resources, if the alleged conduct does not constitute a violation of competition law or if the complainant cannot provide additional information, the case is dismissed. Sampi, Urrutia Arrieta, and Vostroknutova (2024) do not consider these cases.

Reed et al. (2022) use a synthetic difference-in-differences estimator to identify the effect of the commission's rulings on anticompetitive behavior. They control for cases in which an investigation has been initiated, made public, and led to a final decision (often within two years after initiation). This approach identifies separate treatment and control groups for each case.

The methodology compares two effects of enforcement: (1) the average impact on sales, wages, productivity, and operating margins relative to the control group if a case has been initiated, and (2) the additional impact on sales, wages, productivity, and operating margins if a case has been finalized.

Sampi, Urrutia Arrieta, and Vostroknutova (2024) make several assumptions, most notably on the affected market analyzed. (The analysis considers one-digit sectors and regions with size assumptions for Chile, two-digit sectors and regions for Colombia, and four-digit sectors and regions for Uruguay.) They also make assumptions on the impact on firms that are not involved in the investigation (showing market transmission and behavioral effects). Sampi, Urrutia Arrieta, and Vostroknutova (2024) describe these assumptions in more detail. The interventions are assumed to be exogenous based on the process deployed to identify and investigate the cases. In particular, Sampi, Urrutia Arrieta, and Vostroknutova (2024) present evidence that the probability of investigating a firm is uncorrelated with the historical average productivity in the market. Regulations in the three countries apply nationwide and are subject to a rigorous review process, with the final decision dictated by an external competition court that has the authority to dismiss a case if there is insufficient evidence. This process supports the view that the authority's decisions are not guided by local conditions or local political incentives.

box continued next page

Box 3.1

Empirical and identification strategies to clarify the impact of competition policy on productivity *(continued)*

In addition, the case selection and investigation process matter for the empirical analysis. The competition agencies in Chile, Colombia, and Uruguay intervene in the market upon initial complaints by external parties (for instance, private firms or business associations) or by an ex officio procedure following a preliminary investigation. The core function of the investigation is to determine whether the accused party violated competition law, based on evidence obtained and following proper legal recourse. The ultimate decision may include punishment, such as sanctions, or dismissal of the case without charges.

In Chile, once the competition authority prosecutor (Fiscalía Nacional Económica [National Competition Authority]) decides to pursue a case, the evidence must be verified by the Competition Court (Tribunal de Defensa de la Libre Competencia [Competition Court]), which is an independent body specializing in competition matters. The court may order that the anticompetitive behavior cease, or it may impose a sanction, which could include imprisonment. The Supreme Court can overrule the lower court's resolution, in which case the national prosecutor can defend or challenge the court's rulings. These checks and balances ensure that decisions are independent.

In the cases of Colombia and Uruguay, external verification is provided by internal control systems that prevent bias toward specific parties. In addition, the parties involved may request the intervention of civil courts to guarantee the independence of the process. In Colombia, the procedures of the competition authority (Superintendencia de Industria y Comercio [Superintendence of Industry and Commerce]) are overseen by internal and external bodies through the control systems of the Administrative Department of Public Service, the Constitutional Court, and the Attorney General's Office. This last authority supervises the application of the law and how it affects the general interests of society.

In Uruguay, the procedures of the competition authority, a commission within the Ministry of Economy and Finance, may be reviewed externally by the administration or the judiciary. The competition commission requests the approval of external courts for inspections to collect evidence. Inspections are performed by the court itself.

box continued next page

Box 3.1

Empirical and identification strategies to clarify the impact of competition policy on productivity *(continued)*

In Mexico, the Federal Economic Competition Commission is responsible for investigating alleged monopolistic practices and sanctioning firms that act illegally. The commission can initiate investigations or respond to credible complaints from the public. Under the federal Economic Competition Law, agreements to fix prices or divide a market among competitors are deemed absolute monopolistic practices. Parties that engage in such practices must be sanctioned if there is conclusive evidence of wrongdoing. Mexican law identifies other practices, such as vertical restraint, as relative monopolistic practices. Unlike the case of absolute monopolistic practices, defendants have the right in these cases to argue that their practices do not harm or may even benefit consumers. If they can make a compelling argument, they can avoid sanctions.

Since its establishment, the Federal Economic Competition Commission has investigated about 40 percent of all economic activity (weighed by sales) at least once for illegal conduct. Investigations tend to be concentrated in nontradable sectors, such as commerce, transportation, and professional services. Fewer probes target manufacturing, where international trade provides competitive discipline over producer prices.

Source: Reed et al. 2022; Sampi, Jooste, and Vostroknutova 2021; Sampi, Urrutia Arrieta, and Vostroknutova 2024.

a. North American Industry Classification System database, US Census Bureau, Suitland, MD, https://www.census.gov/naics/.

In Chile and Uruguay, Competition Policy Interventions Result in Higher Productivity

Productivity estimates using the Sampi, Jooste, and Vostroknutova (2021) methodology indicate that interventions by competition authorities are followed by a surge in average firm productivity growth in Chile and Uruguay (figure 3.3): 10 percent in Chile, regardless of whether the focus was collusion or abuse of dominance, and 3 percent in Uruguay when the competition policy interventions concerned collusion. The latter result holds in the case of Uruguay if productivity is measured as in Ackerberg, Caves, and Frazer (2015). Moreover, this methodological approach reveals that productivity rises regardless of the type of intervention.[7]

Figure 3.3 Antitrust enforcement raises average productivity

Change in TFPR (%)

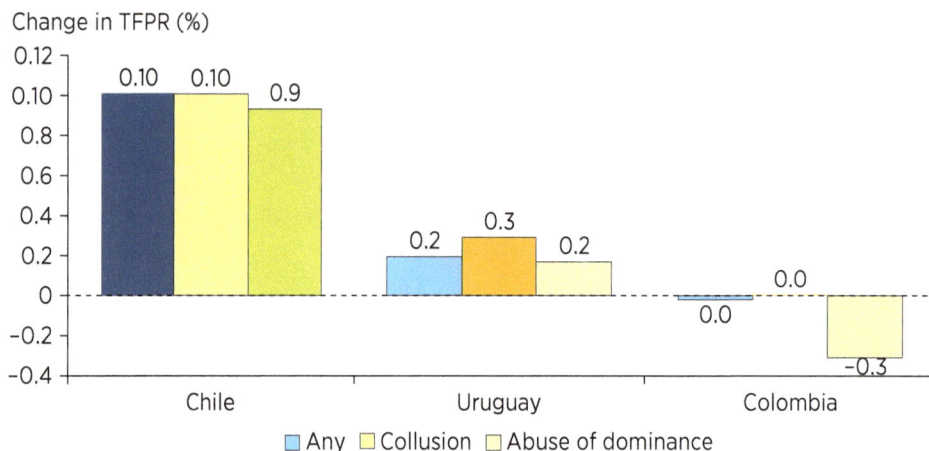

Legend: ■ Any □ Collusion □ Abuse of dominance

Source: Sampi, Urrutia Arrieta, and Vostroknutova 2024.

Note: The figure shows the effect of antitrust enforcement on TFPR by type of abuse in 2007–17. Darker colors indicate significant coefficients. TFPR is estimated using the methodological approach of Sampi, Jooste, and Vostroknutova (2021). TFPR = revenue-based total factor productivity.

Overall, the evidence is not robust to different methodological approaches to the measurement of outcomes. Capturing the positive effects of antitrust enforcement in the region may be difficult because of inadequate microeconomic data and the fact that enforcement activity covers only a fraction of market misbehavior. Isolated interventions may not produce significant changes. Moreover, as shown by the Peruvian case study on subnational governments, competition policy functions in tandem with other regulatory frameworks; if these frameworks do not align well with the policy, they may limit its effectiveness.

Sampi, Urrutia Arrieta, and Vostroknutova (2024) find that, in Uruguay, the impact on revenue productivity is greater if the investigation has been launched ex officio by the competition authority than if it has been undertaken in response to private complaints. This finding is robust across methodological approaches, which suggests that the action of the Uruguayan authority has been targeted appropriately and illustrates the importance of building the internal capacity of competition authorities.

However, measuring the effects of revenue-based total factor productivity (TFPR) has limitations. If the effects of productivity coincide with price changes (a reduction following cartel disbandment, for example), the impact on the physical (output-based) total factor productivity (TFPQ) measure could be greater than the result implied by the TFPR analysis. Only a few cases have involved the complete disbandment of cartels; most investigations have focused on less serious violations that authorities could identify and document. Some cases have involved predatory pricing, whereby prices would rise. Without price data, it is unclear where this sort of error will lead (box 3.2).

Rents complicate the measurement of productivity

One of the chief criticisms in the literature on the effect of trade on productivity is the inadequate measurement of productivity in the absence of price data. In most countries, only revenue-based total factor productivity (TFPR) can be calculated accurately. TFPR is a measure of efficiency in producing physical output that does not distinguish quality and rents, which are both captured by prices. Thus, a rise in productivity measured as TFPR may capture only an increase in rents rather than an increase in efficiency. Matching firm-level data sets with product-level price data allows researchers to distinguish differences between physical (output-based) total factor productivity (TFPQ) and TFPR so that productivity is not mingled with markups.

Using TFPR instead of TFPQ can bias the results upward. For example, in Colombia, there is strong evidence that trade reform has had a positive impact on TFPR, but the use of TFPQ shows a mixed and even diminishing impact (Eslava et al. 2013). Trade liberalization in India lowered input but not output prices, raising rents, which showed up as increased TFPR, but not necessarily a higher TFPQ (De Loecker and Goldberg 2014).

If price data are unavailable, changes in firm-specific markups may be used to help to assess changes in physical productivity. Markups may rise

box continued next page

Box 3.2

Rents complicate the measurement of productivity (continued)

because pure market power or innovation allowed an increase in product quality or a decrease in cost. If markups fell or remained unchanged while TFPR increased, TFPQ must have also increased. However, if there is a simultaneous rise in TFPR, product quality, and markups, what happens to TFPQ would be unclear. It may rise or fall. Additional estimates of product quality or innovation would help to reach a conclusion.

Different types and definitions of innovation, quality upgrading, or technology transfer can yield different impact assessments. Whether negative or positive, the effects of trade on innovation may depend on the type of innovation in question (Hombert and Matray 2018). Technology transfers have been documented in some settings, from foreign entrants to intermediate input producers, domestic firms, and new domestic entrants (Javorcik 2004; Shu and Steinwender 2019).

There are also important nuances explaining the size of the effects at the sector or market level in cases where wrongdoing has been found. These differences exist mainly because of the heterogeneity of firms' capabilities to adapt to competition authorities' interventions.

Antitrust Sanctions Boost Productivity

A distinctive practice in competition law in Mexico allows Reed et al. (2022) to identify the causal effects on economic outcomes of antitrust sanctions or financial penalties on agents involved in illegal conduct. In some jurisdictions, including the United States, researchers may not learn the identity of the relevant market in an antitrust case until after prosecutors bring the case to trial. In contrast, in Mexico, to undertake any investigation, the Federal Economic Competition Commission is obliged to publish in the Official Federal Gazette the identity of the relevant market. This information enabled Reed et al. (2022) to observe changes in the Mexican markets where illegal conduct was suspected but not punished because the cases were closed without a decision. They use these changes as a counterfactual in assessing the impact of sanctions.[8] They find that sanctions in antitrust cases raised sales, wages, and productivity in the investigated industries. Sales grew 5.8 percent in response to sanctions, compared to cases that were closed without a decision, where sales growth fell by 7.1 percentage points (figure 3.4).

Figure 3.4   Antitrust sanctions lead to higher sales, wages, and productivity

Annualized percentage points

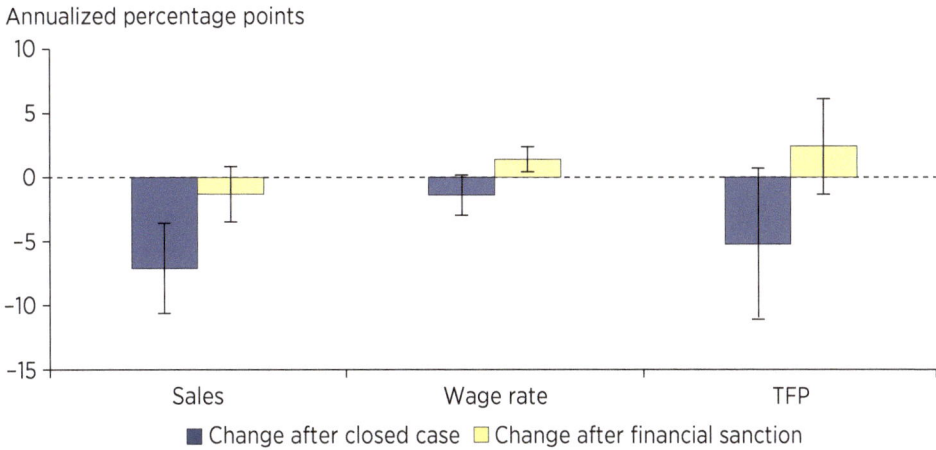

■ Change after closed case   □ Change after financial sanction

Source: Reed et al. 2022, using data from the 1993–2018 Economic Censuses.

Note: The figure shows the effect of antitrust sanctions on sales, wages, and productivity in Mexico, 1993–2018. TFP is industry TFPQ, assuming a constant elasticity of substitution demand function (Hsieh and Klenow 2009). The vertical black lines are 95 percent confidence intervals. The bars are the average percent change in the outcome measured as difference in differences. Sales are total industry sales. Wages are the total remuneration of industry employees divided by total employment. The profit margin is value added minus total remuneration of employees, divided by sales. The percent change in the profit margin assumes a baseline profit margin of 20 percent, similar to the level that many of the firms in the sample achieve. TFP = total factor productivity; TFPQ = physical (output-based) total factor productivity.

The trends among closed cases suggest that industries in which illegal conduct is suspected and investigated tend to be those that are in decline for unrelated reasons.[9] These trends imply that cartels may be more likely to form in industries where demand is falling, as predicted in standard industrial organization theory, as a way to protect profits. The slower decline after sanctions suggests that, although antitrust sanctions cannot reverse declining sales, they may perhaps slow the rate of decline. Although cartels may increase the profits of their members, they reduce demand by charging higher prices. If sanctions force the cartel to cease collusion and prices fall, consumers buy more. Consistent with this mechanism, operating margins also fall after sanctions, whereas they rise on average after cases are closed.

The results on wages and total factor productivity (TFP) illustrate the mechanisms behind this finding. After sanctions, wage rates are estimated to rise by 1.4 percentage points annually, and TFP is estimated to rise by 2.4 percentage points annually. These estimates suggest that antitrust sanctions boost productivity and pass the benefits directly to workers as higher wages. Higher productivity may stem from the more competitive environment obliging firms to improve operations. Consistent with this theory, increases in productivity are broad-based and affect all firms in an industry.

Although this result applies to the entire data set, box 3.3 describes two cases that offer further confirmation. Judges face difficult decisions when evaluating exclusive dealing arrangements offered by dominant firms (Gavil and Salop 2020). Even if an agent refuses an exclusive contract intended to restrict competition, should offering such a contract still be punished? It is likely that such actions will persist with impunity if the Federal Economic Competition Commission decides to drop the relevant investigations. In the Mexican case, the fact that an investigation did not result in a sanction led to a decline in sales and wages and an increase in profit margins. Rising margins accompanied by declining sales and wages could indicate that such industries are experiencing anticompetitive behavior, which would raise markups while reducing dynamism.

Box 3.3

A tale of two antitrust cases in Mexico

In 2007, a complaint was filed in Mexico alleging that real estate broker associations were fixing brokerage rates. After an investigation and lengthy appeals, the Federal Economic Competition Commission ruled in 2014 that the defendants had engaged in price fixing. It imposed a fine equivalent to about US$1.5 million and ordered the end of such practices. The sanction was associated with a 116 percent increase in marketwide sales by real estate brokers, relative to other real estate services (figure B3.3.1).

The second case was launched in 2003 following a complaint alleging monopolistic practices in firms specializing in wedding planning and supply services. The complaint claimed that a dominant firm that organized a wedding supply exhibition conditioned the sale of stands there on the requirement that exhibitors not maintain stands at exhibitions organized by a competitor. In this case, citing evidence that exhibitors had not accepted the exclusive contracts, the commission did not find convincing evidence of harm and closed the case without sanction in 2004. The decision not to sanction was associated with an 88 percent decline in wedding and regional dress sales, relative to a control group (figure B3.3.2).

box continued next page

Box 3.3

A tale of two antitrust cases in Mexico *(continued)*

Figure B3.3.1   Real estate sales increased significantly following the imposition of sanctions

Log of sales

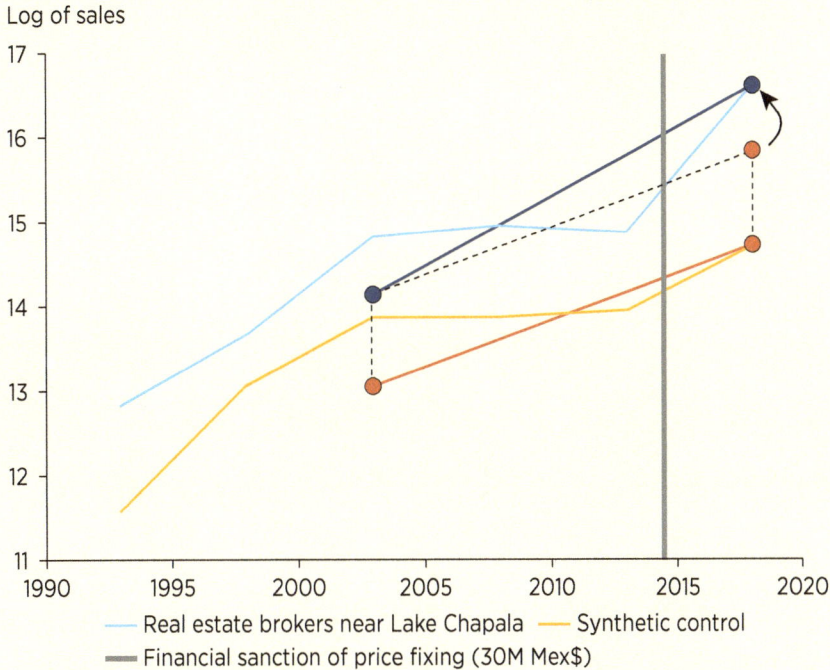

— Real estate brokers near Lake Chapala   — Synthetic control
— Financial sanction of price fixing (30M Mex$)

Source: Reed et al. 2022, using data from the 1993–2018 Economic Censuses.

Note: The figure shows the change in real estate sales, with antitrust sanctions, in Mexico, 1990–2020. Sales in industry #531210, "realtors and real estate brokers," near Lake Chapala are indicated by the light blue line. The thin red line indicates the average national sales in four other six-digit activities from the three-digit subsector #531, "real estate services," where the average is weighted so the industries have a similar pre-trend in (the log of) sales. There are four control industries, each with approximately equal weight. The thick blue line connects the average of (the log of) sales in the treatment industry before and after the sanction. The thick red line connects these same averages in the synthetic control industry. The counterfactual outcome in the treated industry is constructed by shifting the thick red line up along the dotted lines so the pretreatment average control outcome matches the pretreatment average treatment outcome. This counterfactual outcome is indicated with a red dot. The difference in differences connects the observed outcome with this counterfactual. The difference in differences is indicated by the arrow, which is equal to 0.77 log points of sales, or an increase in sales of $(\exp(0.77) - 1) \times 100 = 116$ percent.

box continued next page

Box 3.3

A tale of two antitrust cases in Mexico *(continued)*

Figure B3.3.2   Wedding-related sales declined after the commission decided not to impose sanctions

Log of sales

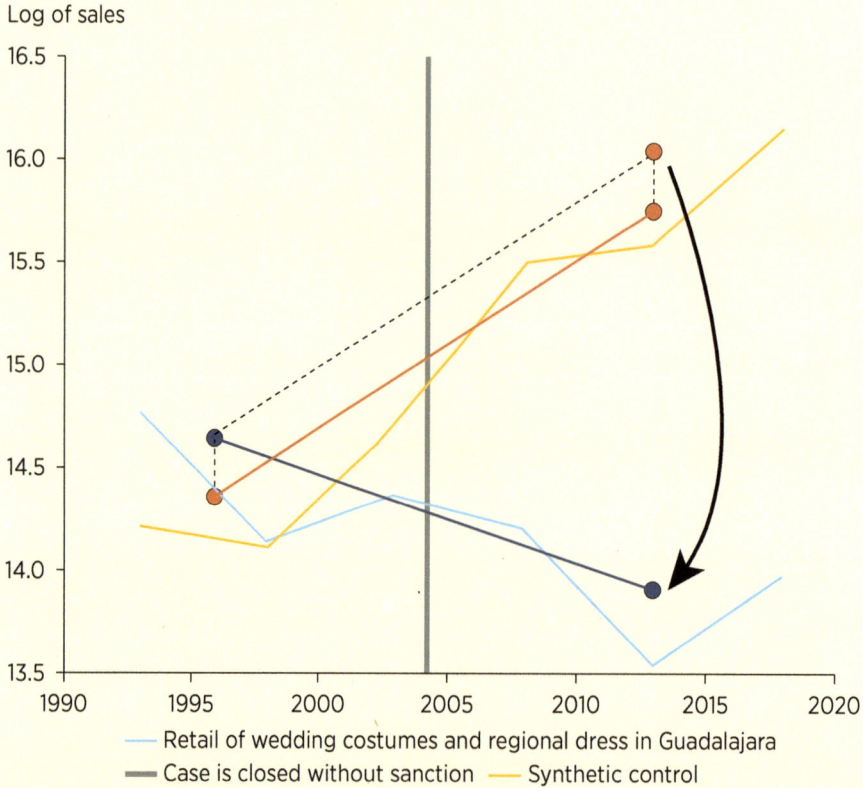

Source: Reed et al. 2022, using data from the 1993–2018 Economic Censuses.

Note: The figure shows the shange in wedding-related sales, without antitrust sanctions, in Mexico, 1990–2020. Outcome changes are estimated using the synthetic difference-in-differences method. Sales in industry #463214, "retail trade of wedding and regional dresses," are indicated by the thin blue line. The thin red line indicates the average sales in four other six-digit activities from the three-digit subsector #463, "retail of textiles, jewelry, clothing accessories, and footwear subsector," where the average is weighted so the industries have a similar pre-trend in (the log of) sales. The difference in differences is indicated by the arrow, which is equal to −2.15 log points of sales, or a decrease in sales of (exp(−2.15) −1) × 100 = −88 percent.

The closing of cases because of a lack of sufficient evidence may reflect the competition authority's inability to gather such evidence (as discussed in chapter 5 of this report). The different outcomes in the two cases highlight the importance of ensuring that national competition authorities have adequate capacity to assess and investigate cases.

Source: Reed et al. 2022.

A long-running debate in advanced antitrust jurisdictions such as the United States concerns the question of false positive and false negative findings of harm from antitrust violations. Using the language of decision theory, Khan (2018) argues that, in cases where they have discretion, judges are biased toward making type II errors (false negatives, or not sanctioning agents when their conduct has harmed competition) because of an incorrect presumption that type I errors (false positives, or sanctioning agents when their conduct has not harmed competition) are more costly. Salop (2017) provides several examples of cases in which false negatives were more costly. The results in Reed et al. (2022) suggest that closing an investigation without sanctions could be a false negative on average because sales, wages, and productivity decline. If there were no false negatives, a uniformly negative or null change in sales, wages, and profit margins would be expected after the commission closes a case without sanction.

This section shows that antitrust sanctions increase the average TFP in the affected market but that TFP falls after a decision not to sanction. The positive effect of sanctions on TFP shows that more sanctions resulting from investigations may be beneficial. By evaluating outcomes after sanctions and closed cases in a similar way, other national competition agencies might understand their capacity and effectiveness.

Both Antitrust Regulations and Their Enforcement Matter for Productivity Outcomes

Arayavechkit, Jooste, and Urrutia Arrieta (2022) study how competition policy enforcement affects productivity (TFPR), the dispersion of markups, product quality, and marginal costs in ICT in Peru.[10] The impact of competition policy enforcement on productivity in ICT is positive among market leaders, which are defined as the top 25 percent of firms in the productivity distribution (estimated as in Sampi, Jooste, and Vostroknutova [2021]), but the aggregate effect is insignificant. In line with other case studies in this report, the increased competitive pressure leads to churning at the lower end of the productivity distribution. For the least productive firms, TFPR and markups both fall after a competition policy case (figure 3.5). However, TFPR increases among the leading firms (figure 3.6). Gains in productivity, often without a commensurate change in markups, suggest that TFPQ productivity improves. This result assumes that marginal costs are not significantly affected.

Figure 3.5 Laggards lose markups following antitrust cases

Effect on markups (%)

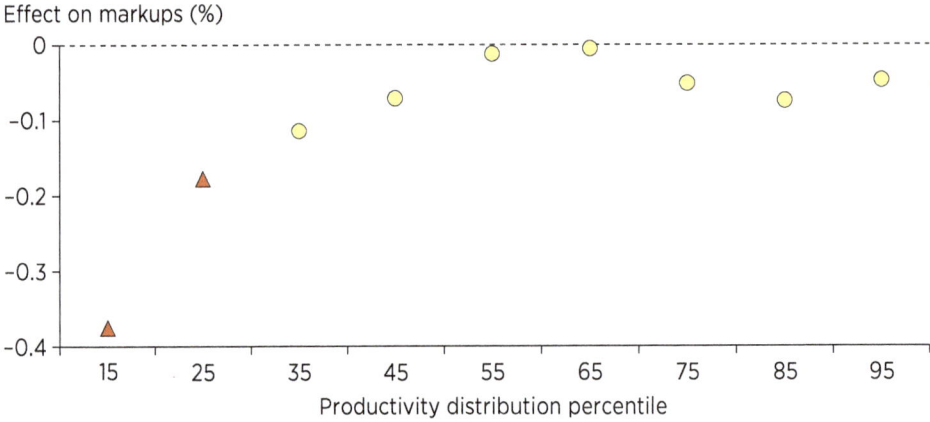

Productivity distribution percentile

Source: Arayavechkit, Jooste, and Urrutia Arrieta 2022.

Note: The figure shows the effect of antitrust cases on markups, relative to firms not ordered to take corrective action, by firm productivity level. Red triangles indicate that the estimates are statistically significant. ICT = information and communication technology; TFPR = revenue-based total factor productivity.

Figure 3.6 Leaders advance and laggards fall further behind following antitrust enforcement

Effect on TFPR (%)

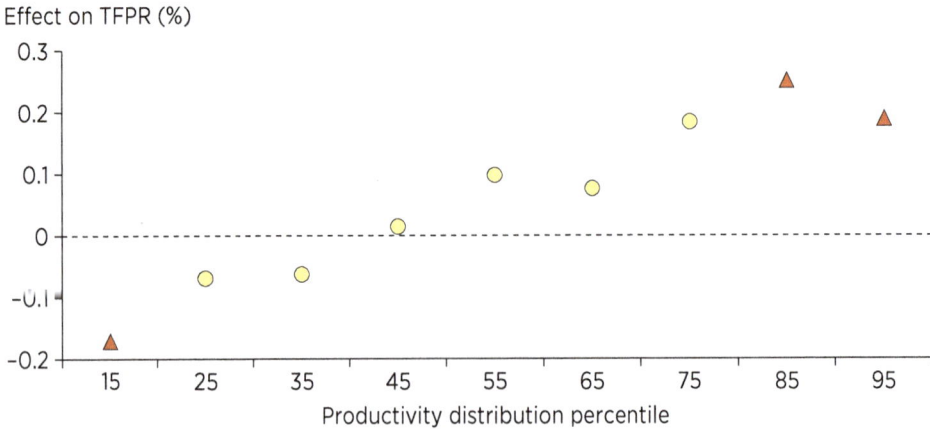

Productivity distribution percentile

Source: Arayavechkit, Jooste, and Urrutia Arrieta 2022.

Note: The figure shows the effect of antitrust enforcement on TFPR, relative to firms not ordered to take corrective action, by firm productivity level. Red triangles indicate that the estimates are statistically significant. ICT = information and communication technology; TFPR = revenue-based total factor productivity.

The aggregate effect is mirrored by the firm age profile. As a group, young and middle-aged firms respond positively to competition policy enforcement. Within that group, the leading young and middle-aged firms show the largest productivity increases (figure 3.7). These results are in line with a theme that emerges across all types of firms in the region. Leading firms—measured by relative productivity—react to competitive pressures, while laggards tend to capitulate. However, there is less consistency in the evidence from the responses of younger versus older firms in the face of competitive pressures. In general, there is evidence that frontier firms in services, particularly in ICT, tend to be younger than frontier firms in manufacturing (Andrews, Criscuolo, and Gal 2015).

Figure 3.7 Enforcement effects on productivity across leaders and laggards are conditional on age

Effect on TFPR (%)

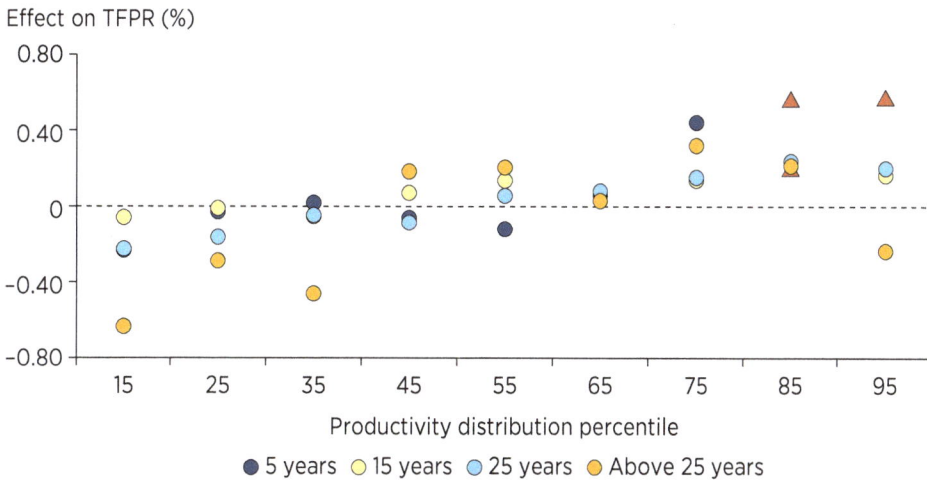

Productivity distribution percentile

● 5 years   ○ 15 years   ○ 25 years   ● Above 25 years

Source: Arayavechkit, Jooste, and Urrutia Arrieta 2022.

Note: The figure shows the effect of enforcement on TFPR, by firm age and productivity level. Red triangles indicate that estimates are statistically significant. TFPR = revenue-based total factor productivity.

Conclusions

This chapter has discussed new empirical evidence of the effectiveness of competition policy interventions in developing countries. Overall, it found that targeting collusion and the abuse of dominance increases productivity in leading firms. However, a positive net impact on overall or market productivity depends on the balance between productivity gains by leading firms that are able to escape competition by boosting their innovation efforts and the decline in productivity and sales suffered by laggard firms.

With the available information, isolating the mechanism through which these effects occur in each country is not empirically feasible. The fact that leading firms respond well to competitive pressure is a strong indication of the association between innovation and the ability to escape competition. However, it does not rule out other channels, such as entry or allocation effects.

Raising the investigative capacity and financial resources of competition authorities would generate broader productivity benefits by making competition policy more effective. This conclusion is based on results reported for Mexico, where cases that were closed without sanctions because of a lack of investigative capacity allowed the targeted firms to continue harming consumers and nondominant firms. In other countries, cases initiated by the competition authorities were more likely to increase productivity, suggesting that increasing the authorities' capacity to investigate more cases may have additional positive effects on productivity. Overall, the evidence suggests that governments in the region would benefit from the pursuit of more aggressive antitrust law enforcement.

Finally, the fact that innovation spurred by antitrust regulation and enforcement occurs mainly among leading firms signals the scope for coordinating reforms to facilitate innovation—access to financing, managerial capabilities, infrastructure for incubation and accelerator centers, and so forth.[11] To amplify the benefits of antitrust efforts, governments need to combine these efforts with complementary policies.

Notes

1. Kang (2023) provides a literature review and discussion on the opposite results involving frontier research and development in the United States. Chapters 1 and 5 of this report discuss the debate over the application of antitrust and patent law in developing countries.
2. Although the impact of factor market regulations on productivity has been studied, the empirical evidence on product markets has mostly involved case studies focused on the effects on equity prices, profits, and consumer prices (Aguzzoni, Langus, and Motta 2013; Besley, Fontana, and Limodio 2021; Bittlingmayer 1993; Duso, Neven, and Röller 2007; Ilzkovitz and Dierx 2015).
3. Bid rigging is excluded because of the lack of data and the small number of cases. Sampi, Urrutia Arrieta, and Vostroknutova (2024) provide detailed descriptions for Chile, Colombia, and Uruguay; and Reed et al. (2022) do so for Mexico.
4. Such conduct is covered in the United States under the conspiracy to monopolize doctrine in the Sherman Act, section 2.
5. These cases are often pursued under laws sanctioning the abuse of dominance.
6. For Chile, the analysis relies on the Longitudinal Survey of Firms collected by the National Institute of Statistics in 2007–17 and the National Statistics Institute's Innovation Survey in 2007–17. Unlike elsewhere, where data on both manufacturing and services are available, in Colombia, the firm database is available only for manufacturing through the Annual Manufacturing Survey conducted by the

National Administrative Department of Statistics for 2007–18. In Uruguay, the analysis uses firm data from the Annual Economic Activity Survey collected by the National Institute of Statistics in 2007–16. In contrast to other countries, Mexico's data set is an economic census, which includes small and sole proprietorship firms. The quinquennial economic censuses of the Instituto Nacional de Estadística, Geografia e Informática [National Institute of Statistics, Geography and Informatics] cover the calendar years 1993–2018.

7. In Colombia, no positive effect is found using the Sampi, Jooste, and Vostroknutova (2021) methodology, and the Ackerberg, Caves, and Frazer (2015) methodology yields evidence of a negative effect on productivity.
8. This approach resolves an issue in earlier analyses of antitrust enforcement wherein the counterfactual is represented by another industry in the same sector with similar cost and demand drivers, rather than a market in which illegal activity is suspected but not punished. If illegal conduct occurs in industries characterized by unique trends that distinguish these industries from others in the same sector, the earlier approach does not work. The new approach also ensures that the counterfactual includes any potential deterrent or encouragement associated with an investigation that acts as a warning shot because its existence is made public to market participants, although the investigation does not lead to a trial.
9. Firms that escape investigation because of a lack of sufficient evidence may bias the results in either direction. If the firms violated competition law and were underperforming (in TFP) compared with peers in the market, then the coefficient would have an upward bias. If the firms were performing similarly to average market peers, the coefficient would be biased downward.
10. This effort consisted of combining firm-level data from the Annual Economic Survey over 2007–17 with applicable laws and regulations decreed during the same period at the four-digit International Standard Industrial Classification (ISIC) code level. Data on regulations were collected from several authorities for different ICT markets. ICT is split into software, hardware, telecommunications, and infrastructure. The appendix in Arayavechkit, Jooste, and Urrutia Arrieta (2022) describes the data and codification steps. For the ISIC, refer to ISIC (International Standard Industrial Classification of All Economic Activities) (dashboard), Statistics Division, Department of Economic and Social Affairs, United Nations, New York, https://unstats.un.org/unsd/classifications/Econ/ISIC.cshtml.
11. Cirera et al. (2020) provide a comprehensive summary of policies aimed at promoting innovation in developing economies.

References

Ackerberg, Daniel A., Kevin Caves, and Garth Frazer. 2015. "Identification Properties of Recent Production Function Estimators." *Econometrica* 83 (6): 2411–51.

Aghion, Philippe, Antonin Bergeaud, Matthieu Lequien, Marc J. Melitz, and Thomas Zuber. 2022. "Opposing Firm-Level Responses to the China Shock: Horizontal Competition versus Vertical Relationships?" NBER Working Paper 29196 rev., National Bureau of Economic Research, Cambridge, MA.

Aghion, Philippe, Nicholas Bloom, Richard Blundell, Rachel Griffith, and Peter Howitt. 2005. "Competition and Innovation: An Inverted-U Relationship." *Quarterly Journal of Economics* 120 (2): 701–28. https://doi.org/10.1093/qje/120.2.701.

Aguzzoni, Luca, Gregor Langus, and Massimo Motta. 2013. "The Effect of EU Antitrust Investigations and Fines on a Firm's Valuation." *Journal of Industrial Economics* 61 (2): 290–338. https://doi.org/10.1111/joie.12016.

Andrews, Dan, Chiara Criscuolo, and Peter N. Gal. 2015. "Frontier Firms, Technology Diffusion, and Public Policy." OECD Productivity Working Paper 2, Global Forum on Productivity, Organisation for Economic Co-operation and Development, Paris. https://doi.org/10.1787/5jrql2q2jj7b-en.

Arayavechkit, Tanida, Charl Jooste, and Ana Francisca Urrutia Arrieta. 2022. "How Regulation and Enforcement of Competition Affects ICT Productivity: Evidence from Matched Regulatory-Production Surveys in Peru's ICT Sector." Policy Research Working Paper 10151, World Bank, Washington, DC. http://hdl.handle.net/10986/37920.

Begazo, Tania Priscilla, and Sara Nyman. 2016. "Competition and Poverty: How Competition Affects the Distribution of Welfare." Viewpoint (April 1), World Bank, Washington, DC.

Besley, Timothy J., Nicola Fontana, and Nicola Limodio. 2021. "Antitrust Policies and Profitability in Nontradable Sectors." *American Economic Review: Insights* 3 (2): 251–65.

Bittlingmayer, George. 1993. "The Stock Market and Early Antitrust Enforcement." *Journal of Law and Economics* 36 (1, Part 1): 1–32. https://doi.org/10.1086/467263.

Cirera, Xavier, Jaime Frías, Justin Hill, and Yanchao Li. 2020. *A Practitioner's Guide to Innovation Policy: Instruments to Build Firm Capabilities and Accelerate Technological Catch-Up in Developing Countries.* Washington, DC: World Bank. https://doi.org/10.1596/33269.

De Loecker, Jan K., and Pinelopi Koujianou Goldberg. 2014. "Firm Performance in a Global Market." *Annual Review of Economics* 6 (1): 201–27.

Duso, Tomaso, Damien J. Neven, and Lars-Hendrik Röller. 2007. "The Political Economy of European Merger Control: Evidence Using Stock Market Data." *Journal of Law and Economics* 50 (3): 455–89. https://doi.org/10.1086/519812.

Eslava, Marcela, John C. Haltiwanger, Adriana Kugler, and Maurice David Kugler. 2013. "Trade and Market Selection: Evidence from Manufacturing Plants in Colombia." *Review of Economic Dynamics* 16 (1): 135–58. https://doi.org/10.1016/j.red.2012.10.009.

Fox, Eleanor M., Harry First, Nicolas Charbit, and Elisa Ramundo, eds. 2016. *Antitrust in Emerging and Developing Countries: Featuring Africa, Brazil, China, India, Mexico—Conference Papers.* 2nd ed. New York: Concurrences Review.

Gal, Michal S., Mor Bakhoum, Josef Drexl, Eleanor M. Fox, and David J. Gerber, eds. 2015. *The Economic Characteristics of Developing Jurisdictions: Their Implications for Competition Law.* Cheltenham, UK: Edward Elgar.

Gavil, Andrew I., and Steven C. Salop. 2020. "Probability, Presumptions, and Evidentiary Burdens in Antitrust Analysis: Revitalizing the Rule of Reason for Exclusionary Conduct." *University of Pennsylvania Law Review* 168 (7): 2107–43. https://scholarship.law.upenn.edu/cgi/viewcontent.cgi?article=9721&context=penn_law_review.

Hombert, Johan, and Adrien Matray. 2018. "Can Innovation Help U.S. Manufacturing Firms Escape Import Competition from China?" *Journal of Finance* 73 (5): 2003–39.

Hsieh, Chang-Tai, and Peter J. Klenow. 2009. "Misallocation and Manufacturing TFP in China and India." *Quarterly Journal of Economics* 124 (4): 1403–48.

Ilzkovitz, Fabienne, and Adriaan Dierx. 2015. "Ex-Post Economic Evaluation of Competition Policy Enforcement: A Review of the Literature." Directorate-General for Competition Staff Paper (June), European Union, Luxembourg.

Javorcik, Beata Smarzynska. 2004. "Does Foreign Direct Investment Increase the Productivity of Domestic Firms? In Search of Spillovers through Backward Linkages." *American Economic Review* 94 (3): 605–27.

Kang, Hyo. 2023. "How Does Price Competition Affect Innovation? Evidence from US Antitrust Cases." Research Paper, Marshall School of Business, University of Southern California, Los Angeles, CA.

Khan, Lina M. 2018. "The Ideological Roots of America's Market Power Problem." *Yale Law Journal Forum* 127: 960–79. https://www.yalelawjournal.org/forum/the-ideological-roots-of-americas-market-power-problem.

Reed, Tristan, Mariana De La Paz Pereira López, Ana Francisca Urrutia Arrieta, and Leonardo Iacovone. 2022. "Cartels, Antitrust Enforcement, and Industry Performance: Evidence from Mexico." Policy Research Working Paper 10269, World Bank, Washington, DC. https://doi.org/10.1596/1813-9450-10269.

Salop, Steven C. 2017. "An Enquiry Meet for the Case: Decision Theory, Presumptions, and Evidentiary Burdens in Formulating Antitrust Legal Standards." Georgetown Law Faculty Publications and Other Works, Georgetown University Law Center, Washington, DC. https://scholarship.law.georgetown.edu/facpub/2007/.

Sampi, James Robert, Charl Jooste, and Ekaterina Vostroknutova. 2021. "Identification Properties for Estimating the Impact of Regulation on Markups and Productivity." Policy Research Working Paper 9523, World Bank, Washington, DC. http://hdl.handle .net/10986/35070.

Sampi, James Robert, Ana Francisca Urrutia Arrieta, and Ekaterina Vostroknutova. 2024. "Antitrust Enforcement, Markups, and Productivity: Evidence for Selected South America Countries." Background paper for this report. World Bank, Washington, DC.

Shu, Pian, and Claudia Steinwender. 2019. "The Impact of Trade Liberalization on Firm Productivity and Innovation." *Innovation Policy and the Economy* 19 (1): 39–68.

4

International Competition, Complementarity, and Capabilities

Introduction

International trade is widely viewed as a long-run driver of aggregate productivity partly because it facilitates creative destruction, that is, the entry of productive firms, competition with technologically superior international firms, and eventual improvements in factor allocation (Aghion et al. 2022; Akcigit and Melitz 2022; Amiti and Konings 2007; Autor, Dorn, and Hanson 2013; Pavcnik 2002).

However, the relationship between greater import competition, productivity, and innovation is not always straightforward among all market participants. It affects firms differently depending on their distance to the global technological frontier and the aggregate response (Aghion et al. 2022). The mixed response of sales and productivity among Chilean and Mexican firms to the Chinese trade shock provides a clear example of this more nuanced view, which is especially relevant for developing countries.[1]

China's World Trade Organization Accession as an Import-Related Competition Shock to Firms

China's accession to the World Trade Organization (WTO) offers a clear and relevant real-world experiment to study the response of firms in the region to the greater competition associated with trade liberalization. This chapter focuses on the effects of this shock on competition in Chile, Mexico, and Peru.

The value of China's overall exports grew from US$62 billion in 1990 to US$1.2 trillion in 2007, a staggering average rate of about 20 percent per year. China entered the WTO in 2001. By 2009, it had become the world's largest exporter and, by 2010, the second-largest economy. Latin America and the Caribbean's share of world imports from China expanded with remarkable speed. Mexico's share surged by a factor of 16 in a single decade. This surge was matched by only a moderate increase in flows in the opposite direction. China's share of imports from Mexico rose by a factor of 1.5 (from 1.9 to 2.8 percent) in 1994–2004.

The China import shock compressed sales of domestic firms in Mexico and was associated with lower sectorwide productivity in Chile. As Cusolito, Garcia-Marin, and Maloney (2021) demonstrate, in Chile, domestic firms that are far from the global productivity frontier face difficulties in relying on innovation to escape competition; therefore, they reduce output. In Chile, the jump in imports from China led to a fall in domestic firms' average output. Similarly, Iacovone, Rauch, and Winters (2013) find that, in Mexico, incumbents' sales fell because of increased import competition.

The absence of positive aggregate effects of trade on productivity in the region may seem counterintuitive in light of the conclusions in the mainstream trade literature (box 4.1).

Box 4.1

The complex impact of trade liberalization

The literature shows that, across Latin America and the Caribbean, greater trade openness is generally supportive of productivity growth. The 2002 trade reforms in Colombia, which reduced average tariffs and tariff dispersion across industries, had strong positive effects on firm exit and productivity. Reflecting improvements in market selection mechanisms, Eslava et al. (2013) and Fernandes (2007) find that physical (output-based) total factor productivity growth rose at the plant, market, and aggregate levels (as discussed in box 3.2, in chapter 3 of this report). Studies find that higher productivity is linked to trade openness in Brazil (Muendler 2004; Schor 2004) and Chile (Cusolito and Maloney 2018; Liu 1993; Pavcnik 2002). In Mexico, where the concentration of local industries is generally associated with lower firm productivity, Rodríguez-Castelán, López-Calva,

box continued next page

Box 4.1

The complex impact of trade liberalization *(continued)*

and Barriga Cabanillas (2020) find that industries with extensive exposure to international markets exhibit higher firm productivity.

The success of export competition in improving productivity is driven by marketwide effects, especially if the foreign market is significantly larger than the domestic market. However, the impact of import competition has been more ambiguous, especially in developing countries. For example, in the early 1980s, the dramatic rise in productivity in the US iron ore industry occurred because of competition with Brazilian plants. The rise was mainly achieved through changes in work practices, which helped to raise labor, material, and capital productivity, as documented by Schmitz (2005). However, increased competition from Chinese imports had an overall negative impact on patenting activity among US manufacturing firms, which is a proxy for innovation and productivity. Autor et al. (2020) confirm that this outcome was driven mostly by the exit of laggards.

Studies of import competition highlight the crucial role of innovation and capacity in coping with trade-induced shocks. Fernandes (2007) documents the link between tariff liberalization and plant productivity in Colombia, and Fernandes and Paunov (2013) document the link in Chile. In line with Aghion et al. (2005), a frequent finding is that responses to competition vary across firms. Stronger firms—more productive, larger, and exporting—are more likely to survive and respond positively to a competition shock. Bloom, Draca, and Van Reenen (2016) analyze imports from China in 12 European countries. They find that, in some sectors, Chinese competition boosted the innovative activity of European firms that survived but decreased employment and lowered the overall chances of firm survival. In heavily exposed sectors, low-technology firms suffered declines in jobs and survival rates, while high-technology firms were relatively safe. Bustos (2011) documents a positive association between competition and technology upgrading in Argentina.

Multiproduct firms that face competitive pressure on one of their products are likely to make internal adjustments to that product, including withdrawing it from the market. Such actions may become important for overall productivity. Bernard, Redding, and Schott (2010) find that the impact of product switching on US manufacturing growth is as large as the impact of the exit and entry of firms. Liu (2010) concludes that, in the United States, an increase in import competition makes firms more likely to drop less important products (those with smaller shares in total sales) but

box continued next page

Box 4.1

The complex impact of trade liberalization *(continued)*

less likely to drop core products (those with the largest shares in sales). Similarly, Eckel and Neary (2010) note that Mexican producers tended to react to the trade liberalization associated with the North American Free Trade Agreement by concentrating on core competencies.

The response of productivity to trade liberalization differs across markets, products, and firms. For instance, Schor (2004) finds that nominal tariff reductions in Brazil were positively correlated with rising productivity, but the effects varied depending on the characteristics of firms, including size, product, and technology; the degree of industry concentration; initial nominal tariffs; and the shares of firms importing and exporting. Chen, Imbs, and Scott (2009) contend that openness to trade squeezes margins and pricing among European firms but typically also raises productivity.

Ultimately, the effect of trade openness on the productivity of domestic firms depends on a plethora of factors: market size and structure, competition, sector, and the presence of market imperfections, such as inadequate access to finance, informality, and pervasive regulations (Autor et al. 2020; Bloom, Draca, and Van Reenen 2016; Campbell and Mau 2021; Keung, Li, and Yang 2016).

Sources: Based on Akcigit and Melitz 2022; Iacovone, Rauch, and Winters 2013; and the studies cited.

Four factors have likely contributed to these results. First, the firm-level data sets used in the literature allow only short-term localized impacts to be measured. Because of its dynamism, however, creative destruction is most powerful and more broad-based in the long run. Moreover, even short-term impacts vary by sector, product, and firm.

The second factor behind the absence of positive aggregate effects of trade on productivity in the region is the generally less positive aggregate impact of import competition relative to the aggregate impact of export competition (box 4.1).

Third, the lack of productivity gains may arise from widely used measures that include not only physical productivity but also rents and quality. Shifts in productivity among leaders may reflect changes in product innovation and quality upgrades rather than a persistent decline in productivity.

Fourth and most important, leader firms that can sway average market outcomes in a positive direction during a trade shock are in short supply in the region. In Chile, only 10 percent or less of domestic firms were able to upgrade quality or innovate in response to the import shock, compared with 50 percent in developed countries in similar circumstances and 25 percent in China (Aghion et al. 2009; Bombardini, Li, and Wang 2017; Maloney and Zambrano 2023). These facts emphasize the strong need for complementary policies, such as innovation systems, which might foster more leaders and increase the resilience of domestic markets in the face of shocks.

Mexico: The China Trade Shock Affected Firms and Markets Differently

This section shows that, relative to competition in output markets, competition in input markets can be more beneficial for domestic firms, but the benefits are more likely to accrue to the most productive firms than other firms. It also shows that, in Mexico, the response to competitive pressure from Chinese firms differs depending on the plant, product, and sector, as well as firm characteristics, such as capacity, size, and skill.

The effects of competition on productivity depend on a firm's capacity and size, the market in which the firm operates, and the quality of the products being introduced. Aggregate sales in a market do not necessarily rise when more firms enter. Instead, existing market shares may be redistributed among the market participants.

Iacovone, Rauch, and Winters (2013) utilize the surge in Chinese exports to Mexico in 1994–2004 as a quasi-natural experiment to investigate the competitive pressure that international competition exerts on Mexican manufacturing firms. They show that forces of creative destruction in the wake of China's accession to the WTO encouraged plant exit, product exit, and sales contraction among less productive domestic firms (laggards) but had positive effects on the sales of capable incumbent firms (that is, leaders in sales). To carry out the analysis, Iacovone, Rauch, and Winters use data from monthly industrial surveys of Mexican plants by the Institute of Statistics of Mexico (Instituto Nacional de Estadística, Geografia e Informática) that cover about 85 percent of all Mexican industrial output. They merge plant product data with Comtrade data at the six-digit level from the World Customs Organization Harmonized System to measure exposure to competition. The exposure variable is the share of Chinese imports in total imports in the market and at the plant level as the weighted average of Chinese imports of the products of each plant, using product sales shares as weights.[2] They include several instruments in the analysis to address potential endogeneity issues in accounting for possible effects on Mexican firms of Chinese exports to Mexico. The estimation also includes fixed effects to control for plant product fixed effects and year fixed effects. The study accounts for potential differences in the treated and control groups before and after the China trade shock. It finds no statistical differences in initial sales among the control and treatment groups, thus supporting the comparability of the groups after the shock.

Competition with Chinese firms led to a reallocation of factors among products within individual plants and across plants. The process of creative destruction and market selection operates at both the plant and product levels. For example, firms making a peripheral product (that is, a product of minor importance in the firm's total sales) are more likely to pull the product from the market if the firm faces strong competition. However, products that are core to a firm's business (products associated with large shares of total output) are less vulnerable to this effect. The probability of being dropped as a result of competition was significantly positive among the less important products of Mexican firms, whereas the probability was significantly negative for core products (figure 4.1).

Figure 4.1 Effects of competition differ for peripheral and core products

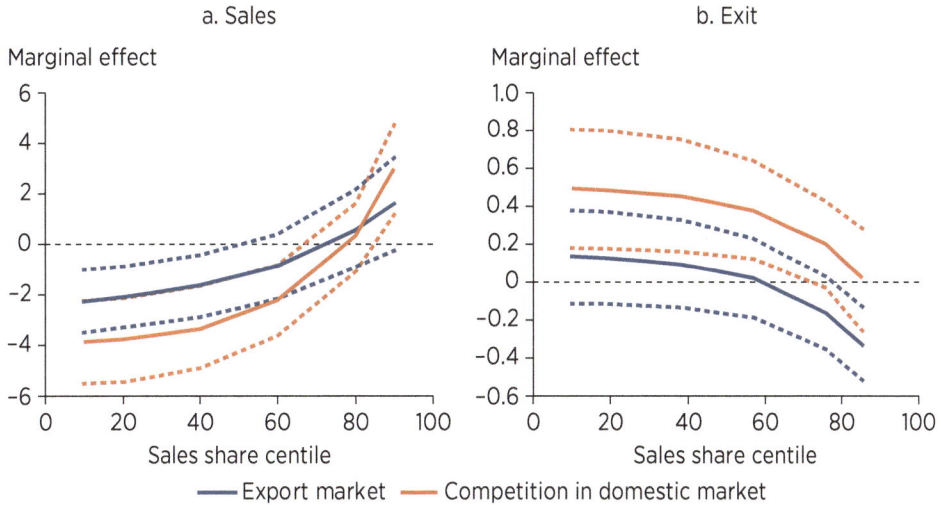

a. Sales

b. Exit

Export market   Competition in domestic market

Source: Iacovone, Rauch, and Winters 2013.

Note: The figure shows the marginal effects of competition on products as coefficients in the regressions. The thin dashed lines show the 95 percent confidence intervals. The x axis shows sales centiles or sales share centiles across plants, controlling for plant-product interaction. Core products have higher sales shares (right-side x axis) than the peripheral products (left-side x axis). The y axis indicates the marginal effect of competition, derived from the corresponding independent variable regressions using the coefficients on competition from China and the interaction term, multiplied by the corresponding plant size.

Access to cheaper and possibly better intermediate inputs as a result of the entry of foreign firms into input markets may benefit all firms along the value chain. Although cheaper inputs may not induce productivity growth in output markets, Tello and Tello-Trillo (2021) show that aggregate productivity outcomes may be enhanced following liberalization in input markets relative to output markets. That larger plants and core products benefit disproportionately from expanded access to cheaper imported intermediate goods lends support to this conclusion. Access to cheaper inputs helps firms to improve the competitiveness of their core products. In sales, the output of core products expands more because of the greater penetration of imported inputs, whereas the output of peripheral products expands less or not at all.

An important distinction in the results on input markets is the absence of product exits. This lack of exits suggests that differences in the ability to use imported intermediate inputs contribute crucially to the variations in the impact of Chinese competition. Thus, the fact that larger plants are better able to use cheaper inputs suggests that capacity matters for productivity outcomes.

Firm size also matters. Sales of peripheral products and sales of the output of smaller plants declined and were more likely to cease altogether following China's accession to the WTO, whereas sales of core products and sales of the output of larger plants seemed to be relatively impervious to the shock. This result implies the existence of reallocation of market shares within firms and across firms. However, the positive effects significantly exceed zero only at the extensive margin (exit and survival) of the top 10 percent of products in the export market and the top 20 percent of products at the intensive margin (sales) in the domestic market (figure 4.2).

Figure 4.2 The impact of competition has been positive among large firms and negative among small firms

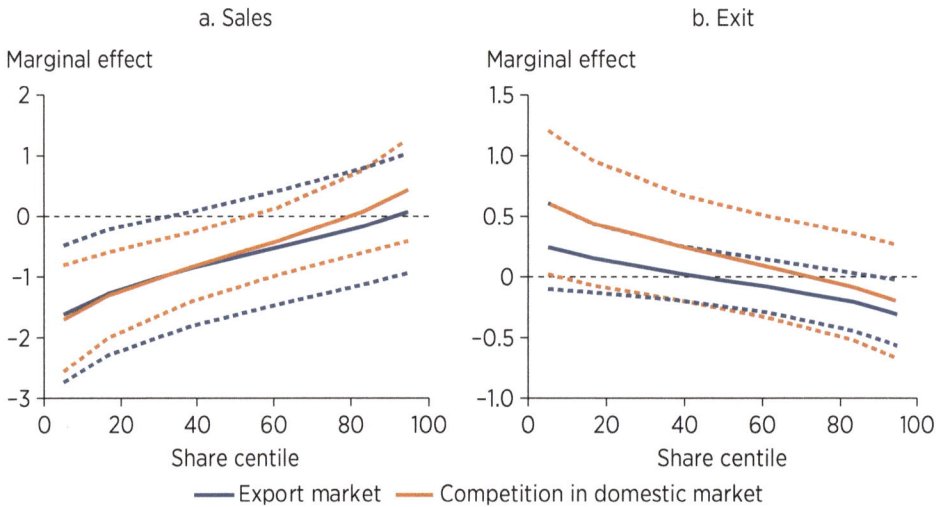

Source: Iacovone, Rauch, and Winters 2013.

Note: The figure shows the marginal effects of competition on plants as coefficients in the regressions. The thin dashed lines show the 95 percent confidence intervals. The x axis shows sales centiles or sales share centiles across plants, controlling for plant-product interaction. The y axis indicates the marginal effect of competition, derived from the corresponding independent variable regressions using the coefficients on Chinese competition and the interaction term, multiplied by the corresponding plant size.

The analysis also highlights the importance of capabilities and skills. Large firms with relatively more skilled workers were more likely to boost sales in response to the shock caused by Chinese imports. In particular, 10 percent of the most productive firms significantly increased sales. In this way, Tello and Tello-Trillo (2021) find direct evidence of sales creation among the leading firms and link this sales creation to skills.

Other studies have also found that innovative activity increased in Mexican plants following China's competition surge. Initiatives such as ISO-2000 certification, just-in-time supply, and worker participation programs became more common in the face of higher competitive pressure from China (Iacovone, Keller, and Rauch 2011). Iacovone (2012) finds that following the trade liberalization associated with the North American Free Trade Agreement, a 10 percent reduction in tariffs spurred productivity growth by 4–8 percent on average. Although this effect was much weaker among lagging firms, sometimes close to zero, the productivity of leading firms rose by 11–13 percent. These differences were due to innovation and managerial efforts rather than merely increases in the use of inputs.

Iacovone, Pereira López, and Schiffbauer (2016) show that Mexican firms possessing information technology used it to increase productivity only if they were faced with competitive pressure from imports. Therefore, import competition may be a catalyst for productivity upgrades by incentivizing incumbents to use existing technologies more effectively.

Overall, these findings show that insulating the domestic market from competition is likely to harm productivity. It may do so because such protection tends to benefit less productive plants and peripheral products. Protection would only partially relieve local economic stress because competitive effects also operate through export markets. Policy reforms should aim to permit and facilitate change by recognizing the centrality of efficient firms in the growth of productivity.

Chile: Leaders Innovate in Response to International Competition

The results illustrated in the previous section highlight the capacity to innovate as a critical quality of market leaders. This section expands on this line of inquiry, exploring the relationship between international competition and innovation in Chile, drawing on the findings of Cusolito, Garcia-Marin, and Maloney (2021). The Chile case study is unique for three reasons. First, it uses a matched production-innovation panel data set that contains information on input and product prices at the firm level and, therefore, allows more accurate measures of markups and physical (output-based) total factor productivity (TFPQ).[3] Second, the data enable studying broader measures of innovation outcomes that are more suitable for a developing country context, such as quality. Third, because Chile did not undertake sector-specific reform at the time of China's WTO accession, the case study allows the direct attribution of results to the international competitive pressures of trade.[4]

In manufacturing, import competition from China generates an average reduced innovation effort in Chile (figure 4.3). However, similar to the case in Mexico, results vary between leading and lagging firms. There are significant increases in the product quality and marginal costs of the leading firms (figure 4.4). Research and development, process innovation, product innovation, and quality all fall among laggards; and the effects are stronger if markups are decreasing. In contrast, among leaders, product innovation and quality rise. This effect is more evident if markups are increasing.

Figure 4.3 Manufacturing plants' innovation fell and product quality rose in Chile

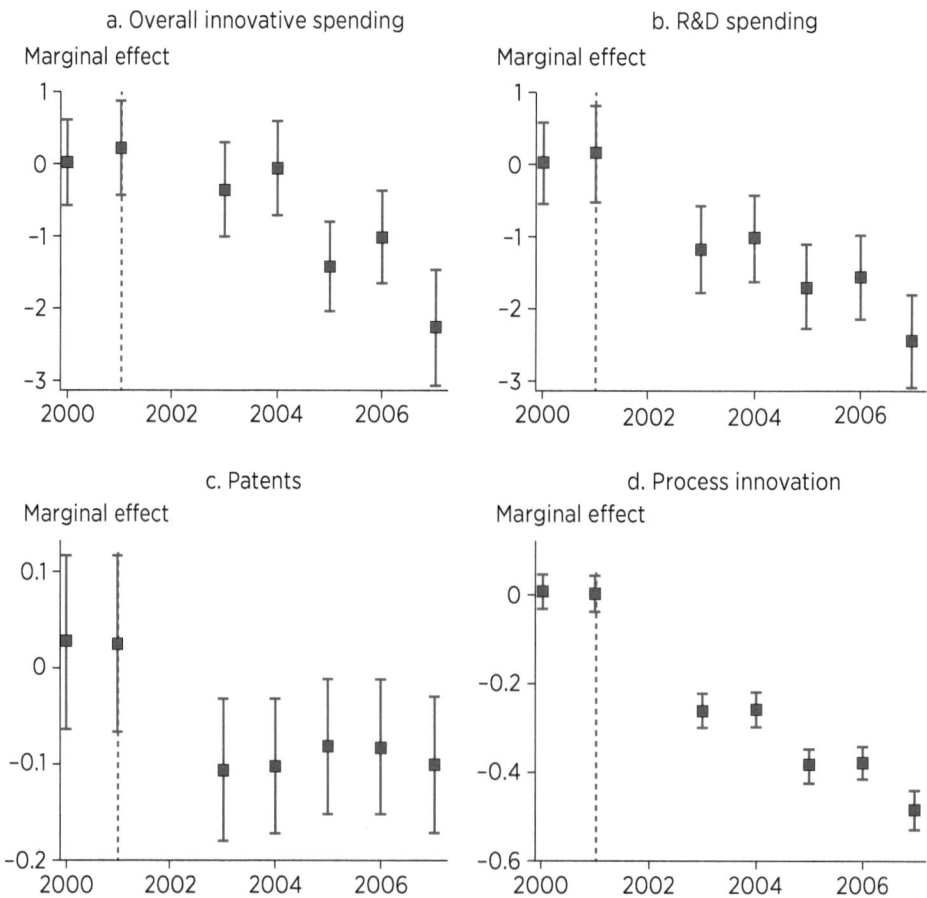

a. Overall innovative spending

b. R&D spending

c. Patents

d. Process innovation

figure continued next page

Figure 4.3 Manufacturing plants' innovation fell and product quality rose in Chile (*continued*)

e. Product innovation

f. Product quality

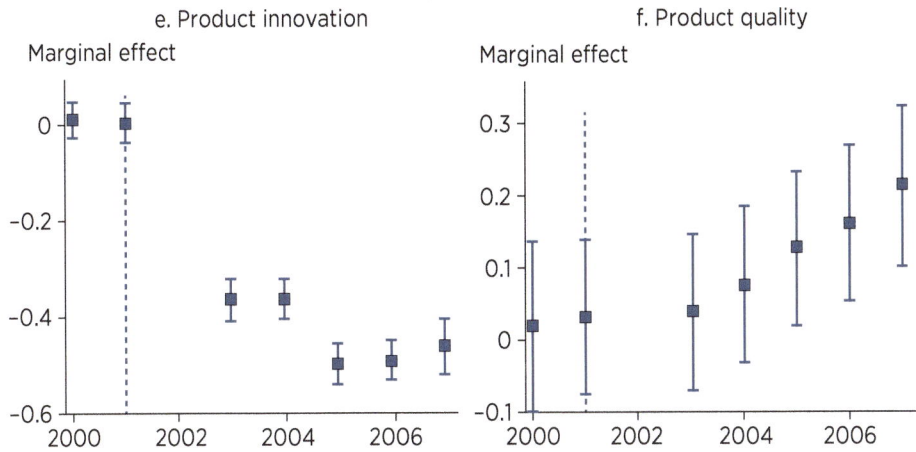

Source: Cusolito, Garcia-Marin, and Maloney 2021.

Note: The figure shows the within-plant trajectories of different innovation outcomes (marginal increases in innovation) before and after China's entry into the WTO in 2001. All results are at the plant level, controlling for plant effects and two-digit sector-year fixed effects. Standard errors (clustered at the three-digit sector-year level) are in parentheses. The vertical lines show the 90 percent confidence intervals. WTO = World Trade Organization.

Figure 4.4 Product innovation and product quality rose among leaders but fell among laggards in Chile

a. Overall R&D spending

b. Process innovation

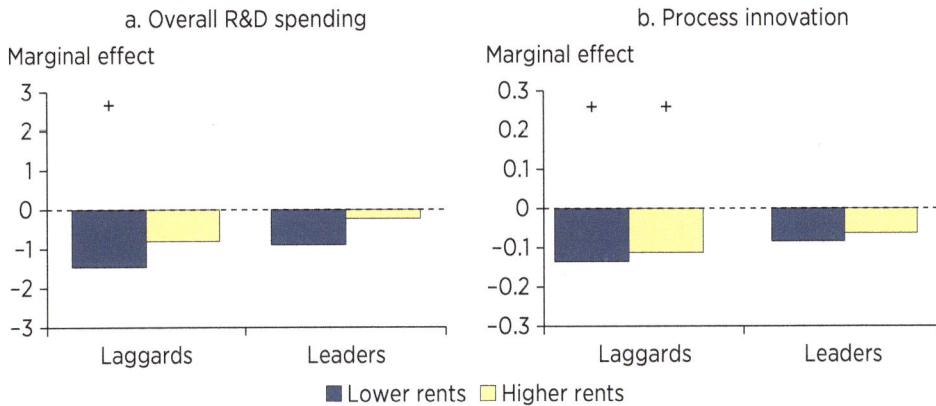

■ Lower rents □ Higher rents

figure continued next page

Figure 4.4 Product innovation and product quality rose among leaders but fell among laggards in Chile (*continued*)

c. Product innovation

Marginal effect

d. Product quality

Marginal effect

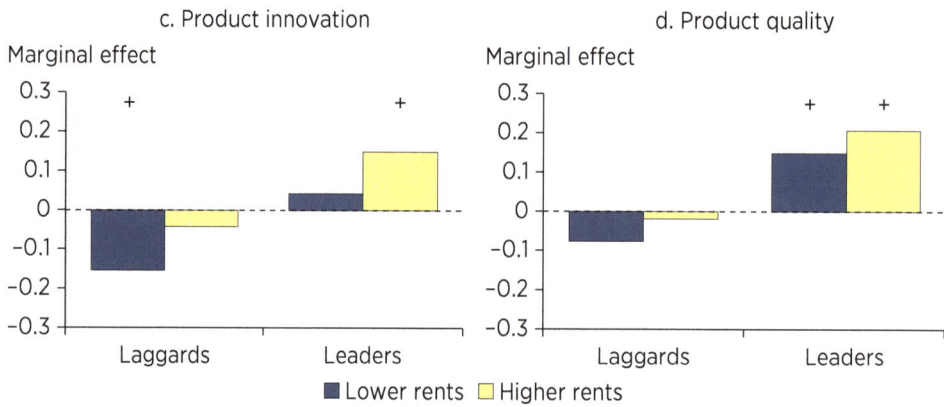

■ Lower rents   □ Higher rents

Source: Cusolito, Garcia-Marin, and Maloney 2021.

Note: The figure shows the effect on different innovation outcomes of the changes in import competition from China. Industry leaders correspond to the top 10 percent of plants with the highest average TFPQ before 2001. Plants with higher (lower) rents because of exposure to import competition are identified by running an auxiliary regression of plant-level markups against instrumented lagged imports from China, industry-year, and plant fixed effects. Thus, the indicator variable considers only the fraction of markups that varies because of increased competition. All regressions are run at the plant-year level, controlling for the logarithm of employment, and include industry-year (at the two-digit level) and plant-level fixed effects. A plus sign (+) above a bar indicates that the corresponding coefficient is statistically significant at the 90 percent level. TFPQ = physical (output-based) total factor productivity; R&D = research and development; WTO = World Trade Organization.

These results are consistent with other recent findings. In a contemporaneous study that dissects the China trade shock, Aghion et al. (2022) find a detrimental effect on the sales and patenting activity of French firms in response to Chinese competition in output markets. The negative impact is concentrated in low-productivity firms, defined as firms achieving below the median in revenue total factor productivity.

Cusolito, Garcia-Marin, and Maloney (2021) find that marginal costs increase among leading firms. Higher marginal costs and higher quality are associated with the higher-quality inputs and more highly skilled labor required to generate the outputs. Market leaders are able to increase total revenues, driven by the sizable rise in output prices, but production is unaffected. The rise in output prices may be the result of increasing product quality. Moving up the quality ladder allows capable firms to escape from competition to another market, which is possibly unaffected by the import shock. Indeed, there is evidence of product quality innovation effort among market leaders, which is consistent with evidence from Costa Rica, where the entry of multinational firms led to a strong, persistent increase in performance among domestic suppliers (Alfaro-Ureña, Manelici, and Vasquez 2022).

The view of Aghion et al. (2005, 2009) that proximity to the frontier is vital and the classical Schumpeterian view of the importance of rents are both confirmed. The literature on quality upgrading is also supported (Shu and Steinwender 2019) (box 4.2). Castellares (2015, 2016) finds that, in Peru, the more productive apparel firms undertake quality upgrades to differentiate their products from low-cost, low-quality Chinese goods, whereas the less productive firms, which cannot increase product quality, react by reducing prices. Castellares also finds evidence that the average quality of Peruvian apparel products increased after China's WTO accession. Medina (2024) shows that Peruvian firms that successfully fended off competition from China had upgraded the quality of their products through within-firm reallocation of specific factors rather than access to new inputs.

Box 4.2

Why leaders succeed: Competitive pressure, managerial capabilities, and internal process improvements

If competition intensifies, some firms become more productive and others do not. Those that are able to innovate, cut costs, or reduce markups become more productive and compete successfully. Others find that doing business in the new environment is too costly or unprofitable. Their productivity falls, they may not be able to sustain lower prices as they lose markups, and some firms give up and exit. As Aghion et al. (2018) and Aghion et al. (2022) conclude, a firm's decision to innovate in response to a change in market conditions depends on whether it can afford to allocate resources optimally within its structure.

A firm may survive competition by upgrading if its size, turnover, and experience allow it to do so (Blaum, Lelarge, and Peters 2019; Criscuolo et al. 2021; Kugler and Verhoogen 2012; Van Biesebroeck 2005). The upgrading may involve raising quality at higher marginal costs or innovating by improving internal processes. This ability to act upon

box continued next page

Box 4.2

Why leaders succeed: Competitive pressure, managerial capabilities, and internal process improvements *(continued)*

changes in the market—sometimes referred to as entrepreneurial ability—is often linked to managerial skills that are correlated with higher productivity or rewarding workers for innovation and technology adoption (Atkin et al. 2017; Bandiera et al. 2020; Bertrand and Schoar 2003). Another important condition is the ability to learn both within and across firms, such as learning by doing (Irwin and Klenow 1994).

Because it is challenging to acquire the capacity to innovate, leading incumbent firms are more likely to possess this capacity. According to Aghion et al. (2004), this capacity depends on the definition of innovation (such as quality upgrading) and assumptions about the nature of the innovation process (such as knowledge capital), as well as firm-specific characteristics. The capacity to innovate is path dependent or linked to past investments, especially in manufacturing, where many types of innovation require heavy investments in machinery. In the view of Arrow (1962), innovation is similar to knowledge capital: it requires time to build up, which is why leaders accumulate more knowledge and capacity over time.

Similarly, the negative effects of distortions may also pile up, for instance, reducing the impact of one-off investments (Lopez-Martin 2016, 2017). The ability to compete or innovate is formed by consumer preferences, production structure, and firm capabilities. However, an ineffective regulatory framework can hold it back. Thus, there is scope for better policy.

Managerial practices are vital for quality upgrading and productivity growth because managers make complex investment decisions that may eventually determine a firm's leader or laggard status. Bloom, Sadun, and Van Reenen (2016) find that these practices account for the large variations in productivity across countries. International competition often leads to better outcomes in countries where skills and capabilities are plentiful and easily accessed, compared to countries lacking these skills. Monfort, Vandenbussche, and Forlani (2008) analyze a relevant experience in Belgium's textile sector in the face of competition from China.

However, not all strategies for improving managerial practices are equal. In a paper on the auto parts manufacturing sector in Colombia, Iacovone,

box continued next page

Box 4.2

Why leaders succeed: Competitive pressure, managerial capabilities, and internal process improvements *(continued)*

Maloney, and McKenzie (2022) test two managerial approaches to productivity: (1) intensive and expensive one-on-one consulting versus (2) inexpensive group consulting. The individual option costs roughly US$30,000 per firm, whereas the group option costs US$10,000 per firm but imparts learning through interactions in a group setting. The dual consulting approach builds on a framework devised by Bloom et al. (2013) but is much larger in scale. Iacovone, Maloney, and McKenzie (2022) find that big firms may prefer the expensive individual option because they have the necessary funds. Small firms, however, might not be able to afford this option. The authors find, however, that both approaches achieve similar improvements in management, at 8–10 percentage points relative to the control group mean. This result indicates that the group consulting approach is more cost-effective. Furthermore, this approach increases firm size, whereas the individual approach has a statistically insignificant effect. The cost-effective intervention would pay for itself through larger firm sales over time.

Firms have access to other mechanisms to increase quality under competitive pressure. Medina (2024) looks at such mechanisms in Peru. Her study applies the country's manufacturing data set to examine quality upgrading to escape competition from China. The upgrading involved within-firm reallocation of factors rather than access to new input products. If faced with competition from low-wage countries such as China, downsizing firms can reallocate idle production factors, leading to quality upgrading. Meanwhile, import competition reduces the returns on fixed factors (capital), which are then reallocated to producing high-quality products. In this way, high-productivity firms intensify their output of high-quality goods. Surviving low-productivity firms follow suit, manufacturing and exporting high-quality goods.

Sources: Based on Iacovone, Maloney, and McKenzie 2022; Verhoogen 2021; and the studies cited.

Only the top 10 percent of Chilean firms, measured by TFPQ, show a positive impact of increased import competition on innovation. This impact is similar to the case of Mexico cited in the previous section, but it contrasts with the pattern in developed countries, where roughly half the firms can innovate in response to international competition. Chile's leading top 10 percent cohort accounts for a quarter of industrial value added. This pattern is consistent with countries that are farther from the frontier and have fewer firms that can compete at this high level.

This result suggests that the larger the share of firms near the frontier is, the larger the potential positive impact of competition is. Thus, raising the capabilities of domestic firms and improving their access to resources may be important complements to policies favoring competition. These complements might include firm-level initiatives such as expanding managerial consulting programs, strengthening local innovation, supporting standards compliance, promoting technology adoption, and ensuring access to longer-term finance (box 4.2).

Domestic competition spurs leading firms toward the domestic technological frontier, where they may eventually compete successfully with international firms (Aghion et al. 2001). Moving toward the frontier may prepare industries for later external trade shocks, such as the one that followed China's WTO accession. Stronger domestic competition will lead to a reallocation of resources from low-productivity plants to high-productivity plants, the entry of more productive plants, and the exit of less productive ones (Melitz and Redding 2021). Cusolito and Maloney (2018) address the impact of competition through churning and show that, during the same period covered by the present study, more than 60 percent of the gains in TFPQ in Chile arose precisely from entry and exit. Liu (1993) finds that, in the early phases of the Chilean reforms, much productivity growth occurred in the extensive margin, thanks to the extraordinary protections and distortions evident at the time.

Peru: Domestic Producers Respond Positively to Input Market Liberalization

Import liberalization has generally been more favorable for domestic producers in input markets than in output markets, primarily because of the impact on marginal costs spread through value chains. This section compares the impacts on input and output markets in Peru and confirms this view.

The empirical literature provides several examples of input market liberalization promoting the productivity growth of domestic producers in the region. The entry of multinational corporations in Costa Rica raised revenue-based total factor productivity among domestic input suppliers by 4–9 percent in 4 years. There was no effect on markups, however, suggesting that there were also improvements in TFPQ (Alfaro-Ureña, Manelici, and Vasquez 2022). In Peru, greater use, variety, and quality of imported intermediate inputs were significantly correlated with higher exports, greater market diversification, and higher export quality at the firm level, even after controlling for unobserved firm heterogeneity (Pierola, Fernandes, and Farole 2018).

Other studies argue that lowering input tariffs gives firms more access to a broader range of cheaper, potentially higher-quality inputs that can help to improve productivity (Amiti and Konings 2007). These benefits may also materialize through learning-by-importing effects and internal quality upgrading, as documented by Medina (2024) in Peru. Empirical results clarify the importance of broad-based policies that promote quality upgrading to support innovation. For example, Bloom, Sadun, and Van Reenen (2016) find that more well-managed firms produce higher-quality products and import a wider range of inputs that are also of higher quality.

Tello and Tello-Trillo (2021) consider the case of Peru, comparing the effects of trade liberalization in output and input markets. Reduced output tariffs on imports from China, the European Union, and the United States cut the overall productivity growth of Peruvian firms (figure 4.5). At the same time, reducing input tariffs on imports from China, the European Union, and the United States had a positive effect across all Peruvian firms (figure 4.6). No significant effects were found to be associated with Peru's free trade agreement with China, suggesting that the increase in competition from China and the reduction in the prices of intermediate inputs from China did not significantly affect firm-level productivity in Peru. In the case of Peru's free trade agreement with the European Union, only the input channel played a positive role in firm-level productivity. Consistent with other evidence from the region, on average, domestic firms were more well-off after input market liberalization.

Figure 4.5 The impact of output market liberalization on productivity is generally negative in Peru

Change in TFP growth in Peru (%)

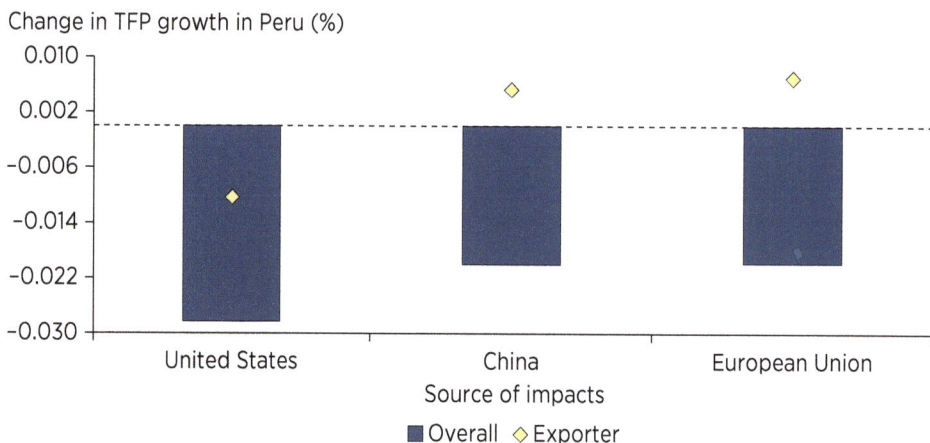

Source: Tello and Tello-Trillo 2021.

Note: The figure shows the effect of a 1 percent tariff reduction on manufacturing firms in Peru. TFP = total factor productivity.

Figure 4.6 The impact of input market liberalization on productivity has been positive in Peru

Change in TFP growth in Peru (%)

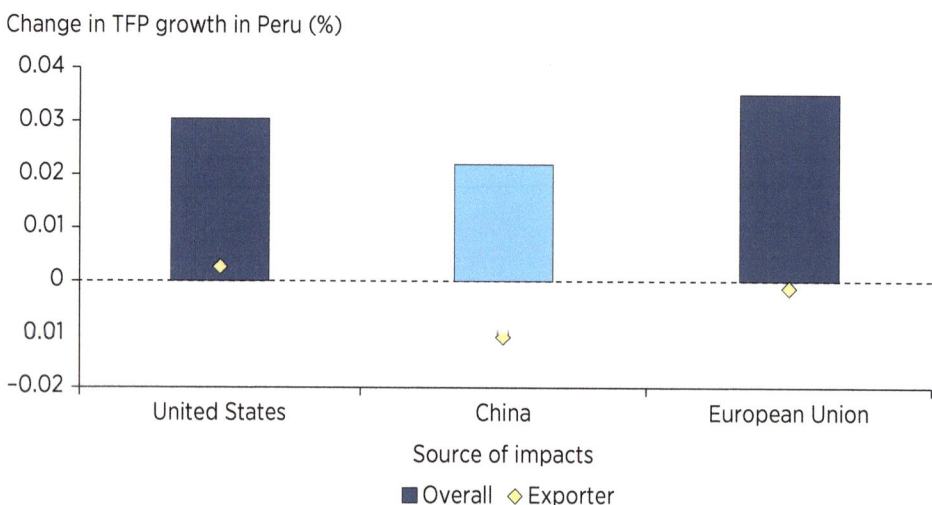

Source: Tello and Tello-Trillo 2021.

Note: The figure shows the effect of a 1 percent tariff reduction on manufacturing firms in Peru. The light blue bar is statistically insignificant. TFP = total factor productivity.

Conclusions

This chapter analyzed the impact of intensified external competitive pressure from imports on sectorwide productivity. The impact on firms ultimately depends on their distance from the global technological frontier. Firms' capacity to innovate in response to greater competition pressures is the key determinant of the positive impact of competition on productivity growth among incumbents. Market leaders—that is, the most productive firms that are also closer to the global technological frontier—will increase innovation and upgrade quality to escape competition. Firms that are unable to innovate will experience lower markups and sales.

At the sector level, whether competition has a positive or negative impact on productivity will depend on the number of firms with the capacity to innovate and the distance of firms from the relevant technological frontier. The more leading firms there are in a sector and the closer these firms are to the frontier, the more likely it is that the sectorwide productivity impacts of competition will be positive. The share of firms capable of innovating in response to an import shock is lower in Chile (10 percent) than in developed countries (25 percent in China and 55 percent in the United Kingdom) (Aghion et al. 2009; Bombardini, Li, and Wang 2017; Maloney and Zambrano 2023).

These findings suggest that complementary policies aimed at enhancing capabilities might magnify the productivity impact of import liberalization.

Notes

1. The analysis explores incumbent responses in the face of international competition. However, because of data limitations, it is not possible to explore the other margins of productivity properly, such as entry margins or market reallocation. Other literature includes interactions with labor market policies, whereby stringent labor regulations rule out employment adjustment following a trade shock (Branstetter et al. 2019).
2. Refer to Harmonized System (dashboard), World Customs Organization, Brussels, Belgium, https://www.wcotradetools.org/en/harmonized-system; UN Comtrade Database (United Nations Commodity Trade Statistics Database), Statistics Division, Department of Economic and Social Affairs, United Nations, New York, https://comtrade.un.org/data/.
3. The study relies on data on manufacturing firms in Chile from 1996 to 2007, with information on product sector and prices. The coverage for Chinese imports is similar. The firm-level information is matched with data from innovation surveys, with the same firm identifications across samples.

4. To allay concerns that Chinese imports are driven by demand factors, this paper uses an instrumental variable based on Chinese import penetration in peer economies—Chilean firms demanding Chinese products rather than actual Chinese market penetration, which is arguably exogenous to Chilean firms.

References

Aghion, Philippe, Stefan Bechtold, Lea Cassar, and Holger Herz. 2018. "The Causal Effects of Competition on Innovation: Experimental Evidence." *Journal of Law, Economics, and Organization* 34 (2): 162–95.

Aghion, Philippe, Antonin Bergeaud, Matthieu Lequien, Marc J. Melitz, and Thomas Zuber. 2022. "Opposing Firm-Level Responses to the China Shock: Horizontal Competition versus Vertical Relationships?" NBER Working Paper 29196 rev., National Bureau of Economic Research, Cambridge, MA.

Aghion, Philippe, Nicholas Bloom, Richard Blundell, Rachel Griffith, and Peter Howitt. 2005. "Competition and Innovation: An Inverted-U Relationship." *Quarterly Journal of Economics* 120 (2): 701–28. https://doi.org/10.1093/qje/120.2.701.

Aghion, Philippe, Richard Blundell, Rachel Griffith, Peter Howett, and Susanne Prantl. 2004. "Entry and Productivity Growth: Evidence from Microlevel Panel Data." *Journal of the European Economic Association* 2 (2-3): 265–76.

Aghion, Philippe, Richard Blundell, Rachel Griffith, Peter Howitt, and Susanne Prantl. 2009. "The Effects of Entry on Incumbent Innovation and Productivity." *Review of Economics and Statistics* 91 (1): 20–32. https://doi.org/10.1162/rest.91.1.20.

Aghion, Philippe, Christopher Harris, Peter Howitt, and John Vickers. 2001. "Competition, Imitation, and Growth with Step-by-Step Innovation." *Review of Economic Studies* 68 (3): 467–92. https://www.jstor.org/stable/2695893.

Akcigit, Ufuk, and Marc J. Melitz. 2022. "International Trade and Innovation." BFI Working Paper 2022-02, Becker Friedman Institute for Economics, University of Chicago, Chicago, IL.

Alfaro-Ureña, Alonso, Isabela Manelici, and José P. Vasquez. 2022. "The Effects of Joining Multinational Supply Chains: New Evidence from Firm-to-Firm Linkages." *Quarterly Journal of Economics* 137 (3): 1495–552. https://doi.org/10.1093/qje/qjac006.

Amiti, Mary, and Jozef Konings. 2007. "Trade Liberalization, Intermediate Inputs, and Productivity: Evidence from Indonesia." *American Economic Review* 97 (5): 1611–38. https://doi.org/10.1257/aer.97.5.1611.

Arrow, Kenneth J. 1962. "The Economic Implications of Learning by Doing." *Review of Economic Studies* 29 (3): 155–73. https://doi.org/10.2307/2295952.

Atkin, David Guy, Azam Chaudhry, Shamyla Chaudry, Amit K. Khandelwal, and Eric A. Verhoogen. 2017. "Organizational Barriers to Technology Adoption: Evidence from Soccer-Ball Producers in Pakistan." *Quarterly Journal of Economics* 132 (3): 1101–64. https://doi.org/10.1093/qje/qjx010.

Autor, David H., David Dorn, and Gordon H. Hanson. 2013. "The China Syndrome: Local Labor Market Effects of Import Competition in the United States." *American Economic Review* 103 (6): 2121–68. https://doi.org/10.1257/aer.103.6.2121.

Autor, David H., David Dorn, Lawrence F. Katz, Christina Patterson, and John Michael Van Reenen. 2020. "The Fall of the Labor Share and the Rise of Superstar Firms." *Quarterly Journal of Economics* 135 (2): 645–709. https://doi.org/10.1093/qje/qjaa004.

Bandiera, Oriana, Andrea Prat, Stephen Hansen, and Raffaella Sadun. 2020. "CEO Behavior and Firm Performance." *Journal of Political Economy* 128 (4): 1325–69. https://doi.org/10.1086/705331.

Bernard, Andrew B., Stephen J. Redding, and Peter K. Schott. 2010. "Multiple-Product Firms and Product Switching." *American Economic Review* 100 (1): 70–97.

Bertrand, Marianne, and Antoinette Schoar. 2003. "Managing with Style: The Effect of Managers on Firm Policies." *Quarterly Journal of Economics* 118 (4): 1169–208. https://doi.org/10.1162/003355303322552775.

Blaum, Joaquin, Claire Lelarge, and Michael Peters. 2019. "Firm Size, Quality Bias, and Import Demand." *Journal of International Economics* 120: 59–83. https://doi.org /10.1016/j.jinteco.2019.04.004.

Bloom, Nicholas, Mirko Draca, and John Michael Van Reenen. 2016. "Trade Induced Technical Change? The Impact of Chinese Imports on Innovation, IT, and Productivity." *Review of Economic Studies* 83 (1): 87–117. https://doi.org/10.1093 /restud/rdv039.

Bloom, Nicholas, Benn Eifert, Aprajit Mahajan, David J. McKenzie, and John Roberts. 2013. "Does Management Matter? Evidence from India." *Quarterly Journal of Economics* 128 (1): 1–51. https://doi.org/10.1093/qje/qjs044.

Bloom, Nicholas, Raffaella Sadun, and John Michael Van Reenen. 2016. "Management as a Technology?" NBER Working Paper 22327, National Bureau of Economic Research, Cambridge, MA.

Bombardini, Matilde, Bingjing Li, and Ruoying Wang. 2017. "Import Competition and Innovation: Evidence from China." Paper presented at the Hitotsubashi Conference on International Trade and FDI 2017, Hitotsubashi University, Tokyo, December 9–10. https://www7.econ.hit-u.ac.jp/cces/trade_conference_2017/paper/matilde _bombardini.pdf.

Branstetter, Lee G., Brian K. Kovak, Jacqueline Mauro, and Ana Venâncio. 2019. "The China Shock and Employment in Portuguese Firms." NBER Working Paper 26252, National Bureau of Economic Research, Cambridge, MA. http://www.nber.org /papers/w26252.

Bustos, Paula. 2011. "Trade Liberalization, Exports, and Technology Upgrading: Evidence on the Impact of MERCOSUR on Argentinian Firms." *American Economic Review* 101 (1): 304–40.

Campbell, Douglas L., and Karsten Mau. 2021. "On 'Trade Induced Technical Change: The Impact of Chinese Imports on Innovation, IT, and Productivity.'" *Review of Economic Studies* 88 (5): 2555–59. https://doi.org/10.1093/restud/rdab037.

Castellares, Renzo. 2015. "Competition and Quality Upgrading in Export Markets: The Case of Peruvian Apparel Exports." Working Paper 2015-010, Banco Central de Reserva del Perú, Lima.

Castellares, Renzo. 2016. "Productividad y competencia de las firmas peruanas en los mercadosde exportación de prendas de vestir." In *Productividad en el Perú: medición, determinantes, e Implicancias*, edited by Nikita Céspedes, Pablo Lavado, and Nelson Ramírez Rondán, 173–91. Lima, Peru: Universidad del Pacífico.

Chen, Natalie, Jean Imbs, and Andrew Scott. 2009. "The Dynamics of Trade and Competition." *Journal of International Economics* 77 (1): 50–62.

Criscuolo, Chiara, Peter Gal, Timo Leidecker, and Giuseppe Nicoletti. 2021. "The Human Side of Productivity: Uncovering the Role of Skills and Diversity for Firm Productivity." OECD Productivity Working Paper 29, Organisation for Economic Co-operation and Development, Paris. https://doi.org/10.1787/5f391ba9-en.

Cusolito, Ana Paula, Alvaro Garcia-Marin, and William F. Maloney. 2021. "Proximity to the Frontier, Markups, and the Response of Innovation to Foreign Competition: Evidence from Matched Production-Innovation Surveys in Chile." Policy Research Working Paper 9757, World Bank, Washington, DC. https://documents1.worldbank.org /curated/en/356601629742092693/pdf/Proximity-to-the-Frontier-Markups-and-the -Response-of-Innovation-to-Foreign-Competition-Evidence-from-Matched -Production-Innovation-Surveys-in-Chile.pdf.

Cusolito, Ana Paula, and William F. Maloney. 2018. *Productivity Revisited: Shifting Paradigms in Analysis and Policy*. Washington, DC: World Bank.

Eckel, Carsten, and J. Peter Neary. 2010. "Multi-Product Firms and Flexible Manufacturing in the Global Economy." *Review of Economic Studies* 77 (1): 188–217.

Eslava, Marcela, John C. Haltiwanger, Adriana Kugler, and Maurice David Kugler. 2013. "Trade and Market Selection: Evidence from Manufacturing Plants in Colombia." *Review of Economic Dynamics* 16 (1): 135–58. https://doi.org/10.1016/j.red.2012.10.009.

Fernandes, Ana Margarida. 2007. "Trade Policy, Trade Volumes, and Plant-Level Productivity in Colombian Manufacturing Industries." *Journal of International Economics* 71 (1): 52–71. https://doi.org/10.1016/j.jinteco.2006.03.003.

Fernandes, Ana Margarida, and Caroline Paunov. 2013. "Does Trade Stimulate Product Quality Upgrading?" *Canadian Journal of Economics* 46 (4): 1232–64.

Iacovone, Leonardo. 2012. "The Better You Are, the Stronger It Makes You: Evidence on the Asymmetric Impact of Liberalization." *Journal of Development Economics* 99 (2): 474–85. https://EconPapers.repec.org/RePEc:eee:deveco:v:99:y:2012:i:2:p:474-485.

Iacovone, Leonardo, Mariana De La Paz Pereira López, and Marc Tobias Schiffbauer. 2016. "Competition Makes IT Better: Evidence on When Firms Use IT More Effectively." Policy Research Working Paper 7638, World Bank, Washington, DC.

Iacovone, Leonardo, Wolfgang Keller, and Ferdinand Rauch. 2011. "Innovation Responses to Import Competition." Working Paper, Princeton University, Princeton, NJ.

Iacovone, Leonardo, William F. Maloney, and David J. McKenzie. 2022. "Improving Management with Individual and Group-Based Consulting: Results from a Randomized Experiment in Colombia." *Review of Economic Studies* 89 (1): 346–71. https://doi.org/10.1093/restud/rdab005.

Iacovone, Leonardo, Ferdinand Rauch, and L. Alan Winters. 2013. "Trade as an Engine of Creative Destruction: Mexican Experience with Chinese Competition." *Journal of International Economics* 89 (2): 379–92. https://doi.org/10.1016/j.jinteco.2012.09.002.

Irwin, Douglas A., and Peter J. Klenow. 1994. "Learning-by-Doing Spillovers in the Semiconductor Industry." *Journal of Political Economy* 102 (6): 1200–27. https://www.jstor.org/stable/2138784.

Keung, Lorenz, Nicholas Li, and Mu-Jeung Yang. 2016. "The Impact of Emerging Market Competition on Innovation and Business Strategy." NBER Working Paper 22840, National Bureau of Economic Research, Cambridge, MA.

Kugler, Maurice David, and Eric A. Verhoogen. 2012. "Prices, Plant Size, and Product Quality." *Review of Economic Studies* 79 (1): 307–39. https://doi.org/10.1093/restud/rdr021.

Liu, Lili. 1993. "Entry-Exit, Learning, and Productivity Change: Evidence from Chile." *Journal of Development Economics* 42 (2): 217–42.

Liu, Runjuan. 2010. "Import Competition and Firm Refocusing." *Canadian Journal of Economics* 43 (2): 440–66.

Lopez-Martin, Bernabe. 2016. "Informal Sector Misallocation." Banco de México Working Paper 2016-09, Banco de México, Mexico City.

Lopez-Martin, Bernabe. 2017. "From Firm Productivity Dynamics to Aggregate Efficiency." *World Bank Economic Review* 30 (Supplement 1): S57–S66. https://doi.org/10.1093/wber/lhw021.

Maloney, William F., and Andrés Zambrano. 2023. *Optimal Protection for Innovation: Revisiting Industrial Policy*. Washington, DC: World Bank.

Medina, Pamela. 2024. "Import Competition, Quality Upgrading, and Exporting: Evidence from the Peruvian Apparel Industry." *Review of Economics and Statistics* 106 (5): 1285–1300. https://doi.org/10.1162/rest_a_01221.

Melitz, Marc J., and Stephen J. Redding. 2021. "Trade and Innovation." NBER Working Paper 28945, National Bureau of Economic Research, Cambridge, MA.

Monfort, Philippe, Hylke Vandenbussche, and Emanuele Forlani. 2008. "Chinese Competition and Skill-Upgrading in European Textiles: Firm-Level Evidence." LICOS Discussion Paper 198/2008, LICOS Centre for Institutions and Economic Performance, Katholieke Universiteit Leuven, Leuven, Belgium.

Muendler, Marc-Andreas. 2004. "Trade, Technology, and Productivity: A Study of Brazilian Manufacturers 1986–1998." CESifo Working Paper 1148, Munich Society for the Promotion of Economic Research, Center for Economic Studies, Ludwig Maximilian University and Ifo Institute for Economic Research, Munich, Germany.

Pavcnik, Nina. 2002. "Trade Liberalization, Exit, and Productivity Improvements: Evidence from Chilean Plants." *Review of Economic Studies* 69 (1): 245–76. https://doi.org/10.1111/1467-937X.00205.

Pierola, Martha Denisse, Ana Margarida Fernandes, and Thomas Farole. 2018. "The Role of Imports for Exporter Performance in Peru." *World Economy* 41 (2): 550–72.

Rodríguez-Castelán, Carlos, Luis F. López-Calva, and Oscar Eduardo Barriga Cabanillas. 2020. "The Effects of Local Market Concentration and International Competition on Firm Productivity: Evidence from Mexico." Policy Research Working Paper 9210, World Bank, Washington, DC. http://hdl.handle.net/10986/33604.

Schmitz, Jr., James A. 2005. "What Determines Productivity? Lessons from the Dramatic Recovery of the U.S. and Canadian Iron Ore Industries Following Their Early 1980s Crisis." *Journal of Political Economy* 113 (3): 582–625. https://doi.org/10.1086/429279.

Schor, Adriana. 2004. "Heterogeneous Productivity Response to Tariff Reduction: Evidence from Brazilian Manufacturing Firms." *Journal of Development Economics* 75 (2): 373–96. https://EconPapers.repec.org/RePEc:eee:deveco:v:75:y:2004:i:2:p:373-396.

Shu, Pian, and Claudia Steinwender. 2019. "The Impact of Trade Liberalization on Firm Productivity and Innovation." *Innovation Policy and the Economy* 19 (1): 39–68.

Tello, Mario D., and Cristina J. Tello-Trillo. 2021. "Trade Liberalization, Input Tariffs, Output Tariffs, and Productivity: Evidence from Peru." World Bank, Washington, DC.

Van Biesebroeck, Johannes. 2005. "Firm Size Matters: Growth and Productivity Growth in African Manufacturing." *Economic Development and Cultural Change* 53 (3): 545–83. https://doi.org/10.1086/426407.

Verhoogen, Eric A. 2021. "Firm-Level Upgrading in Developing Countries." NBER Working Paper 29461, National Bureau of Economic Research, Cambridge, MA.

5

Getting It Right: Making Competition Work

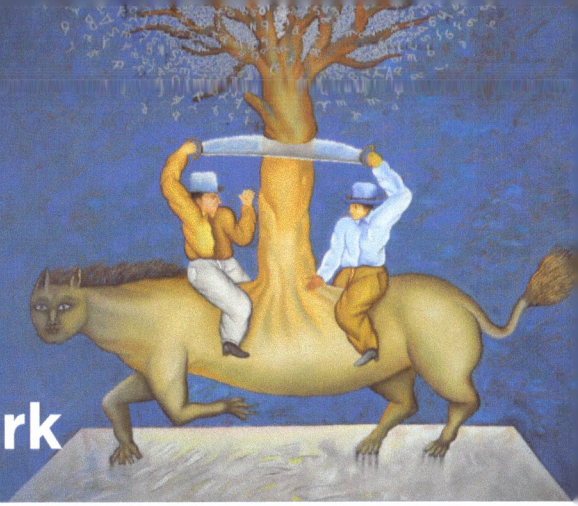

Introduction

Empirical evidence shows that competition policy can play a critical role in boosting productivity growth. It also shows that different firms respond differently to competitive pressure, suggesting that sound competition policy needs to be complemented with other policies, including innovation policies, to boost aggregate productivity growth.

This chapter touches on issues in implementation reform, particularly policy complementarities and the capacity of implementing institutions, because certain reforms will miss the targets desired without the prior or simultaneous implementation of other reforms (Loayza and Woolcock 2020). It investigates the core elements of competition policy, highlighting areas where governments in the region might consider changes. It discusses interactions and trade-offs with other policy areas, including innovation and international trade policy, drawing on the empirical evidence gathered in chapters 1 to 4 of this report and other regional and global experiences. It explores the factors that make competition work, through a summary of competition policy in Latin America and the Caribbean. In accomplishing this, the chapter reviews and nuances the material in chapters 1 to 4 and adds insights.

An Effective Competition Policy Framework

An effective competition policy framework is built on three pillars: (1) the implementation of pro-competition regulations to facilitate the entry and operations of new firms; (2) a competitive neutrality principle affecting private market players directly, but also public players; and (3) effective enforcement of laws and regulations on competition (World Bank and OECD 2017).

Competitive neutrality provides that all enterprises, public or private, domestic or foreign, should face the same set of rules and that government ownership or involvement in the marketplace in fact or in law does not confer an undue competitive advantage on any actual or potential market participant.

Reforming government regulations and practices that, by accident or design, restrict market competition or the effectiveness of competition policy is necessary to enhance the functioning of markets. Coordination of policy across public and private entities to generate a truly competitive business environment and promote contestable and open markets is vital to enhancing entrepreneurship and creating pressure to innovate.

Table 5.1 captures the key elements of an effective competition policy framework supported by established competition law.

Table 5.1 Key elements of an effective competition policy framework

Fostering competition in markets

Pillar 1: Pro-competition regulations and government interventions: opening markets and removing anti-competitive sectoral regulation	Pillar 2: Competitive neutrality and non-distortionary public assistance	Pillar 3: Effective competition law and antitrust enforcement
Implement the reform of policies and regulations that strengthen dominance, such as restrictions on the number of firms, statutory monopolies, bans on private investment, and lack of access regulations favoring essential facilities	Control government assistance to avoid favoritism and minimize distortions of competition	Tackle cartel agreements that raise the costs of key inputs and final products and reduce access to a broader variety of products
Eliminate government interventions that foster collusive outcomes or increase the costs of competing, such as controls on prices and other market variables that increase business risk	Ensure competitive neutrality, including relative to SOEs	Prevent anti-competitive mergers
Reform government interventions that discriminate against or otherwise harm competition on the merits, such as interventions that tilt the playing field or promote high levels of discretion	Reform government interventions that discriminate against or otherwise harm competition on the merits, such as interventions that tilt the playing field or promote high levels of discretion	Strengthen the general antitrust and institutional framework to combat anti-competitive conduct and abuse of dominance

Sources: World Bank and OECD 2017; adapted from Kitzmuller and Licetti 2013.

Note: SOEs = state-owned enterprises.

Competition authorities—the national agencies responsible for enforcing competition law—and sectoral agencies that implement regulations that promote competition play a crucial role in fostering dynamic markets. A healthy competitive environment not only relies on well-designed laws and regulations aimed at an economy or individual sectors but also depends on effective enforcement. The capacity of competition authorities to investigate, prosecute, and prevent anticompetitive behavior is critical (box 5.1).

Box 5.1

A brief history of competition authorities in Latin America and the Caribbean

Many countries in the region are relative latecomers in the establishment of competition laws and competition authorities. Compared with Organisation for Economic Co-operation and Development (OECD) members, the passage of competition laws lags in the region by almost 23 years, and the establishment of competition authorities lags by about 19 years.

There are marked differences across the region. Although a competition law was adopted in Argentina in 1923, followed by Chile and Colombia by the end of the 1950s and Brazil in 1962, half of the 16 countries in the region included in the OECD CompStats database adopted competition policy only in the current century.[a] The establishment of competition authorities follows closely the establishment of competition policies (OECD 2022). The young age of most competition regimes in the region likely reduces the level and effectiveness of competition enforcement.

Building on experience, many countries have significantly changed their competition laws and enforcement regimes in the past 20 years. These changes include institutional changes, such as concentrating all enforcement powers in a single authority and increasing the organization's autonomy. Changes in existing laws have involved the introduction or reform of merger control or leniency regimes and the strengthening of investigative and sanctioning powers.

Despite these efforts, competition enforcement is still considered weak in many countries in the region. This weakness may arise because of the limited

box continued next page

Box 5.1

A brief history of competition authorities in Latin America and the Caribbean *(continued)*

resources of the competition authority and shortcomings in the law. For example, nearly one-third of the countries in the region included in the OECD database still lack an operational legal framework governing competition (World Bank 2021a).

Source: Based on OECD Competition Statistics (OECD CompStats) Survey 2024 (web page), Organisation for Economic Co-operation and Development, Paris, https://survey.oecd.org/index.php?r=survey/index&sid=371986&lang=en; OECD 2022.
Note: The OECD CompStats database compiles general statistics on competition agencies, including data on enforcement and resources and information on advocacy initiatives. The data are collected annually and currently cover 2015–21. The database includes data from 79 jurisdictions, including 16 in Latin America: Argentina, Barbados, Brazil, Chile, Colombia, Costa Rica, the Dominican Republic, Ecuador, El Salvador, Mexico, Nicaragua, Panama, Paraguay, Peru, Trinidad and Tobago, and Uruguay. OECD Competition Trends (portal), Organisation for Economic Co-operation and Development, Paris (https://www.oecd.org/fr/corruption/oecd-competition-trends.htm).

a. OECD Competition Statistics (OECD CompStats) Survey 2024 (web page), Organisation for Economic Co-operation and Development, Paris, https://survey.oecd.org/index.php?r=survey/index&sid=371986&lang=en.

Although empirical findings mostly support reforms in pillars 1 and 3 of the competition framework, this chapter includes broad policy discussions on pillar 2, based on chapters 1 to 4 of this report and policy research by the World Bank, including papers prepared for this report, consistent with the World Bank Markets and Competition Policy Assessment Toolkit (table 5.1).[1]

Reducing Regulatory Barriers, Improving Contestability

As discussed in chapters 1 to 4 of this report, competition in countries in Latin America and the Caribbean is considerably restricted by entry and expansion barriers and, in some sectors, concentration in market structures. The barriers inhibit new firms from entering markets and incumbents from reacting, adapting to competitive pressure, and thriving. The barriers not only are costly but also have important implications for productivity.

Table 5.2 provides an effects-based classification of qualitative restrictions identified in the data on product market regulation according to the World Bank Markets and Competition Policy Assessment Toolkit.

In addition, oligopolistic market structures remain prominent in some sectors. For instance, the latest Enterprise Survey data confirm the existence of substantial monopoly, duopoly, and oligopoly market structures in manufacturing, which is normally a competitive sector in which a natural monopoly is not justified.[2] Concentrated market structures may emerge naturally regardless of the level of competition, for example, in small markets or in an environment of large economies of scale. They may also result from failure to enforce competition regulations or because government policies restrict entry, facilitate dominance, or create a tilted playing field.

Poorly designed policies can damage competition and delay the adoption of technology. There is evidence indicating that eliminating such government-related barriers can spur productivity growth (as discussed in chapter 2 of this report). By the same token, improving competition policy design and strengthening competition authorities' enforcement capacity may boost productivity growth.

Policy reform represents an effective means to reduce obstructions to both creative destruction (market churning) and firm growth. Fundamental to boosting productivity in the region, creative destruction allows the entry of productive firms and the exit of less productive firms, freeing resources for use by more productive firms. Incumbent firms that perceive the entry of new enterprises and the resulting greater competition as a threat may be induced to become more productive through innovation, technology adoption, or better management.

Eliminating Rules That Restrict Entry and Reinforce Dominance

Governments sometimes curtail competition in markets by imposing rules that explicitly limit entry. These rules include the assignment of monopoly rights and absolute bans on entry; relative bans on entry and expansion; protection of incumbent rights through entry decisions, restrictive licenses, and permits; and impediments to switching providers. In network industries, the level of restriction varies by country. The energy sector seems to be the most highly restricted across the region. In transportation, such as water and road transportation, there are restrictions on entry and growth, such as capacity limitations, national flag requirements, and cabotage prohibitions.[3]

Table 5.2   Examples of restrictive regulations in Latin America and the Caribbean

General typology	Specific typology	Examples of specific existing restrictions identified from the PMR questionnaires (for example, of countries with relatively high and/or many restrictions)
Rules that reinforce dominance or limit entry	Monopoly rights and absolute ban on entry	Laws or other regulations restrict the number of competing firms allowed to operate a business (for example, by establishing a legal monopoly or duopoly, or a limited number of operators) in all or some sectors, such as electricity, gas, telecom, rail freight transportation, and others. (Brazil, Costa Rica, Mexico, and Peru)
		There are goods or services such as gasoline, LPG and/or other nonspecified goods and services that can be sold only in outlets operating under a local or national legal monopoly. (Argentina, Colombia, and Costa Rica)
Rules that reinforce dominance or limit entry	Relative ban on entry and expansion of activities	An authorization is always required to establish a retail outlet for selling clothing and for selling food and beverages. (Costa Rica, Mexico, and Peru)
		The professional titles of business professionals are protected by the law, and they have exclusive rights or shared exclusive rights of certain tasks. (All observed LAC countries)
		In the water sector, the rights or entitlements to abstract ground and surface water cannot be traded, leased, or transferred; and those rights are not regularly reallocated. (Argentina, Brazil, Colombia, Costa Rica, and Peru)
		Education requirements, mandatory examinations, practices, or membership in a professional organization is needed for an individual to practice a business profession legally or obtain a professional title. (All observed LAC countries)
	Incumbent rights protected by entry decision	The public procurement regulatory framework requires or permits that a percentage of the contract is reserved for domestic firms in public tenders for the provision of goods and services in all or most sectors. (Argentina, Colombia, and Mexico)

table continued next page

Table 5.2   Examples of restrictive regulations in Latin America and the Caribbean *(continued)*

General typology	Specific typology	Examples of specific existing restrictions identified from the PMR questionnaires (for example, of countries with relatively high and/or many restrictions)
	Requirements for registry (licenses and permits)	An entrepreneur starting up a limited liability company, a personally owned enterprise with no employees, or a personally owned enterprise with up to nine employees must complete many or several steps (registrations, licenses, notifications, and others) to be able to operate, and may need to contact many public and private bodies to start such a company or enterprise. (Argentina, Brazil, and Costa Rica)
		The government does not publish online a list of primary laws or a list of subordinate regulations to be prepared, modified, reformed, or repealed in the next six months or more on the internet. (All observed LAC countries)
		There are no single-contact points (one-stop shops) for obtaining information on all notifications, permits, and licenses that are required to open up a business (except for industry-specific notifications and licenses, including environmental ones). (Brazil, Colombia, Costa Rica, and Peru)
Rules that reinforce dominance or limit entry	Impediments to switch provider	Fixed number portability is not mandated. (Argentina)
		Gas companies are not required to include clear information on customers' annual consumption and the retail tariffs they are charged in the bills they send to their households and small commercial customers. (Mexico)
Rules that are conducive to collusive outcomes or increase the costs of competing in the market	Rules that reduce firms' ability to choose their strategic variables	There are no ongoing mechanisms by which the public can make recommendations to modify, provide feedback, or dispute specific existing laws and regulations. (Brazil, Chile, Colombia, and Peru)

table continued next page

Table 5.2 Examples of restrictive regulations in Latin America and the Caribbean *(continued)*

General typology	Specific typology	Examples of specific existing restrictions identified from the PMR questionnaires (for example, of countries with relatively high and/or many restrictions)
	Restrictions on types of products and services/format and location	Air carriers that offer domestic transportation services cannot freely choose key variables, such as the routes they wish to serve, the frequency of the flights they wish to offer on each route, or the size/capacity of the aircrafts on the routes they serve (subject to technical constraints). These carriers need approval by a public body. (Argentina and Peru)
		All or some form of advertising and marketing is prohibited for certain professions (for example, lawyers, notaries, accountants, and estate agents). (Argentina, Brazil, Colombia, and Costa Rica)
		On retail sale of prescription and nonprescription medicines, there are restrictions on where a pharmacy can be located, who can own a pharmacy (only pharmacists are allowed), the number of pharmacies that the same owner can have (restricted to a maximum of three), and the opening and closing hours of pharmacies. (Argentina)
	Price control	Retail prices are subject to price controls for products such as staple goods (for example, milk, bread, and corn), gasoline, and LPG. There may be price restrictions (fees and tariffs are regulated) in the market for business professions such as legal, notaries, accounting, civil engineering, architecture, and estate agents. (All observed LAC countries)
Rules that discriminate and protect vested interests	Discriminatory application of rules and standards	All or some foreign companies providing long-distance international passenger transportation services by coach cannot provide cabotage services. (All observed LAC countries)
	Discretionary application of rules	Airports are not subject to any form of regulatory ex ante or ex post supervision on the level of their charges or revenues by an independent public body. (Argentina, Chile, Colombia, Costa Rica, and Mexico)
		Liner-conferences in the water freight transportation sector are totally exempted from the application of antitrust rules. (Chile and Mexico)

table continued next page

Table 5.2   Examples of restrictive regulations in Latin America and the Caribbean *(continued)*

General typology	Specific typology	Examples of specific existing restrictions identified from the PMR questionnaires (for example, of countries with relatively high and/or many restrictions)
		In water services, when there are more than five local providers (whether private or public) in a jurisdiction (usually monopolists in different geographic locations), comparable data on each firm's efficiency and performance level (for example, tariffs, quality of water, and security of supply) are not collected by an independent body or regulator. (Argentina and Mexico)
		When developing regulation, regulators are not required to identify and assess the impacts of the preferred regulatory option, or the baseline or "do nothing" option, or alternative regulatory options. (Argentina, Costa Rica, and Peru)
		Regulators are not formally required to consider consultation comments received from the stakeholders when developing the final primary law, or the final subordinate regulation. (Argentina, Brazil, Chile, Colombia, Costa Rica, and Peru)
Rules that discriminate and protect vested interests	Lack of competitive neutrality relative to government entities	In some sectors, SOEs benefit from other favorable treatments that are not available to private firms. (Argentina, Colombia, and Costa Rica)
		National, state, or provincial governments hold equity stakes in the largest firm in the electricity, gas, railway transportation, and air transportation (passenger domestic and airport operations) sectors. (Argentina, Brazil, and Costa Rica)
		In none of the sectors is the public body that exercises the ownership rights in SOEs different from the public body or bodies that regulate the sector in which the firm operates. (Argentina and Brazil)
	State aid/incentives distorting a level playing field	SOEs have access to financing that is not available to private companies in all sectors or some sectors. (Argentina, Chile, Colombia, Costa Rica, and Mexico)

Sources: Miralles, Dauda, and Zipitria 2021; Markets and Competition Policy (dashboard), World Bank, Washington DC, https://www.worldbank.org/en/topic/competition-policy. Elaborated by FCI Markets and Technology global unit based on the application of the World Bank Markets and Competition Policy Assessment toolkit (MCPAT) effect-based rule classification to OECD and OECD–World Bank Group PMR questionnaires.

Note: LAC = Latin America and the Caribbean; LPG = liquefied petroleum gas; OECD = Organisation for Economic Co-operation and Development; PMR = Product Market Regulations indicator; SOEs = state-owned enterprises.

Reducing or eliminating explicit restrictions to market entry is a priority, especially in network industries such as information and communication technology (ICT). Recommendations to facilitate entry in network industries in countries in the region include loosening regulations that (1) inhibit third-party access and participation by gas subsector firms; (2) control entry in the transportation sector, especially by foreign parties; and (3) limit prices.

Reforming entry requirements and reducing administrative costs would be positive steps in promoting entry by new firms. The administrative burdens targeting limited liability start-ups are substantial in several countries, mainly because of complex licensing and permitting requirements (figure 5.1). Periodic reviews of regulations to assess necessity, proportionality, and transparency may represent an effective tool for correcting the distortions created by regulations or eliminating unnecessary regulations that add to the administrative burden (box 5.2).

One-stop shops are effective means to smooth market entry. They offer a multitude of administrative services in a single location, saving business owners considerable time and effort. Entrepreneurs in the region generally must visit multiple agencies to start a business. Only Chile and Mexico have one-stop shops to provide the relevant authorizations and permits.[4] Colombia has a shop, but it provides information on requirements only. Meanwhile, simplifying rules to implement the principle that "silence means consent" can streamline entry and foster administrative efficiency. Such a mechanism exists only in Costa Rica and Mexico. Adopting such a rule more widely would enhance contestability by reducing uncertainty and delays in issuing the licenses and permits needed for market entry.

Eliminating Regulations That Unnecessarily Raise the Cost of Competition

Governments in the region apply a variety of price controls that may have important implications for restricting competition. Therefore, it is critical to evaluate the impact of price controls in retail markets and the potential to introduce or reform pricing mechanisms in sectors characterized by dominant or monopolistic actors. Unnecessary price controls on certain products, paired with the absence of pricing mechanisms in regulated sectors, may distort the incentives of market operators and affect their ability to compete and provide better goods and services.

Figure 5.1 In several countries in LAC, regulations significantly restrict competition

Product Market Regulations indicator

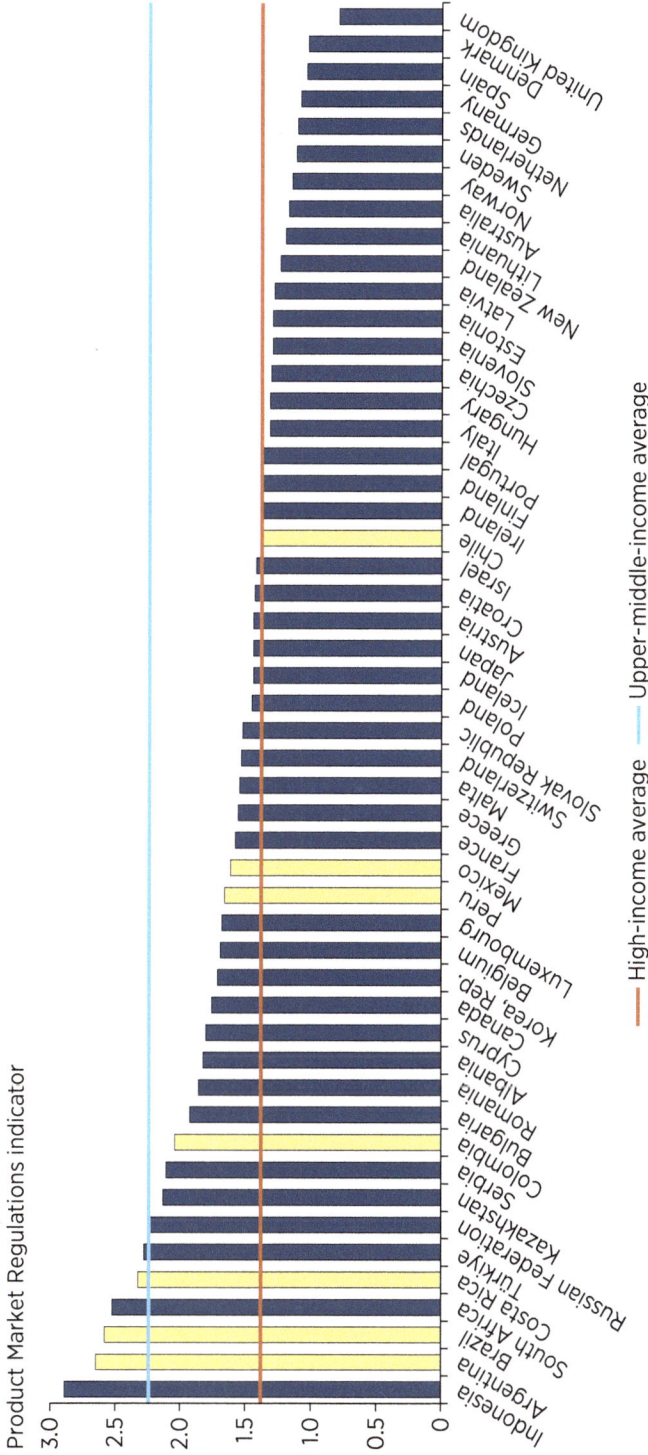

Source: Miralles-Murciego 2021 based on OECD and OECD–World Bank Group Product Market Regulation Database, 2018–20.

Note: Yellow bars indicate LAC countries. LAC = Latin America and the Caribbean; OECD = Organisation for Economic Co-operation and Development; PMR = Product Market Regulations indicator.

Box 5.2

Ex ante assessments of regulations may be vital

In an assessment centering on telecommunications and the pharmaceutical industry in Peru, Coronado et al. (2021) analyze regulations that were approved by Congress in 2015–21 on the mandates of national agencies and local governments. Their methodology is similar to an ex ante regulatory impact assessment—a forecast of likely effects—based on opinions offered by Peru's National Institute for the Defense of Competition and the Protection of Intellectual Property (Indecopi) and other specialized regulators, and considering the criteria of the Organisation for Economic Co-operation and Development's Competition Assessment Toolkit.[a]

Coronado et al. (2021) use this methodology in the belief that Peru's specialized competition and regulatory agencies have adopted a solid technical approach to policy making and that the views of these entities, therefore, likely reflect a credible forecast of the future effects of regulation. They find that most of the regulations they reviewed introduced entry or expansion barriers through the associated requirements, such as licenses and permits (46 percent) or firms' consequent strategic decisions on associated issues, including pricing, advertising, and quality standards, which reduced firms' ability to compete (47 percent).

They also considered complaints that private sector actors filed with the Elimination of Bureaucratic Barriers Commission in 2015–21, claiming that regulations amounted to bureaucratic barriers. The complaints typically focused on transportation, manufacturing, and telecommunications. Most of the barriers in transportation involved permitting requirements to operate passenger services between departments and provinces. In telecommunications, the barriers tended to restrict the construction of mobile telephone antennas or fiber optic networks.

Given that almost half of the reviewed regulations created barriers to competition, these results confirm the value of ex ante and ex post assessments of the impacts of regulations on competition, not only regulations that originate with Indecopi but also those that are adopted by other areas of government.

Source: Coronado et al. 2021.

a. Competition Assessment Toolkit (dashboard), Organisation for Economic Co-operation and Development, Paris, https://www.oecd.org/daf /competition/assessment-toolkit.htm.

A subindicator on government involvement in business operations captures price controls and other factors, such as command-and-control regulations, which may limit competition. In the region, the subindicator values are weakest in Argentina and Brazil, followed by Costa Rica and Mexico.

Reforming Government Interventions That Are Biased and Harm Competition

Vertical integration has been increasing in logistics, raising concerns about the harm to market competition. Entrepreneurs in other industries that depend on networks have expressed concern about the growing incidence of unfair practices in logistics.[5] Many of the worries focus on unequal access to transportation facilities, with demands that the loading and unloading times on schedules governing trucks' access to ports be distributed fairly and respected among all road carriers. There is also concern that vertically integrated firms are using profitable business segments to subsidize unproductive segments. In gas production and delivery, entry may be constrained by the limited separation between transmission and distribution and upstream and downstream markets.

Leveling the Playing Field to Boost Market Entry and Expansion

State-owned enterprises (SOEs) are not as important in the region as they are in other middle-income regions. However, their size and relevance are still significant, which presents an issue because the SOEs operate in markets in which the private sector is also active. For instance, the private sector includes network industries, actors in non-infrastructure markets, and participants in subsectors such as shipbuilding and ship repair and the manufacture of aircraft and spacecraft.[6] Compared with Organisation for Economic Co-operation and Development (OECD) countries, the region has relatively weak governance of SOEs and public procurement—both key elements in implementing an effective competitive neutrality framework.

Controlling Government Assistance

Several reforms would help to level the playing field between public and private actors as well as domestic and foreign operators, thereby boosting market entry and expansion.

Governments in the region would benefit if they took steps to minimize the distortions in competition arising from government support measures. This support may be warranted to tackle market failures or offset the negative effects of shocks, such as the COVID-19 pandemic, but it should be designed in a transparent manner as a temporary measure to address short-term shocks. Several governments adopted support packages to manage health risks and other harmful outcomes of the pandemic. However, they lacked mechanisms to control and evaluate the effects of these policies on competition. Transparency in granting and monitoring support, including the use of the support by beneficiaries, is essential to ensuring competitive neutrality, avoiding favoritism, and minimizing distortions in competition.

Ensuring Competitive Neutrality

Adoption of structures that support competitive neutrality facilitates a level playing field between public and private operators as well as between domestic and foreign actors. Initiatives in SOE governance that would advance this objective include (1) limiting the spread of unincorporated SOEs and subjecting those that exist to private law, (2) separating the commercial and noncommercial activities of SOEs and the costs and revenues of commercial and noncommercial activities, (3) reducing the regulatory privileges and exemptions benefiting SOEs, and (4) inhibiting the ability of SOEs to obtain financing under better conditions relative to private sector competitors.

The principles of competition should become embedded in public procurement, which accounts for up to 20 percent of gross domestic product in some countries in the region, considerably above the level in OECD countries (an average of 13 percent in 2015). It is vital that procurement policies and procedures be transparent and nondiscriminatory to establish fair competition and facilitate the entry of worthy enterprises into the market for public contracts. Attention should be paid to SOEs' access to public tenders and their treatment during the procurement process. More reliance on public-private partnerships could reduce distortions in the process.

In fostering competitive neutrality in public procurement, governments in the region should consider three principles. First, the reference prices of public tenders should be disclosed. Although most of the countries in the region allow the disclosure of these prices, some restrict disclosure, including Argentina in goods and services contracts, Mexico in public works contracts, and Costa Rica in both. Second, entry requirements and the time allotted for bidding on tenders should be proportional to the size or value of the tenders. Only the governments of Chile, Colombia, and Peru now follow this principle. The government of Argentina considers the tender's complexity in setting deadlines, but only in public works contracts. Third, the use of e-procurement should be encouraged to facilitate entry and bidding. In Brazil, for instance, there is no requirement that tender documents be published online or that bids may be submitted online.

Governments in the region should dedicate more effort to promoting competition in procurement. Explicit discrimination in favor of local firms in public tenders exists in all sectors in Argentina and Mexico, and this approach is applied in some sectors in Colombia. In Chile, foreign firms are required to participate in joint ventures with domestic firms to undertake contracts. In Mexico, there must be domestic content in tenders on goods and services and on public works.

Strengthening Implementation and Enforcement

Strengthening competition policy is crucial to realizing the development aspirations of countries in the region. However, policies to foster competition and dismantle cartels, if they exist, are weakly enforced. Progress was severely impeded during the pandemic. As the region recovers, it is important to resume strengthening reforms promoting competition and the enforcement of competition laws.

Tools to Tackle Cartel Agreements

Cartels burden consumers with higher prices, limit newcomers' entry, and reduce the growth opportunities among competitors outside the cartel agreements. Cartels fix prices at above-market levels, restrict output, and split markets among the cartel members. Over the past four decades, more than 300 cartels have been identified and dismantled in markets for critical goods and services in the region.[7] This is progress, but most cartels remain largely undetected: cartel activity in the economy is estimated to be at least 10 times the observed level. In the aftermath of the COVID-19 crisis, corporate consolidation and state intervention in markets may have drastically increased the risk that such anti-competitive behavior would spread to more markets.

To confront this danger, competition authorities need adequate staffing, but they should also follow through on warnings and sanctions. The risk of being caught must be sufficiently high to prevent firms from undertaking such behavior. In addition, if firms are caught, the competition authority and the judiciary must have the power and capacity to investigate and sanction the behavior.

Detection of Anticompetitive Behavior

The secretive nature of cartels represents a challenge for competition authorities seeking to detect them. Therefore, many investigations are reactive in that they result from complaints from competitors or consumers or from firms admitting to an offense in an application for amnesty or leniency. In some cases, competition authorities have been more proactive and opened ex officio investigations to identify abuse of dominance or pinpoint firms that have formed a cartel.

The reason a case is initiated may affect the relationship between competition and productivity. In Uruguay, cases initiated by the competition agency ex officio are more likely to bolster productivity than cases originating from a complaint by a firm, which is often a competitor of the accused firm (Sampi, Urrutia Arrieta, and Vostroknutova 2024).

Leniency Programs

Leniency programs are meant to break the code of silence among cartel conspirators. Following the pioneering introduction of a leniency program in the United States in 1978, many countries added similar incentives to their detection toolboxes. The goal is to induce cartel members to self-report their conduct and cooperate with an investigation by providing insider evidence about clandestine meetings, communication, and agreements (OECD 2019). Incentives typically include a potential reduction in fines or sentences, less restrictive corrective orders, and even immunity from prosecution.

The past 20 years or so have witnessed rapid growth in the number of leniency programs.[8] Before 2000, fewer than 10 jurisdictions worldwide had adopted such programs; by 2010, the number had risen to more than 60 and, by 2017, to 89 (Araujo and Meester 2023, based on OECD data).

Experience shows that such programs are effective in uncovering conspiracies that would otherwise go undetected. In the United States, following revisions in the leniency program in 1993 to clarify and enlarge the scope of amnesty, the number of leniency applications rose to more than 20 per year, and these applications led to several convictions and fines, totaling more than US$1 million (Araujo and Meester 2023). The governments of OECD member countries that have established leniency programs have a newfound ability to detect and punish cartels (Araujo and Meester 2023, based on OECD data).

Governments in Latin America and the Caribbean make less use of leniency programs, compared to governments in Europe, Asia and the Pacific, and OECD countries (figure 5.2). The numbers are low in Latin America and the Caribbean partly because few leniency programs are used actively, although a large number have been established. Only six countries had at least one leniency application between 2015 and 2021, and only three had at least one per year. Another explanation is the relatively young age of leniency programs in the region. Often, a decade passes before a new program receives its first application (Araujo and Meester 2023).

Figure 5.2 LAC countries make less use of leniency programs compared to other countries

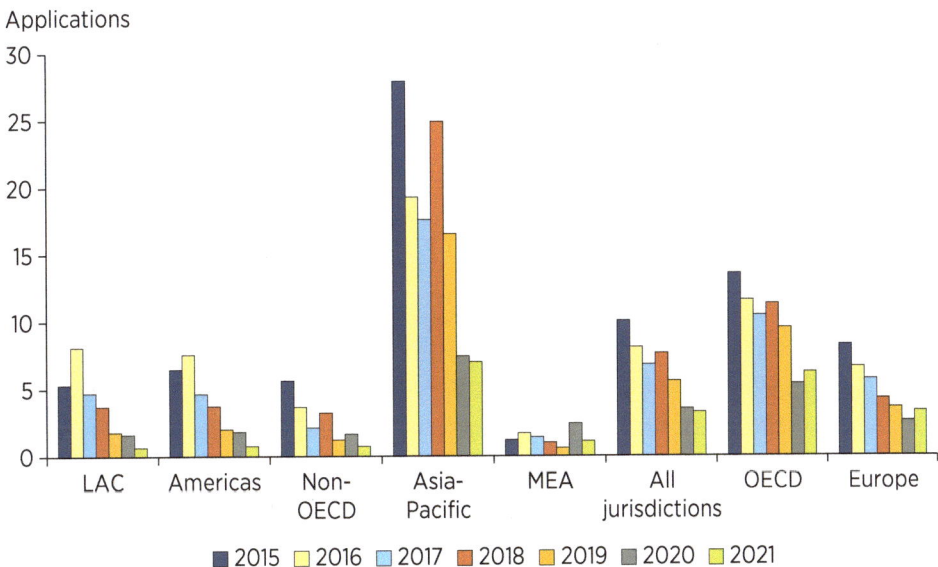

Source: Araujo and Meester 2023, based on Competition (portal), Organisation for Economic Co-operation and Development, Paris, https://www.oecd.org /competition/.

Note: The figure shows leniency applications per agency for selected regions and country groups in 2015–21. Regions are named following the original data source. LAC = Latin America and the Caribbean; MEA = Middle East and Africa; OECD = Organisation for Economic Co-operation and Development.

Globally, although leniency has gained currency, the average number of leniency applications has been steadily declining (figure 5.2). The literature offers several possible explanations, including uncertainties about the correct definition of a cartel, the substantial administrative burden on the company coming forward to participate, the often-long duration of cartel investigations, and the risk that other parties may use an admission of cartel participation to extract damages in court (Araujo and Meester 2023).

Competition authorities in the region should rely more frequently on leniency programs by creating new incentives and ensuring that leniency applicants are adequately protected. Authorities could do so by extending the leniency benefit to subsequent cooperating individuals or entities on a diminishing basis and setting the evidence thresholds required for application relatively low for first applicants. Verbal applications should also be allowed, accompanied by special measures to ensure confidentiality.

Proactive Ex Officio Investigations

In addition to following up on complaints and leniency applications, most competition authorities proactively identify the sectors or markets that are particularly prone to cartel activity. They may investigate specific firms that they suspect of participating in a cartel. These ex officio investigations depend on data collection. Because preliminary investigations leading to ex officio cases are costly and require significant technical capacity, the region's competition authorities require more resources to carry out these crucial investigations properly.

Latin America and the Caribbean significantly underperforms compared to other regions in the average number of ex officio investigations launched against cartels per agency per year (OECD 2024) (figure 5.3). Although this number might imply that the industrial sector in the region is smaller, evidence suggests that many cartels go undetected. The low number of ex officio investigations reduces the attractiveness of leniency applications. It likewise fails to deter firms from turning to anti-competitive behavior in the first place. The competition authorities are spread thin, but they are obligated to follow up on any complaints from the private sector and often prioritize them over ex officio investigations, which demonstrates that there is room for improvement. Because ex officio investigations are more effective at increasing productivity, the use of the limited resources must be reprioritized.

Figure 5.3 Competition agencies in the region launch fewer ex officio investigations of cartels compared to other regions

Investigations

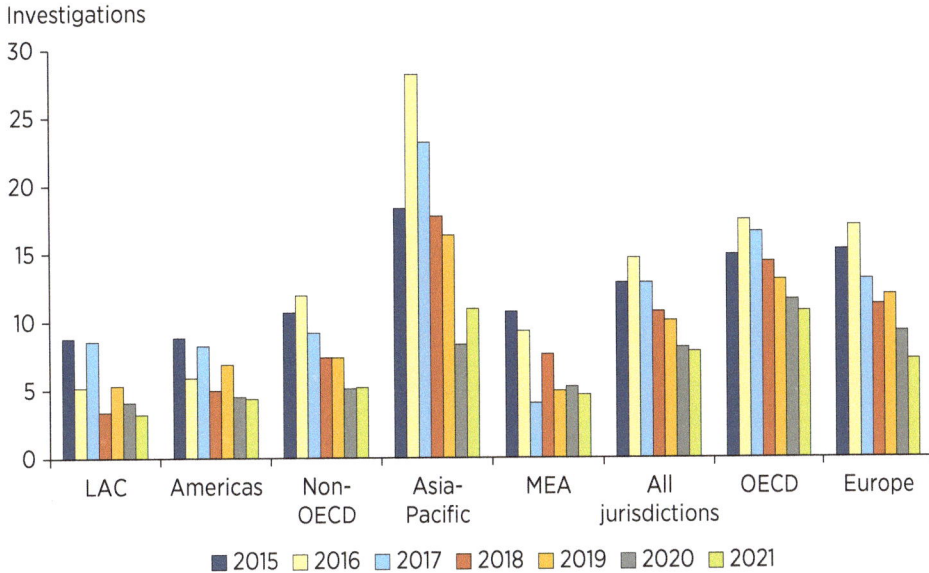

■ 2015 □ 2016 ■ 2017 ■ 2018 ■ 2019 ■ 2020 □ 2021

Source: Araujo and Meester 2023, based on the Competition (portal), Organisation for Economic Co-operation and Development, Paris, https://www.oecd.org/competition/.

Note: The figure shows ex officio cartel investigations per authority for selected country groups in 2015–21. Based on 79 jurisdictions that contributed in 2023. Regions are named following the original data source. LAC = Latin America and the Caribbean; MEA = Middle East and Africa; OECD = Organisation for Economic Co-operation and Development.

Unannounced Inspections

After leniency programs, the most effective tool to obtain both direct and circumstantial evidence on firms that form cartels or otherwise adopt anti-competitive behavior is unannounced inspections, including dawn raids (OECD 2018, 2020). On average, 85-90 percent of unannounced inspections involve detecting cartels, and the remainder are abuse of dominance investigations.

Across all regions of the world, competition authorities conduct the fewest dawn raids and other unannounced inspections in Latin America and the Caribbean (figure 5.4). Moreover, the number of such inspections appears to be decreasing. One reason for this outcome is that among the competition authorities in the region, only the authorities in Brazil, Chile, Colombia, Mexico, and Peru have sufficient legal power.

Figure 5.4 Competition authorities in LAC countries conduct the fewest dawn raids

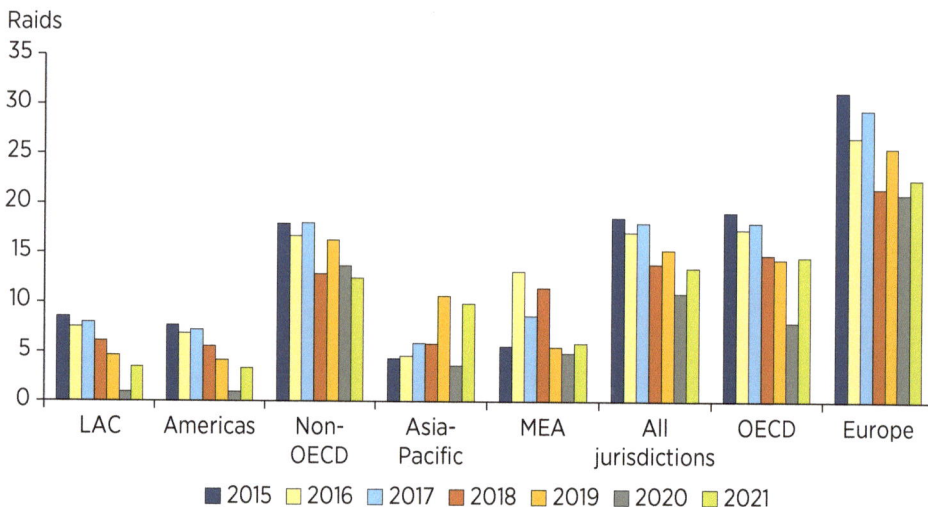

Source: Araujo and Meester 2023, based on Competition (portal), Organisation for Economic Co-operation and Development, Paris, https://www.oecd.org/competition/.
Note: The figure shows the number of dawn raids, adjusted by the economic size of jurisdictions. Economic size is adjusted by calculating the number of dawn raids per € trillion of gross domestic product. Regions are named following the original data source. LAC = Latin America and the Caribbean; MEA = Middle East and Africa; OECD = Organisation for Economic Co-operation and Development.

Another challenge is the lack of expertise among competition authority personnel to undertake digital forensics or apply other information technology tools.[9] Nonetheless, the development and use of particular investigative tools should be proportionate to the competition authority's resources and capacity and the sophistication of any cartel activity in a country. Deploying investigative tools is costly. Applying new tools without the establishment of adequate procedural fairness and confidentiality standards may weaken the business and investment climate.

Sanctions

The risk of hefty fines is a deterrent among firms that are tempted to resort to anti-competitive behavior. A company will choose to behave anticompetitively only if the expected gains are greater than the expected costs, including fines.

Monetary sanctions are substantially lower in the region than in OECD jurisdictions (figure 5.5).[10] Fines are equivalent to only 3 percent of the benefits that cartel members in the region can expect to gain by colluding (World Bank 2021a). This amount may be considered the lower bound based on evidence from OECD countries indicating that fines, expressed as a share of cartel gains, vary substantially, ranging from 3 to 189 percent across these countries (OECD 2002).

The gap in fines between Latin America and the Caribbean and other regions has been widening. On average, cartel fines increased globally by 56 percent in 2015–19, mainly driven by OECD countries. Latin America and the Caribbean is the only region where cartel fines declined, by 11.5 percent annually over the same period (OECD 2022). More recently, several cases in network sectors in the region have involved greater sanctions, showing that competition authorities are moving in the right direction (box 5.3).

Figure 5.5 Sanctions are lower on average in LAC countries compared to OECD countries

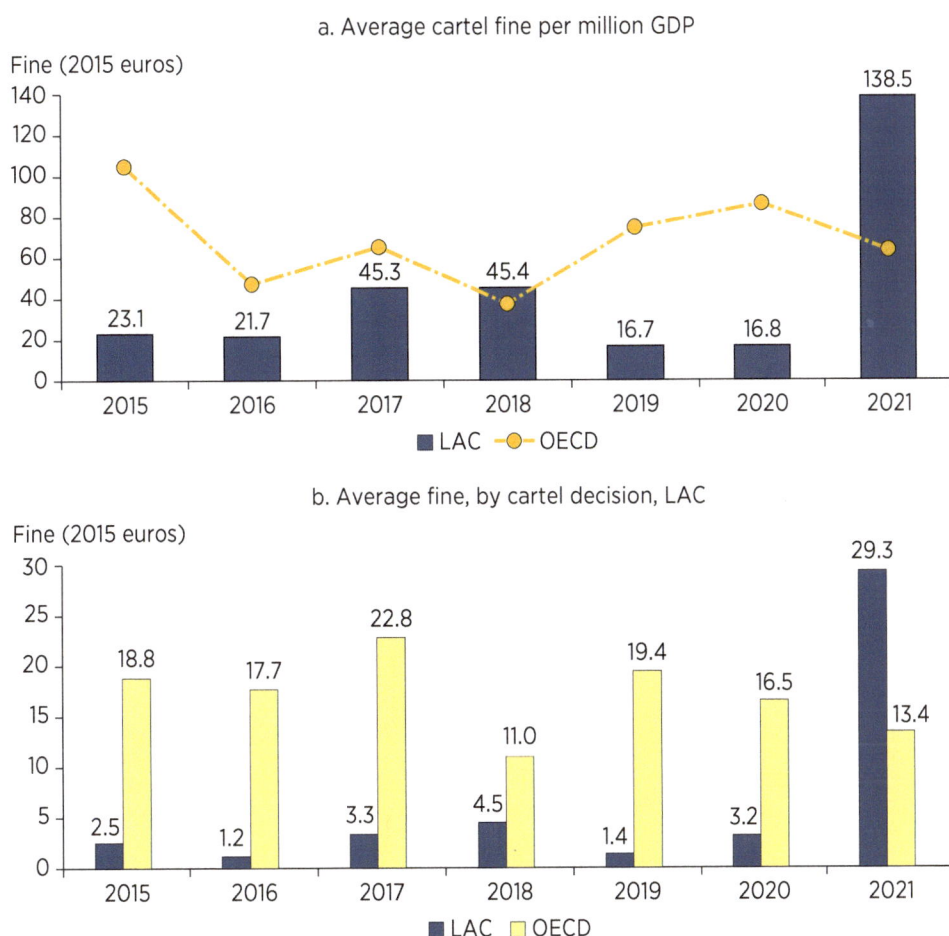

a. Average cartel fine per million GDP

b. Average fine, by cartel decision, LAC

Sources: Araujo and Meester 2023, based on Competition (portal), Organisation for Economic Co-operation and Development, Paris, https://www.oecd.org/competition/; OECD 2024.

Note: The figure shows average cartel fines in LAC and OECD countries in 2015–21. Values are calculated using 2015 exchange rates. The data are robust if they are presented in nominal and real terms or if the number of sanctioned cases is used instead of the amounts. The increase in 2021 derives from the incident in Peru described in box 5.3 and a record fine in that country in a case involving a cartel in the construction sector (Rafferty 2021). LAC = Latin America and the Caribbean; OECD = Organisation for Economic Co-operation and Development.

Box 5.3

Enforcement has recently targeted utilities and other network industries

Many areas in utilities and infrastructure in Latin America and the Caribbean were once dominated by state-owned or state-sanctioned monopolies. There was no change in the regulatory regime following privatization. The private sector was allowed to assume a concentrated market structure. The dominant firm, operating in a theoretically competitive market, often sought to obstruct the introduction of more competition, and it frequently faced little pushback. Antitrust authorities are now targeting these industries, focusing on abuse of dominance.

In 2021, the National Institute for the Defense of Competition and the Protection of Intellectual Property (Indecopi), Peru's competition authority, fined Sociedad Eléctrica del Sur Oeste, the incumbent electricity supplier in central and southern Peru, the equivalent of about US$1.2 million for abusing its dominant position in the electricity supply market to keep and exploit customers. Users in the regulated market were offered an exemption from a one-year notice requirement to change their status to the free market, but only if they retained Indecopi as a supplier in the free market. The company was also fined for similar conduct in northern Peru.

In 2021, the Court for the Defense of Free Competition (Tribunal de Defensa de la Libre Competencia) in Chile upheld abuse of dominance claims brought by the mail company Envía against Correos de Chile, a state-owned postal service provider, and imposed a fine equivalent to about US$4.5 million. It was determined that Correos de Chile had offered Envía customers special discounts that were not justified by cost or other objective considerations. Correos de Chile was not found to have engaged in predatory pricing, but the tribunal ruled that it had engaged in unfair competition by putting pressure on customers to accept an exclusive dealing arrangement.

In 2022, the Federal Economic Competition Commission, Mexico's chief competition authority, imposed a fine equivalent to about US$42 million on the Mexico City International Airport for preventing a luxury bus company from providing services to and from Puebla City. The authority noted that the airport was a repeat offender, previously subject to sanctions for monopolistic practices.

In 2022, Brazil's national competition regulator, the Administrative Council for Economic Defense (CADE), fined telecommunications operators,

box continued next page

Box 5.3

Enforcement has recently targeted utilities and other network industries *(continued)*

including Claro, Oi, and Telefónica, the equivalent of US$152 million for forming a cartel in a 2015 tender issued by Empresa Brasileira de Correios e Telégrafos, the state-owned postal service, to connect all its offices. CADE took the view that the consortium artificially reduced competition in the tender, meaning that bids were higher than they would have been otherwise.

The size and frequency of these cases highlight the utility of pursuing antitrust policy in network sectors.

Source: Cheng 2022.

Criminal Enforcement

In addition to monetary sanctions, enforcement officials in some countries in the region may seek criminal sanctions. Approximately two-thirds of the region's competition regimes in 2020 included criminal penalties for individuals, and almost half allowed such penalties in both cartel and bid-rigging cases.[11] Brazil, Chile, Mexico, and Peru are among the countries where both penalties are permitted. In Colombia, criminal penalties may be assigned only in cases of bid-rigging. Legal systems in other countries, including Argentina and Costa Rica, bar criminal sanctions on individuals in competition cases.

Strengthening the Antitrust and Institutional Framework

The region's antitrust and institutional framework needs to be strengthened along three key dimensions: (1) capacity, (2) independence, and (3) collaboration and monitoring.

Capacity

As discussed in chapter 2 of this report, competition authorities in the region tend to be small and underresourced. In recent years, however, they have gained more autonomy and now operate as specialized bodies with reinforced sanctioning capacity. Competition enforcement is still weak, however, with limited budgeting and staffing. The OECD framework has not yet been fully integrated.

In Mexico, the Federal Economic Competition Commission is effectively pursuing its mandate, but it would be more effective with increased resources for investigations.[12] This is a pattern in the region. Competition authorities across Latin America require more funding and more personnel to undertake more cases and end the long-standing practice of dropping viable investigations because of a lack of resources to gather sufficient evidence. Increased resources would enhance the detection of cartels and anti-competitive practices by allowing competition authorities to investigate markets that exhibit potentially harmful conduct.

Independence

Institutional and budgetary factors may affect the ability of a government to implement competition policy reform. Powerful vested interests, such as cartel members, often seek to hinder the enforcement of competition law through lobbying and political influence, derailing reform efforts. There is nonetheless usually broad public support for policies that promote competition, which strengthens government legitimacy and improves the odds of reform success.

According to a recent World Bank study, Brazil, Chile, Colombia, Mexico, and Peru have "pursued sequenced and gradual reform programs and fostered a high-level political consensus around the importance of detecting, addressing, and preventing the establishment of cartels" (World Bank 2021a, 6).

However, the study also notes that "recent successes among competition authorities in [the region] are at risk of ending abruptly due to threats to their independence stemming from political influence" (World Bank 2021a, 9).

From a political economy and institutional reform standpoint, two policy directions are critical:

- *Seeking robust political consensus and strong institutional buy-in to enhance the sustainability of competition reform.* Recent successes in competition policy in the region demonstrate that building political support for enforcement is fundamental. Dismantling cartels and deterring the formation of new cartels should be a nonpartisan policy goal across the region. Effective competition policies typically enjoy broad-based public support, and their implementation bolsters the government's legitimacy.

- *Strengthening the independence of the competition authority.* Despite periods of successful competition enforcement in Argentina, El Salvador, and Peru, the independence of agencies that initiate competition investigations (the prosecutorial units) and decide cases (the adjudicatory units) should be enhanced, particularly to engage the public in accepting the legitimacy of the decisions of competition authorities.

Several steps can be taken to safeguard the political independence of competition authorities. They include (1) delinking the appointment of the leadership of the competition authority from the political cycle, (2) expanding the appointment process to involve institutions outside the executive branch, (3) adopting merit-based appointment procedures, (4) establishing two-stage appointment processes involving independent bodies, (5) establishing mandates to ensure that officials cannot be removed summarily or pressured with the threat of removal, (6) creating rules to prevent conflicts of interest and limit the ability of private sector actors to exercise undue influence over public officials, (7) enabling the competition authority to request budget allocations directly from the legislature and to self-finance through merger notification fees and other revenue streams, (8) ensuring that adjudicatory units do not have authority over the budget or the composition of prosecutorial units and that the two sets of units are supported by separate technical teams, and (9) shielding the prosecutorial and adjudicatory units from interference by executive branch officials outside the competition authority.

Collaboration and Monitoring

Collaboration between sectoral regulators and competition authorities can bolster the integration of competition principles into regulatory governance. In the region, only Colombia, Mexico, and Peru have embedded the principles of competition in all stages of the regulatory life cycle. This approach can eliminate rules that, by design or chance, encourage the formation of cartels. Removing regulatory obstacles to competition requires a proactive approach among sectoral regulators in close collaboration with competition authorities within a national competition policy framework that effectively enables reform in favor of competition.

For example, regulating even the ICT industry's less sophisticated subsectors would be complex. The impacts of a relevant regulatory regime would likely vary across firms, which would influence the success of the process of quality upgrading. Effective regulation requires that competition authorities possess exceptional technical expertise in data regulation, financial sector infrastructure, and other areas.

High-quality research and analysis are fundamental to building political consensus and identifying an appropriate policy response to regulatory restrictions and anti-competitive behavior. In partnership with sectoral regulators and relevant ministries, this response can lead to more well-targeted activities by competition authorities and raise awareness of the relevance of competition policy within the economic policy agenda. Countries in Latin America and the Caribbean could make a strategic commitment to the regular monitoring of key markets, especially given the evidence of the changes in market dynamics and cartel formation associated with the COVID-19 pandemic. Market studies are extremely useful in gathering intelligence and meeting the information needs of pro-competition policies. In the region, they have been conducted only sporadically, and multiple studies are often undertaken simultaneously as a poor substitute for a commitment to regular market monitoring.[13] The pandemic prompted massive turnover in numerous markets, induced temporary and permanent shifts in consumer demand, and sparked government interventions that may have facilitated collusion among firms. Market studies may represent a powerful signal that a vigilant competition authority is proactively gathering information on potential cartel activity.

For these reasons, a forward-looking research agenda focusing on using data, adopting regulations, monitoring market performance, and organizing logistics solutions can help to address the remaining significant gaps in logistics regulation. A fundamental issue is the use of big data to evaluate the impacts of various regulatory arrangements and market structures on logistics. As more sources of data become available, addressing this sort of issue should become a short-term priority (World Bank 2021b).

Enhancing Enforcement Capacity

The preceding analysis indicates that competition enforcement can be improved in many countries in the region by increasing resources, implementing new tools, and using the tools that are already available more effectively. The following policy directions would help to enhance the enforcement capacity of competition authorities:

- *Strengthen capacity and resources for regulatory reform and competition enforcement*. Relevant steps might include hiring additional staff and training current staff on new challenges.

- *Reinforce leniency programs*. Leniency programs are a cost-effective method of enhancing competition. Competition authorities should ensure that program applicants are adequately protected. They might do so by extending the leniency benefit to subsequent cooperators on a diminishing basis and setting evidence thresholds comparatively low for the initial applicants. Leniency programs should also allow verbal applications supported by measures to guarantee confidentiality.

- *Ensure effective sanctioning of anti-competitive behavior*. The administrative fines for anti-competitive practices are relatively small in the region. Added to the already low probability of detection of cartels, firms face little risk that any cartel activity will result in a financial loss. Fixing fines as a percentage of turnover rather than as a nominal amount would tie the fines more closely to the financial harm caused by collusion.

- *Increase the use of sophisticated investigation tools, such as digital forensics and dawn raids.* Some countries in the region have never relied on dawn raids or other unannounced inspections. Only the competition authorities in Brazil, Chile, Colombia, Mexico, and Peru have access to such tools.

Harnessing Complementary Policies

The impact of competition on productivity can be boosted through policy complementarities. One source of policy complementarity examined here is between trade policy and competition policy, which can be mutually reinforcing, especially through tariff liberalization and preferential trade agreements. Another is the competition-innovation nexus, whereby competition both fuels and is boosted by innovation.

Trade Policy: Preferential Trade Agreements Foster Competition

Trade liberalization through tariff reduction is an important area of complementarity between trade policy and pro-competition reform. Tariff liberalization can generate gains in productivity and growth (as discussed in box 4.1, in chapter 4 of this report). Such impacts are more evident in input markets than in output markets, highlighting the need for competition policies along the value chain to enhance the positive effects in output markets.

Preferential trade agreements (PTAs) represent another avenue for trade and competition policy complementarity. They may support the implementation and enforcement of domestic competition policy. Modern trade agreements are becoming deeper in that they now often encompass a wider range of provisions that are related not only to tariff rates and customs procedures but also to behind-the-border regulations, such as those governing competition, investment, and subsidies (Mattoo, Rocha, and Ruta 2020). For example, PTA commitments might cover the adoption of a competitive neutrality framework in national legislation on competition, subsidies, and SOEs, as well as the expansion of the mandate of competition authorities to encompass government assistance and SOEs. Licetti, Miralles, and Teh (2020) review the competition provisions in more than 200 multilateral, regional, and bilateral trade agreements, using a new global database on deep trade agreements.[14] They find that 84 percent of the agreements include competition-related provisions, defined as any national or regional competition requirement, whether regulatory or institutional.

PTAs in the region have followed the overall global trend by including an increasing number of competition-related provisions: 80 percent of the PTAs in Latin America and the Caribbean (66 of 82) have at least some provisions on competition policy. Competition-related commitments are at the core of multilateral PTAs in the region, with only a few exceptions, such as the Global System of Trade Preferences among Developing Countries, the Latin American Integration Association, and the Pacific Alliance (Rocha and Ruta 2022).[15] Although substantive competition provisions are standard in the architecture of regional integration, the coverage of competitive neutrality provisions varies, and no multilateral agreement regulates government assistance. The regulation of monopolies, undertakings that involve exclusive rights, and anti-competitive behavior by SOEs has been incorporated into PTAs between Central America and the European Union and in the Trans-Pacific Strategic Economic Partnership Agreement, whereas other agreements tend to focus on monopolies or SOE regulation.[16] Among intraregional agreements, the Southern Common Market has the most comprehensive coverage of competition issues, regulating collusive practices, the abuse of dominance, monopolies, and anti-competitive practices by SOEs.[17]

A critical issue relative to competition-related provisions in PTAs and PTA provisions in general is the ability to enforce these provisions. Licetti, Miralles, and Teh (2020) examine the enforceability of competition-related provisions, using dispute settlement language in the agreements. They classify provisions according to six levels of enforceability,[18] and find that substantive competition commitments exhibit high levels of enforceability. Specifically, in competition-related provisions in PTAs, binding commitments exist in 64 percent on regulating monopolies, 55 percent on prohibiting or regulating the abuse of a dominant position, 49 percent on regulating cartels and concerted practices, and 47 percent on regulating the anti-competitive behavior of SOEs.

Even if PTAs do not directly guide domestic policies that affect competition, they may play an essential role in enhancing policy transparency. They may act as a commitment tool by promoting regulatory cooperation and supplying an institutional framework to bring together relevant actors and engage the private sector. These indirect channels through which PTAs affect domestic competition may be at least as effective as direct requirements and perhaps more so.

If they are deep agreements, PTAs can play a critical role in promoting competition in domestic markets and boosting productivity through direct and indirect channels. However, unleashing these effects is conditional on the existence of low tariffs and nontariff measures in trade relations with countries that are not members of the agreements. If the incidence of these tariffs and nontariff measures is substantial, the impact of the PTAs on domestic competition is limited (Lee 2022).

The Competition-Innovation Policy Nexus

Innovation is one mechanism that firms may use to survive competition or counter the threat of new competitors' entry. Competition may thus fuel the needs and desires that propel a firm to innovate.

However, innovation is costly. It requires a concerted effort from all parts of a firm and represents an investment risk because the returns are uncertain. It also requires skilled and motivated managers and other capable personnel to be successful, particularly at the global technological frontier, where competition can erode the rents deriving from innovation. This reality spurs the policy debate in industrialized countries over whether embracing antitrust legislation and investigations or pursuing patents is more effective in the quest for development and a healthy economy.

Aghion et al. (2009) offer an answer. They show that competition and innovation policies can be complementary if incumbents and entrants are encouraged to innovate. From the perspective of a developing country, the trade-off between antitrust initiatives and patents arises only if frontier innovation has become the main engine of productivity growth (box 5.4). Such a trade-off is not relevant to most countries in Latin America and the Caribbean.

Box 5.4

Is the antitrust versus patents debate relevant in developing countries?

Although the rents from innovation at the global technological frontier may be high, the investments in research and development (R&D) that are required to achieve such innovation are also substantial. Competition may erode the rents from innovation at the frontier to the point that they become insufficient to cover the costs of R&D. For example, in contrast to the findings of this report on countries in the region, Kang (2023) shows that patent applications fell significantly after the dismantling of cartels in the United States. Frontier innovation there must be protected by patents. If it is not, innovators may not be able to recoup their expenditures, and nobody would innovate at the technological frontier, even if they could.

A monopolist whose business is not threatened would seem to have few incentives to make the sacrifices required to innovate, such as significant investments in skilled labor and improvements in internal processes or products (Arrow 1976). Yet the same monopolist might have more resources and capacity to innovate and a more remarkable ability to harvest the total value of the resulting benefits (Schumpeter 1942).

box continued next page

Box 5.4

Is the antitrust versus patents debate relevant in developing countries? *(continued)*

This trade-off is the core of the antitrust versus patent policy debate in industrialized countries. Too much market power reduces the incentive to innovate and, therefore, reduces productivity. In this case, antitrust policy will raise productivity. Too much competition may destroy the monopoly rents that firms receive by patenting their inventions; therefore, competition may reduce the effort to innovate. In this case, antitrust policies will reduce productivity. However, policies that increase firms' rents from patenting will increase productivity.

Aghion et al. (2009) show that complementarities exist between innovation and competition policies. When innovation occurs at the frontier, such as in the Republic of Korea or the United States, the antitrust versus patent debate is centered on the trade-off between competition (antitrust) policies that boost competition and policies that maintain the rents from patents, thereby attracting innovators. From the policy perspective, the complementarity between competition and innovation means that competition (antitrust) policies are needed to ensure churning and provide incentives to escape competition through innovation. Patent protection is needed to extend the lifespan of the benefits that innovating firms reap from technical upgrading.

However, patent-worthy frontier innovation is scarce in developing countries, particularly in Latin America and the Caribbean. Most developing countries do not possess the technological capacity to generate global patentable innovation that is at or near the global technological frontier. The sort of innovation that dominates in most developing countries consists of introducing technology that has already been created and produced elsewhere or realizing improvements in domestic technological capacity. This catch-up innovation is of three types: (1) acquisition of tacit knowledge in the process of technology transfer from elsewhere, (2) imitation, and (3) process innovation.

The acquisition of tacit knowledge plays an essential role in technological upgrading in developing countries because it is a necessary step in transferring technology from elsewhere. Foreign technology must be adapted to the local environment so that local firms can use it. Tacit knowledge is critical in this process. It is not codifiable and can be transfered only through tacit, intangible means. Yet, without it, foreign technologies are useless to local firms. The acquisition of tacit knowledge

box continued next page

Box 5.4

Is the antitrust versus patents debate relevant in developing countries? *(continued)*

thus represents an advance in the technological capacity of a developing country. Moreover, it may also require R&D, which adds to technological capacity.

Imitation may be much more than directly reproducing or copying a technology. Imitation may also represent a time-consuming and costly approach. Imitating a technology may account for up to 65 percent of the original innovation costs and 70 percent of the time spent on the original R&D. Imitation may sometimes cost more than the original innovation. New R&D may be required to understand and replicate the product. Imitation in a developing country may not be innovative in the global sense; however, it may contribute to the country's technological capacity and constitute an innovation in the local environment.

If developing countries achieve genuine innovation in the global sense, it is more likely to involve process innovation rather than product innovation. It is possible to discover a new, more efficient way to make a product during the engagement in production. The creation of a new product, meanwhile, is likely to require dedicated R&D effort, which is rare in developing countries.

Innovation in Latin America and the Caribbean is still mostly catch-up, not frontier innovation. It has been chiefly based on imitation and technology transfer, such as acquiring machinery, other equipment, or disembodied technology. In many cases, R&D is prohibitively costly in terms of both financial cost and human capital. The number of patent applications is negligible in most countries in the region.

The complementarity between innovation and competition policies is still important in the region because competition is an incentive for the adoption of productive technology, and innovation capabilities lead to better productivity outcomes when firms compete with each other.

Sources: Based on Aghion et al. 2001; Anlló and Suárez 2009; Cheng 2022; Cirera and Maloney 2017; Navarro et al. 2010; Competition and Innovation (dashboard), Organisation for Economic Co-operation and Development, Paris, https://www .oecd.org/competition/the-relationship-between-competition-and-innovation .htm; and the authors cited.

Complementarities between Competition and Innovation in the Region

Competition policy alone will not effectively raise productivity without broad innovation at the firm level. This report concludes that firms' capability to innovate is critical to increasing productivity under competitive pressure. Competition of the kind described by Schumpeter (1942) intensifies the choice among firms between innovating or shutting down. This report documents the destruction at the lower end of the productivity distribution in Chile and Mexico, following competition with firms at the global frontier. A striking finding in both countries is that only 10 percent or less of domestic firms could undertake quality upgrading or innovation, compared with 50 percent in developed countries in similar circumstances and 25 percent in China (Aghion et al. 2009; Bombardini, Li, and Wang 2017; Maloney and Zambrano 2023). The innovation paradox examined in the next subsection sheds light on this result. The number of firms with sufficient capacity to escape competition has essential implications for the marketwide impacts of competitive pressure. It determines how creative the creative destruction will be.

Innovation policy alone cannot raise productivity without the competitive pressure to make firms want to innovate. The literature finds that the effectiveness of technology adoption in enhancing productivity is greater in an environment of competitive pressure. For example, in Mexico, many firms have employed ICT technology but achieved only minimal gains in productivity. Only firms under substantial competitive pressure have used technology to increase their productivity significantly and escape competition (Iacovone, Pereira López, and Schiffbauer 2017). The response was driven by complementary investments in innovation and the organizational changes necessary to improve the effectiveness of ICT technologies, such as using computers to improve production processes instead of only for internet connection. Moreover, recent research on firms in the region shows that market competition strengthens the propensity of firms to innovate and the intensity of investment in innovation (Álvarez, Benavente, and Crespi 2019; Pelaez, Hurtado, and Avila-Maecha 2024). Benavente and Zúñiga (2021) find strong evidence that innovation policy in Chile and Peru shores up the innovation investment of beneficiary firms, but only in highly competitive sectors. Competition creates incentives for firms that have already deployed technology to use the technology to increase productivity.

Therefore, the competition-innovation policy debate is not the same in developing countries as in developed countries (as described in box 5.4). There are still strong complementarities between competition and innovation policies in developing countries, and the complementarities go both ways. Increased exposure to competition, through domestic competition policy reform or trade liberalization, will boost innovation more the closer firms are to the technological frontier. Innovation policy that increases firms' capabilities to innovate, resulting in a higher share of leaders, might thus enhance aggregate productivity in response to competitive pressures. The success of competition policy in raising productivity will depend on how well innovation policy has supported firms. Providing access to technologies or enhancing innovation capabilities alone will not generate productivity growth in middle-income countries. Without competitive pressure, firms will not use new technologies to increase productivity. Therefore, the success of an innovation policy also hinges on the presence of a good competition policy.

Policy makers in the region have an opportunity to build on the potential synergies between competition and innovation policies. Getting competition policy right in both design and enforcement is critical. A well-designed and well-enforced competition policy will ensure that firms constantly have incentives to innovate and escape from competition. Building strong innovation systems is required to ensure that firms, once motivated to do so, have the resources and technological capacity they need to escape the competitive pressure.

Competition May Help to Offset the Innovation Paradox

The innovation paradox—the coexistence in developing countries of low levels of innovation-related investment and potentially high returns on such investment—helps to clarify why firms in the region face difficulty in upgrading or innovating. Cirera and Maloney (2017) explain the paradox by way of (1) weak managerial and organizational capabilities at the firm level, (2) missing complements to innovation-related investments in physical and human capital, and (3) weak government capacity to implement innovation policy. Ensuring that the missing complementarities are provided and enhancing capabilities across firms and government are thus critical to fostering innovation.

Weak firm capabilities are a pervasive deterrent to innovation at the firm level. As Cirera and Maloney (2017) show, firms in developing countries lag significantly in managerial capabilities. The countries in the region are roughly in the middle of the distribution, with management scores that are well below the scores of the OECD countries in the sample. Managerial quality plays a major role in firms' acquisition of these capabilities, and this quality is influenced by the educational attainment of managers, ownership structure of firms (such as family or government ownership), openness to trade, exposure to multinational enterprises, and degree of participation in global value chains (Bloom and Van Reenen 2007). Box 4.2, in chapter 4 of this report, offers some considerations for improving managerial quality based on recent research by the World Bank.

The absence of crucial complementary inputs to technological upgrading, particularly adequate human capital, may deter innovation—human capital matters at all levels, from frontline workers to engineers and scientists. The complementarity of various aspects of successful productivity-increasing innovation is highlighted in figure 5.6, which shows that, even with the substantial human capital in the region, firms' absorption of technology is low. Poor managerial quality may contribute to low absorption if firms cannot use workers productively. Managerial quality arises not only from the formal educational attainment of managers but also from on-the-job upskilling and foreign experience that exposes managers to more advanced practices. Interaction with other policies is also important; for example, significant public sector research and development can boost private sector efforts. Other factors that increase technology absorption include a good enabling environment external to the firm, including competitive markets, access to finance, and adequate supplies of knowledge and human capital (Arza et al. 2023; Cirera, Comin, and Cruz 2022).

Figure 5.6 Absorption of technology is low in some countries, even if human capital levels are similar

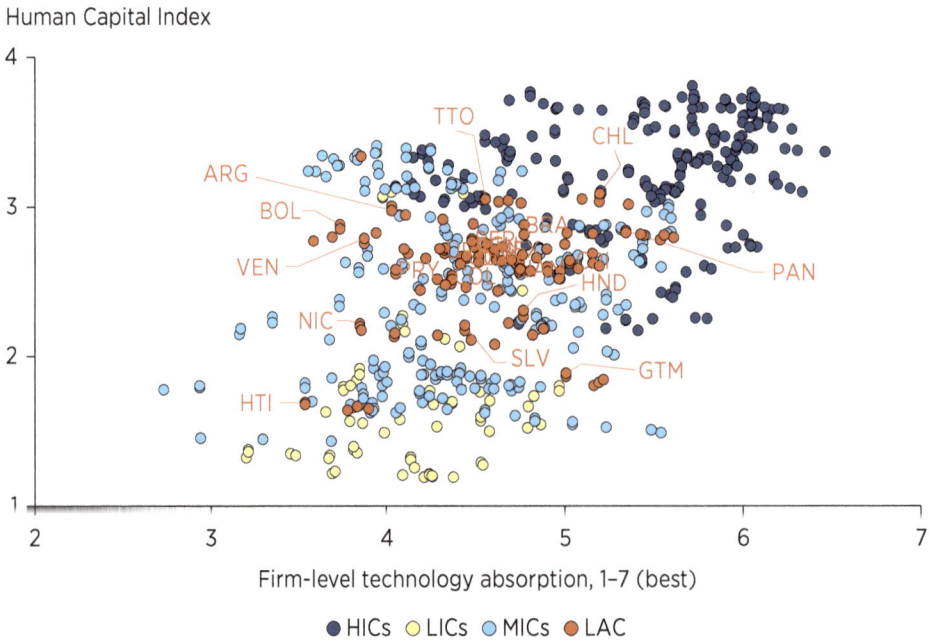

Human Capital Index

Firm-level technology absorption, 1–7 (best)

● HICs ○ LICs ● MICs ● LAC

Sources: Penn World Table (database version 10.1); Groningen Growth and Development Centre, Faculty of Economics and Business, University of Groningen, Groningen, Netherlands, https://www.rug.nl/ggdc/productivity/pwt/; Schwab 2019; World Development Indicators (Data Catalog), World Bank, Washington, DC, https://datacatalog.worldbank.org/search/dataset/0037712; Human Capital Index (HCI), World Bank, Washington, DC, https://datacatalog.worldbank.org/int/search/dataset/0038030/human-capital-index.

Note: The figure shows human capital and technology absorption for 1950–2019. For a list of country codes, go to https://www.iso.org/obp/ui/#search. HICs = high-income countries; LAC = Latin America and the Caribbean; LICs = low-income countries; MICs = middle-income countries.

Figure 5.7 The capabilities escalator

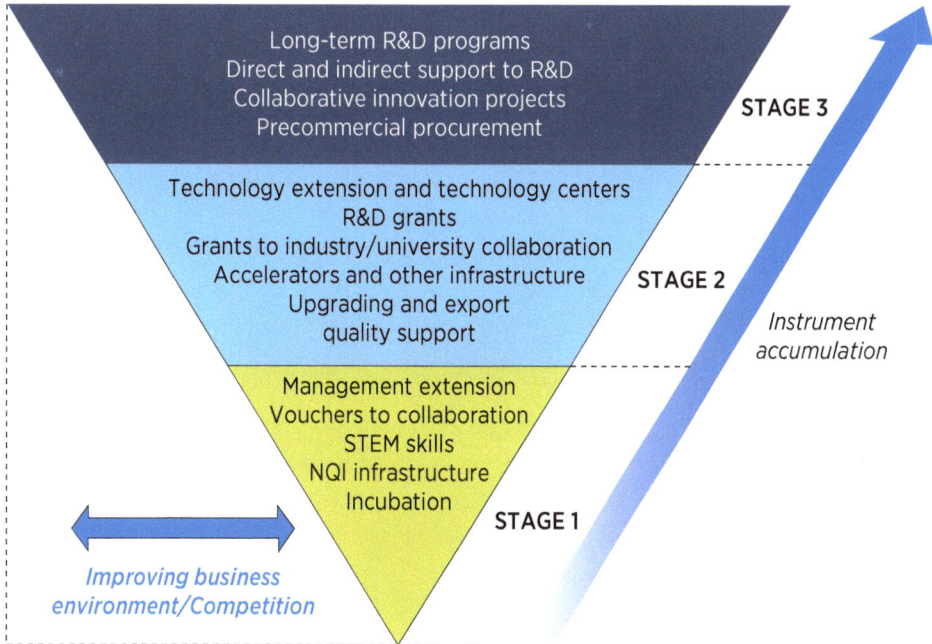

Long-term R&D programs
Direct and indirect support to R&D
Collaborative innovation projects
Precommercial procurement

STAGE 3

Technology extension and technology centers
R&D grants
Grants to industry/university collaboration
Accelerators and other infrastructure
Upgrading and export
quality support

STAGE 2

Instrument accumulation

Management extension
Vouchers to collaboration
STEM skills
NQI infrastructure
Incubation

STAGE 1

Improving business environment/Competition

Source: Cirera and Maloney 2017.

Note: NQI = national quality infrastructure; R&D = research and development; STEM = science, technology, engineering, and mathematics.

The process of innovation policy reform may be illustrated by the stages of the capabilities escalator, which depicts the sequencing from less to more sophisticated pro-innovation policies (figure 5.7). Competition and the business environment are at the base. An increasingly sophisticated innovation system is required to ascend the escalator. Cirera and Maloney (2017) stress that, to complete the escalator, governments must develop their capabilities in designing, implementing, and coordinating innovation policy. They note that political commitment is crucial to maintaining the long-term perspective required for successful investments in innovation.

Barriers to competition may impede managerial and organizational upgrading. A lack of competition makes the survival of inefficient, poorly managed firms more likely, and dampens firms' incentives to strengthen their capabilities. Confronted by the pressure of competition, however, capable firms adopt measures to increase productivity through innovation and greater efficiency in resource allocation and use.

Conclusions

Four broad, cross-cutting policy directions emerge from the analysis in this chapter. They are related to competition policy design and implementation, policy trade-offs, and complementarities.

First, the interface between competition policy and the broader regulatory framework is critical. Ill-conceived product market regulations, for example, may reduce contestability and dampen competition by creating barriers to entry, facilitating collusion, and tilting the playing field. To succeed, competition policy reform may require prior or accompanying regulatory reform.

Second, competition and innovation are generally mutually complementary, but there are situations in which pro-competition policies may conflict with innovation. In particular, the distribution of firms according to productivity or distance from the technological frontier matters for the success of competition-innovation reform. A firm's desire to escape competition will be triggered only among firms that can innovate, and innovation policy can lead to productivity growth only if there is also a competition policy. Development policy design thus becomes more complex if the complementarities and trade-offs are considered.

Third, capabilities matter for both private sector firms and public sector competition authorities. Strong organizational and managerial capabilities are necessary among firms if pro-competition policies, such as import liberalization, are also to be pro-innovation. Government capacity will determine the scope and prioritization of each country's competition and innovation policies. To use limited capabilities and resources to the greatest effect, the competition authorities in most countries in the region should prioritize addressing cartels and dominance abuse.

Fourth, institutional independence and political support are vital for the success of pro-competition reform. Reform is more likely to succeed if there is a robust political consensus in its favor and the competition authorities are beholden to no one in the political or business world.

Notes

1. The toolkit provides a typology for assessing the potentially adverse impact on competition of regulations and rules that (1) reinforce dominance or limit entry, (2) promote the formation of cartels or increase the cost of competing in the market, and (3) tilt the playing field. Refer to Markets and Competition Policy (dashboard), World Bank, Washington DC, https://www.worldbank.org/en/topic/competition -policy, and Miralles, Dauda, and Zipitria (2021).
2. World Bank Enterprise Surveys (dashboard), World Bank, Washington, DC, https://www.enterprisesurveys.org/en/enterprisesurveys.

3. For instance, Brazil, Costa Rica, and Mexico bar foreign competition in railway freight services. Brazil and Chile ban such competition in passenger railway services. Except in Costa Rica, to provide freight transportation services between ports within the region, vessels must fly the local national flag and be owned by a domestic company. In air transportation, Brazil and Costa Rica do not take part in regional service agreements. In road transportation, cabotage in bus services is prohibited, except in Peru, and no country in the region allows cabotage in freight. Only in Argentina are foreign road transportation firms permitted to pick up freight without restrictions. Chile and Peru allow it only in the case of selected destination countries. Open skies agreements among countries in the region involve restrictions on the fifth to ninth freedoms of the air. Refer to Freedoms of the Air (web page), International Civil Aviation Organization, Montreal, Canada, https://www.icao.int/pages/freedomsair .aspx.

4. Constitución de Sociedad por Acciones Simplificada (one-stop online shop), Secretariat of Economy, Mexico City, https://www.gob.mx/tramites/ficha /constitucion-de-sociedad-por-acciones-simplificada-sas/SE2568; Tu Empresa en un Día (one-stop online shop), Ministry of Economy, Development, and Tourism, Santiago, Chile, https://www.registrodeempresasysociedades.cl/Default.aspx.

5. Examples include the smaller forwarders who face pressure to use road carriers associated with integrated operators to access scarce shipping capacity or obtain more favorable commercial conditions, such as longer detention times, that is, the time lapse between the retrieval of a full container at a port and the return to the port of the empty container (World Bank 2021b).

6. Pineda and Musacchio (2020) show that SOEs in Latin America and the Caribbean are large relative to the size of the economies in which they operate. The average ratio of SOE assets to gross domestic product is 16 percent in the region. In Chile, Colombia, Costa Rica, Ecuador, Jamaica, Mexico, Panama, and Uruguay, the ratio is 20 percent or more.

7. Merger control and enforcement to reduce the abuse of dominance are antitrust tools that complement anticartel enforcement. However, these tools are less well developed and not uniformly applied across the region.

8. All 12 of the region's active leniency programs were established in the 2000s, as were most in Europe. The first was in Brazil (2000), followed by Mexico (2006), Uruguay (2007), El Salvador and Peru (2008), Chile and Colombia (2009), Ecuador (2016), Argentina (2018), Costa Rica (2019), and Nicaragua and the Dominican Republic (2021).

9. For instance, because of capacity limitations and weaknesses in the legal framework, competition authorities in Costa Rica, Honduras, and Paraguay have never carried out dawn raids.

10. The gap in cartel fines between Latin America and the Caribbean and the OECD is even larger by median value because two countries in the region impose larger fines than the rest of the region.

11. Worldwide jurisdictions in the OECD CompStats database, covering 79 OECD and non-OECD jurisdictions. Refer to OECD Competition Trends (portal), OECD, Paris, https://www.oecd.org/fr/corruption/oecd-competition-trends.htm, and OECD (2020).

12. Reed et al. (2022) provide more insights into the experience in Mexico. Their evidence shows that the competition authority sometimes may not sanction harmful conduct because investigators lack adequate resources to prove their cases conclusively. Because enforcement by the competition authority is popular among consumers and labor, Reed et al. (2022) conclude that enforcement could be readily reinforced following an increase in investigative resources.

13. Competition authorities in the region conducted fewer than 10 studies per year in 2010 and 2011, but then published almost 40 in 2017. The competition authority in

Honduras conducted 15 studies within the first four years of its operation, but only three in the six subsequent years.

14. Deep Trade Agreements: Data, Tools, and Analysis (dashboard), World Bank, Washington, DC, https://datatopics.worldbank.org/dta/table.html.

15. Refer to GSTP (Global System of Trade Preferences among Developing Countries) (dashboard), UN Trade and Development, Geneva, https://unctad.org/topic/trade -agreements/global-system-of-trade-preferences; LAIA (Latin American Integration Association) (homepage), LAIA, Montevideo, Uruguay, https://www.aladi.org /sitioaladi/; Pacific Alliance (Alianza del Pacífico) (homepage), https://alianzapacifico .net/en/.

16. TPSEP (Trans-Pacific Strategic Economic Partnership Agreement) (website), New Zealand Foreign Affairs and Trade, Wellington, New Zealand, https://www.mfat.govt.nz/en /about-us/who-we-are/treaties/trans-pacific-strategic-economic-partnership.

17. MERCOSUR (Southern Common Market) (dashboard), MERCOSUR, Montevideo, Uruguay, https://www.mercosur.int/en/.

18. Based on approaches developed by Hofmann, Osnago, and Ruta (2017) and Horn, Mavroidis, and Sapir (2010), the six levels of enforceability are nonbinding (level 0); best effort (level 1); binding, but not subject to dispute settlement (level 2); binding with state-to-state dispute settlement (level 3); binding with private-state dispute settlement (level 4); and binding with both private-state and state-to-state dispute settlement (level 5).

References

Aghion, Philippe, Richard Blundell, Rachel Griffith, Peter Howitt, and Susanne Prantl. 2009. "The Effects of Entry on Incumbent Innovation and Productivity." *Review of Economics and Statistics* 91 (1): 20–32. https://doi.org/10.1162/rest.91.1.20.

Aghion, Philippe, Christopher Harris, Peter Howitt, and John Vickers. 2001. "Competition, Imitation, and Growth with Step-by-Step Innovation." *Review of Economic Studies* 68 (3): 467–92. https://www.jstor.org/stable/2695893.

Álvarez, Roberto, José Miguel Benavente, and Gustavo Atilio Crespi. 2019. "Innovation in the Global Economy: Opening-Up Latin American Innovation Systems." IDB Discussion Paper IDB-DP-00729, Integration and Trade Sector, Competitiveness, Technology and Innovation Division, Inter-American Development Bank, Washington, DC.

Anlló, Guillermo, and Diana Suárez. 2009. *Innovación, Algo más que I+D; Evidencias Iberoamericanas a partir de las encuestas de innovación: Construyendo las estrategias empresarias competitivas.* Buenos Aires: Economic Commission for Latin America and the Caribbean.

Araujo, Sonia, and Wouter Meester. 2023. *Competition Authorities in LAC: Resources and Activity: An International Benchmark*. Washington, DC: World Bank and Organisation for Economic Co-operation and Development.

Arrow, Kenneth J. 1976. "The Rate of Discount for Long-Term Public Investment." In *Energy and the Environment: A Risk-Benefit Approach*, edited by Holt Ashley, Richard L. Rudman, and Christopher G. Whopple, 113–40. New York: Pergamon Press.

Arza, Valeria, Xavier Cirera, Emanuel López, and Agustina Colonna. 2023. "Explaining Differences in the Returns to R&D in Argentina: The Role of Contextual Factors." *Economics of Innovation and New Technology* 32 (6): 751–82. https://doi.org/10.1080 /10438599.2021.2024075.

Benavente, José Miguel, and María Pluvia Zúñiga. 2021. "The Effectiveness of Innovation Policy and the Moderating Role of Market Competition: Evidence from Latin American Firms." IDB Discussion Paper IDB-DP-890, Institutions for Development Sector,

Competitiveness, Technology, and Innovation Division, Inter-American Development Bank, Washington, DC.

Bloom, Nicholas, and John Michael Van Reenen. 2007. "Measuring and Explaining Management Practices across Firms and Countries." *Quarterly Journal of Economics* 122 (4): 1351–408.

Bombardini, Matilde, Bingjing Li, and Ruoying Wang. 2017. "Import Competition and Innovation: Evidence from China." Paper presented at the Hitotsubashi Conference on International Trade and FDI 2017, Hitotsubashi University, Tokyo, December 9–10. https://www7.econ.hit-u.ac.jp/cces/trade_conference_2017/paper/matilde _bombardini.pdf.

Cheng, Thomas K. 2022. *Competition and Innovation Policy Nexus in Developing Countries*. Washington, DC: World Bank.

Cirera, Xavier, Diego A. Comin, and Marcio Cruz. 2022. *Bridging the Technological Divide: Technology Adoption by Firms in Developing Countries*. Washington, DC: World Bank.

Cirera, Xavier, and William F. Maloney. 2017. *The Innovation Paradox: Developing-Country Capabilities and the Unrealized Promise of Technological Catch-Up*. Washington, DC: World Bank. https://doi.org/10.1596/978-1-4648-1160-9.

Coronado, Javier, Ivo Gagliuffi, María Isabel Alvarado, and Fiorella Senno. 2021. *Research Consultancy on the Productivity and Competition Report in Latin America*. Lima, Peru: Garrigues.

Hofmann, Claudia, Alberto Osnago, and Michele Ruta. 2017. "Horizontal Depth: A New Database on the Content of Preferential Trade Agreements." Policy Research Working Paper 7981, World Bank, Washington, DC.

Horn, Henrik, Petros C. Mavroidis, and André Sapir. 2010. "Beyond the WTO? An Anatomy of EU and US Preferential Trade Agreements." *World Economy* 33 (11): 1565–88.

Iacovone, Leonardo, Mariana De La Paz Pereira López, and Marc Tobias Schiffbauer. 2017. "ICT Use, Competitive Pressures, and Firm Performance in Mexico." *World Bank Economic Review* 30 (Supplement 1): S109–S118. https://doi.org/10.1093/wber/lhw023.

Kang, Hyo. 2023. "How Does Price Competition Affect Innovation? Evidence from US Antitrust Cases." Research Paper, Marshall School of Business, University of Southern California, Los Angeles, CA.

Kitzmuller, Markus, and Martha Martínez Licetti. 2013. "Competition Policy: Encouraging Thriving Markets for Development." ViewPoint Public Policy for the Private Sector 331, Finance and Private Sector Development Vice Presidency, World Bank, Washington, DC.

Lee, Woori. 2022. *Role of Deep Trade Agreements in Improving Competition in LAC*. Washington, DC: World Bank.

Licetti, Martha Martínez, Graciela Miralles, and Robert Teh. 2020. "Competition Policy." In *Handbook of Deep Trade Agreements*, edited by Aaditya Mattoo, Nadia Rocha, and Michele Ruta, 505–52. Washington, DC: World Bank.

Loayza, Norman V., and Michael Woolcock. 2020. "Designing Good Policies Is One Thing, Implementing Them Is Another." *Let's Talk Development* (blog), March 5, 2020. https://blogs.worldbank.org/en/developmenttalk/designing-good-policies -one-thing-implementing-them-another.

Maloney, William F., and Andrés Zambrano. 2023. *Optimal Protection for Innovation: Revisiting Industrial Policy*. Washington, DC: World Bank.

Mattoo, Aaditya, Nadia Rocha, and Michele Ruta, eds. 2020. *Handbook of Deep Trade Agreements*. Washington, DC: World Bank.

Miralles, Graciela, Seidu Dauda, and Leandro Zipitria. 2021. *Barriers to Competition in Product Market Regulation: New Insights on Latin American Countries*. Washington, DC: World Bank.

Navarro, Antonio, Fernando Losada, Emilio Ruzo, and José A. Díez. 2010. "Implications of Perceived Competitive Advantages, Adaptation of Marketing Tactics and Export Commitment on Export Performance." *Journal of World Business* 45 (1): 49–58.

OECD (Organisation for Economic Co-operation and Development). 2002. "Hard Core Cartels: Harm and Effective Sanctions." Policy Brief, OECD Observer, Public Affairs Division, Public Affairs and Communications Directorate, OECD, Paris. https://www .oecd.org/competition/cartels/21552797.pdf.

OECD (Organisation for Economic Co-operation and Development). 2018. "Investigative Powers in Practice, Break-Out Session 1: Unannounced Inspections in the Digital Age." Issues Note by the Secretariat, Global Forum on Competition, Report DAF/COMP /GF(2018)7, Competition Committee, Directorate for Financial and Enterprise Affairs, OECD, Paris.

OECD (Organisation for Economic Co-operation and Development). 2019. *Review of the Recommendation of the Council Concerning Effective Action against Hard Core Cartels [OECD/LEGAL/0294]: Report by the Secretariat.* Report DAF/COMP(2019)13 (July 4). Paris: Competition Committee, Directorate for Financial and Enterprise Affairs, OECD.

OECD (Organisation for Economic Co-operation and Development). 2020. *Competition Trends 2020.* Paris: OECD.

OECD (Organisation for Economic Co-operation and Development). 2022. *Competition Trends 2022.* Paris: OECD. https://web-archive.oecd.org/2022-03-21/624967-oecd -competition-trends-2022.pdf.

OECD (Organisation for Economic Co-operation and Development). 2024. *OECD Competition Trends 2024.* Paris: OECD.

Pelaez, Sergio, Bryan Hurtado, and Javier Avila-Maecha. 2024. "Taxation and Innovation: Evidence from Colombia." *Economics of Innovation and New Technology* 33 (1): 166–84.

Pineda, Emilio, and Aldo Musacchio. 2020. "Solving the State-Owned Enterprises Puzzle in Latin America and the Caribbean." *Recaudando Bienestar* (blog), January 18, 2020. https://blogs.iadb.org/gestion-fiscal/en/solving-the-state-owned-enterprises -puzzle-in-latin-america-and-the-caribbean/.

Rafferty, Olivia. 2021. "Peru Imposes Largest-Ever Fine on Construction Cartel." *Global Competition Review*, November 24. https://globalcompetitionreview.com/article /peru-imposes-largest-ever-fine-construction-cartel.

Reed, Tristan, Mariana De La Paz Pereira López, Ana Francisca Urrutia Arrieta, and Leonardo Iacovone. 2022. "Cartels, Antitrust Enforcement, and Industry Performance: Evidence from Mexico." Policy Research Working Paper 10269, World Bank, Washington, DC. doi:10.1596/1813-9450-10269.

Rocha, Nadia, and Michele Ruta, eds. 2022. *Deep Trade Agreements: Anchoring Global Value Chains in Latin America and the Caribbean.* Washington, DC: World Bank. http://hdl.handle.net/10986/37655.

Sampi, James Robert, Ana Francisca Urrutia Arrieta, and Ekaterina Vostroknutova. 2024. "Antitrust Enforcement, Markups, and Productivity: Evidence for Selected South America Countries." Background paper for this report. World Bank, Washington, DC.

Schumpeter, Joseph Alois. 1942. *Capitalism, Socialism, and Democracy.* New York: Harper and Brothers.

Schwab, Klaus, ed. 2019. *Insight Report: The Global Competitiveness Report 2019.* Geneva: World Economic Forum. http://www3.weforum.org/docs/WEF_TheGlobal CompetitivenessReport2019.pdf.

World Bank. 2021a. *Fixing Markets, Not Prices: Policy Options to Tackle Economic Cartels in Latin America and the Caribbean.* Washington, DC: World Bank.

World Bank. 2021b. *World Development Report 2021: Data for Better Lives.* Washington, DC: World Bank.

World Bank and OECD (Organisation for Economic Co-operation and Development). 2017. *A Step Ahead: Competition Policy for Shared Prosperity and Inclusive Growth.* Washington, DC: World Bank.

6
Concluding Remarks

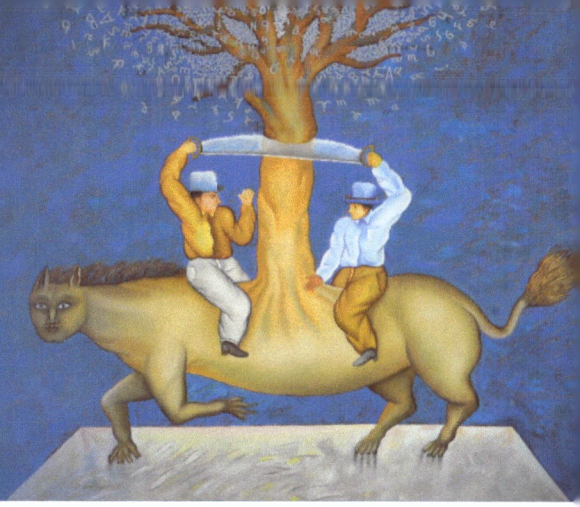

Summary

There are many possible explanations for the decades of lackluster growth in Latin America and the Caribbean: macroeconomic volatility, low savings and investment rates, underdeveloped institutions, resource misallocation across sectors and firms, and others. Another critical factor stands out: the low competitive pressure among firms, which fails to stimulate the forces of creative destruction and provides inadequate incentives for innovation.

Creative destruction in the region is hobbled by entry barriers that protect inefficient, unproductive firms from competition and enable them to collect rents. Barriers to firm growth and expansion into new markets sap the strength of productive firms. These barriers are both regulatory and market based. They weaken competitive pressure, causing low entry rates, high markups, slower growth of firms, and weak innovation efforts, all of which contribute to low productivity growth.

Could more intense competition accelerate productivity growth in the region? The empirical studies commissioned for this report suggest that the answer is yes. National competition authorities have fostered competition that, in turn, has cultivated productivity growth by encouraging firms with the capabilities to innovate. It is not only newcomers that innovate but also incumbents. Although incumbents may have the requisite resources, such as savings and access to technology, they may need to be pushed to innovate, by the prospect of losing business through competitive pressure.

The empirical evidence presented in this report shows that reducing entry barriers and enforcing antitrust laws can incentivize leading incumbent firms to innovate, resulting in improved sales and productivity.

Through analysis of the short-term impacts of import liberalization, the report highlights the crucial role of competition policy in preparing countries for inevitable external shocks. However, the ultimate success of competition policy in raising productivity depends on complementary policies that amplify the benefits of competition for productivity. The report emphasizes that the competition-innovation nexus is critical. Countries need coordinated progress in their competition policy frameworks and national innovation systems. The region requires fresh reforms to boost productivity and hasten the shift toward private sector–led growth. Competition policy must play a major role by leveling the playing field for market participants, unblocking the creative destruction process, and providing highly productive enterprises with new incentives to grow and innovate, while enabling unproductive enterprises to exit the market. Better enforcement of antitrust laws and overhauling the regulatory framework might enhance competitive pressures. Reforms must be explicitly evaluated for their effect on productivity to enable evidence-based policy making.

Competition policy cannot be expected to act in a vacuum. Institutions and the capacity of competition authorities and private firms are also important. Competition authorities need greater human and financial resources to supervise markets because investigations of suspected competition law violations can occur only with commitments of staff and time. Competition authorities also need institutional and policy autonomy to avoid capture by vested interests. In addition, private firms must have strong organizational and management skills to succeed as innovators.

The findings of this report demonstrate why competition policy should be designed, implemented, and evaluated not in isolation but as a central component of consistent, comprehensive national development strategies.